Chicken Soup for the Soul.

Chicken Soup for the

Preteen Soul.

21st Anniversary Edition

Chicken Soup for the Preteen Soul 21st Anniversary Edition
An Update of the 2000 Classic
Jack Canfield, Mark Victor Hansen, Patty Hansen, Irene Dunlap and Amy Newmark

Published by Chicken Soup for the Soul, LLC www.chickensoup.com
Copyright ©2021 by Chicken Soup for the Soul, LLC. All Rights Reserved.

The publisher gratefully acknowledges the many publishers and individuals who granted Chicken Soup for the Soul permission to reprint the cited material.

Front and back cover illustrations of star swooshes courtesy of iStockphoto.com/lenm (©lenm), illustrations of individual stars courtesy of iStockphoto.com/OlgaYakovenko (©OlgaYakovenko)
Interior illustrations of star swooshes courtesy of iStockphoto.com/lenm (©lenm)

Cover and Interior by Daniel Zaccari

Distributed to the booktrade by Simon & Schuster. SAN: 200-2442

Publisher's Cataloging-In-Publication Data
(Prepared by The Donohue Group, Inc.)

Names: Canfield, Jack, 1944- compiler.
Title: Chicken soup for the preteen soul, 21st anniversary edition : an
    update of the 2000 classic / [compiled by] Jack Canfield [and 4 others].
Description: 21st anniversary edition. | Cos Cob, CT : Chicken Soup for
    the Soul, LLC, [2021] | Interest age level: 009-013. | Summary:
    "Stories to help today's preteens be the happiest, best versions of
    themselves"--Provided by publisher.
Identifiers: ISBN 9781611590807 (paperback) | ISBN 9781611593204 (ebook)
Subjects: LCSH: Preteens--Conduct of life--Literary collections--Juvenile
    literature. | Preteens--Conduct of life--Anecdotes--Juvenile literature.
    | CYAC: Conduct of life--Literary collections. | Conduct of
    life--Anecdotes. | LCGFT: Anecdotes.
Classification: LCC BJ1631 .C465 2021 (print) | LCC BJ1631 (ebook) | DDC
    158.1/083--dc23
Library of Congress Control Number: 2021937451

PRINTED IN THE UNITED STATES OF AMERICA
on acid∞free paper

30 29 28 27 26 25 24   06 07 08 09 10

Chicken Soup for the

Preteen Soul.

21st Anniversary Edition

An Update of the 2000 Classic

Jack Canfield, Mark Victor Hansen,
Patty Hansen, Irene Dunlap and Amy Newmark

Chicken Soup for the Soul, LLC
Cos Cob, CT

Chicken Soup for the Soul

Changing lives one story at a time®
www.chickensoup.com

Table of Contents

❶
~Achieving Dreams~

❷
~Friendship~

3

~Family~

4

~Love~

5

~Death and Dying~

❻
~Attitude and Perspective~

❼
~Overcoming Obstacles~

8

~Choices~

9

~Tough Stuff~

10

~Changes~

⑪

~Eclectic Wisdom~

Foreword

This is real life — in a book.

Y'all know that life may not be perfect, right? But no matter how complicated or challenging life might be for you, you are one of the blessed and lucky ones! From this point on, you have a manual for life!

Finding out what others have gone through during their preteen years can help you realize that you're not alone and maybe even keep you from going through the same things. Be open-minded enough to let their experiences help make your transition into teenage-hood a smoother one. At least this way you'll have some shortcuts!

Be kind to others, even the people who you may not like. You might find that they're dealing with the same stuff as you. Remember that everyone has something to offer to this world.

Above all, go for your dreams. The world will be a better place when you give life your best and follow your heart.

God Bless,
— Kenan Thompson —
Film and television actor

Introduction

At a certain time, between the ages of nine and twelve, experiences seem to be extra hard. It's like being half into dolls and half into make-up. For girls, every little thing you say seems to make us cry — most of all, comments about clothes, boys and weight. The boys I know try to hide their feelings, but they seem to have most of the same problems.

I am eleven years old, and I have nearly all of these troubles. When I try to be grown-up, people tell me I'm too young. When I do something wrong, people tell me to grow up. I don't understand. I guess we're always going to be too big for some things, and too young for others. That's just how the world is.

Relax, it's just your preteen years.

~Michelle Richard

The preteen years are the true age of personal empowerment — old enough to move, shake and change the world and too young to be caught up in the belief that it can't be done. At the same time, you might be feeling mood swings, hormone surges and a growing interest in romance. While you are facing these physical and emotional changes, events like divorce, changing friendships, permanent loss due to the death of a loved one, and moving or having a close friend move can be extra difficult during these already challenging years.

In addition to all of these issues, you are also filled with questions — questions about your place in the world, your beliefs, who you are and how you fit in to the greater scheme of things, as this poem written by Megan Brown, age twelve, addresses:

Sometimes I wonder if we all see the same colors.
Or if someone is colorblind and they just don't know it!
What's beyond our universe?
I wonder if there are other worlds.
Is there a heaven? I know there is, but... really is there?
I wonder if when we sleep,
Our dreams are actual places we are going to.
I think we may be living in someone's dream right now.
I think that mirrors lie.
What are we?

Back when we were putting together our first book for preteens, we heard from Aubrey Nighswander. She said, "I'm twelve years old, and in my opinion, it's one of the toughest times in anyone's life. We are just at the age when we're no longer kids, but not yet teenagers. We want to have rights and responsibilities, and yet we're not ready to accept the roles of adults. At times, we want to be grown-up. But, at others, we want to be a two-year-old again, without any worries other than when we're going to have to take a nap! Some may consider thirteen to be the age of a teenager, but I personally think we're still preteens until about the age of fourteen. So for all those preteens out there, who are going through the same mood swings, feelings and thoughts, who are struggling to push into the role of a teenager — enjoy every millisecond of your life, and don't grow up too fast. And remember, you're NOT alone."

Not being alone. That is super important. When you read these stories about the experiences of other kids your age, you'll realize you share many experiences and emotions. That is so empowering and comforting. And that's why this collection of stories for preteens has become a classic, one of our most popular books ever. We published it for the first time in the year 2000, and now we present it to you updated for its 21st anniversary. We've pulled out some stories that seem out of date these days. We moved some stories that we found too mature for this collection into one you may read in a few years, the new 25th anniversary edition of *Chicken Soup for the Teenage Soul*.

And we included brand-new stories for you — ones about being a kid during the pandemic, social media and technology, and many other modern-day issues.

Chapter 1

Achieving Dreams

If it were all up to me
The poor would have riches
And the blind man would see
The hungry would eat
And the weak would be strong
And the people with hatred would all get along
The ones who are greedy would start to share
And unfriendly people would start to care
The thirsty would drink
And the deaf person hear
And sorrow and sadness would all disappear
And that is how the world would be
If it were all up to me.

—Sara Alfano, 11—

The Turnaround

*Some people want it to happen, some wish it would
happen, and others make it happen.*
~Michael Jordan

My knees started shaking, yet my body froze; it felt as though my soul departed my body and I had no control over it. Anxiously, I looked through the roster posted on the wall of the locker room; my heart was beating harder and harder as I slowly saw all my friends' names on that list but could not find mine. *John, Bryce, Ro,* I thought, *everybody is on here except me.* At that moment, I froze; I just could not accept that all my friends were on the team but I was not.

I was so convinced there was a mistake that I went and found the coach, "Hey coach, are you sure that the roster you posted is correct?" I asked anxiously, dreading his answer.

"Yes, the names on the list are finalized. Sorry if you did not make it this year buddy. There is always next year," the coach replied without the slightest bit of remorse.

I could feel the hot, bitter tears building in my eyes, and I ran out of the room as fast as I could. As soon as I walked out, I saw my friends crowding into the locker room to look at the finalized team list. I heard them shouting and laughing as I slowly walked away, every one of them jumping around with exuberance after seeing that they made the team. Trying to forget about the situation, I headed over to the cafeteria to buy some food, but my friend Dan caught up to me on the way.

"Hey, what's up! Everybody is coming over to my house to celebrate making the team! Will you be there?" he jubilantly asked.

"I... I didn't make the team," I stammered, nervous about how he would react.

"Oh, I didn't know. I guess you can still come after school if you want. Well, I got to go now," he hesitated, his voice a mixture of pity and surprise.

Dan walked away, leaving me in despair. I felt dead inside, like nothing mattered. I trudged through the rest of school; walking was such a burden that it felt as if I had a 100-pound weight tied to my backpack. My mind was also blank for the rest of the school day; everything my teachers said went in one ear and out the other.

After school, as I walked to the parking lot to get picked up, I saw all my friends gathered near the rear of the lot, celebrating and joking around. I detoured around the side of the school to avoid them, trying not to think about being one of the only people in our friend group to not make the team.

I saw my father's familiar red Mazda pull up near the school lot, and I walked up to the car and got in. He smiled at me, played the radio, and started driving home, oblivious to the fact that something was wrong. Then when we got home, he noticed my sullen walk and gloomy face, and asked me what was wrong.

"Nothing. Well, it's just that all my friends made the school team. Everyone! Except me..." I stammered, not knowing how he would react.

"Well, what are you going to do about it? Are you just going to sit there?" he asked.

Surprised, I didn't know what to say, and I just shook my head and went into my room. I thought hard for thirty minutes about what my dad said, and it started making sense to me. Nobody was going to give me a spot on that team. I would have to earn it. Having made this mental breakthrough, I decided to work toward my goal of making the team. Conveniently, there was a gym near my school, so as soon as the bell rang for school to end, I biked to the gym and trained for two hours. I ran, dribbled, and shot until I collapsed on the hardwood floor every single day.

There were moments when I didn't think I could keep on going, but I powered through it. *After all,* I thought, *hard work beats talent when talent doesn't work hard.*

After almost a year of practicing and training, I tried out for my seventh-grade team. "Step, dribble, shoot," I said to myself, "You got this!" After the tryout, I felt confident and congratulated myself. Regardless of the outcome, I knew that I had worked hard and learned something about mental toughness.

The next day, I found out I made the team; seeing my name printed in large bold letters felt as though all my dreams came true in one wondrous moment. The greater the effort, the sweeter the reward, and by making the team, I had officially made a turnaround.

— Kaiwen Zhang—

Trash Bags Are
for Trash

What do we live for if not to make life less
difficult for each other?
~George Eliot

I walked through the den on my way to get ready for bed and looked once again at the amazing mountain of duffel bags. Each bag had a stuffed animal, a luggage tag and a note from me inside it. The pile of bags went from floor to ceiling, more than five thousand bags, enough for each and every foster-care kid in three states. My dream was coming true — big time.

After I went to bed, right before I went to sleep, I closed my eyes and thought back to when it all started… when I got the idea for my dream…

I had been in second grade when I went with my two brothers and my parents to Paris, France. My brothers, Brock and Cory, and I had entered an essay contest about what we were going to do to change the world to make it a better place to live. We won and were chosen as three of ten kids who would represent the United States at the Children's World Summit. Nine hundred kids from around the world were chosen to meet with each other and talk about world issues. We exchanged ideas on solving the problems in our world today and had lots of fun during the days we were together.

While I was there, I met two foster-care kids. They were two boys, and after getting to know them, I learned a lot about what foster-care kids go through. They told me that when kids go into the foster-care system, they don't just lose their parents and their home, sometimes they are also separated from their brothers and sisters. Not every foster-care home wants to care for an entire family of kids. Foster-care kids also lose most of their toys and clothes. They told me that when the kids are picked up from their home by a social worker, they are given only a trash bag to put their few belongings into. This trash bag is what foster-care kids carry with them when they are moved from home to home.

I felt really sad when I heard this. I couldn't even imagine what life would be like without my family and home — much less what it would be like to have to live out of a trash bag. Trash bags are for trash, not for kids to carry their belongings in.

After I came home from France, I saw an after-school movie that was about a girl living in foster care. It was just like what the boys had described to me at the Children's World Summit, and it made me cry. Right then I decided that I wanted to help foster-care kids. These kids needed my help because they were not being respected like they should be.

My whole family is into volunteering. Brock and Cory had started a project after they saw a show on television about some kids who died in a fire. The kids had died because the fire department didn't have this special camera that can see through smoke to find people in a burning house. My brothers began Project Rescue Vision in 1996 to raise needed money for our town's fire department. Of course, I helped too. I was only four years old, and I was the "President of the Art Department." My job was to hand-color all of the information envelopes that were given out. I helped them until I was seven. Then I began my own project for foster-care kids.

I started by asking my mom to stop at garage sales when I saw suitcases or duffel bags for sale. I would tell the person who was having the garage sale what I wanted to do with the bags, and most of the time they gave me the bags for free. I tried to put myself into the mind of a foster-care kid, and I decided that the kids should have a stuffed animal in the bag, too. I figured that if I was in that situation I would want a cuddly friend to hug when I was sad and felt lonely for my parents. People often gave those to me for free, too.

In October 1998, I helped organize a luggage drive during our local "Make a Difference Day." Some congresspeople and senators showed up to give their support, and I came up with this idea for everyone to get their hand painted and then put their handprint on a big banner to show that they had made a difference that day. I got all these kids to help paint people's hands. It was really funny to watch these important people have their hands painted.

The senators and congresspeople went back to Washington and told other people about my project, and then a company named Freddie Mac set up a grant for me and donated fifteen thousand dollars. I am the youngest person they have ever granted money to. Because of this grant, I had a story about my project and me on the cover of *The Washington Post*. Then the most amazing thing happened. President and Mrs. Clinton read about me and wanted to meet me. I was really excited! They were so nice, and I gave the President one of my bags with a Beanie Baby in it to give to any foster kid that he might meet. A few days later, he sent some bags to me from his own collection to give to foster-care kids, so I did.

My project really started growing because of all the media attention. Radio stations called me for interviews about what I was doing and some TV shows had me on. More people then heard about me from the TV and radio interviews and from word-of-mouth, and they called me to offer help.

Every week I called my friends and family to see if they wanted to come and put together bags. I always had help from many people. My class even helped, too. My teacher announced to my class what I was doing, and everybody started bringing stuffed animals and duffel bags to school. One of my friends brought in ten big bags full of stuffed animals!

On each bag, I put a luggage tag designed by me. On the front of each luggage tag is a picture of a girl and a suitcase with wheels on it. In each bag, I put a cuddly stuffed animal and a special note I wrote, letting them know that I love and care about them. My mom helped me type this note:

> Dear Friend,
>
> Hi, my name is Makenzie Snyder. I am nine years old, and I'm in the third grade. I collect suitcases and duffel bags as an act of kindness for those who are in need of them. God told me you could use a duffel bag and a cuddly friend so I sent this with love to you. I want you to always know that you are loved, especially by me. And, always remember to be positive, polite and never give up.
>
> Love, your friend,
> Makenzie Snyder

After the bags are stuffed, I call social workers to tell them they can come and pick up the bags to hand out to the foster-care kids. I have had a lot of support from several big companies, schools, churches, organizations and individuals who have donated money, or sent me bags and stuffed animals. I've even been on the *Rosie O'Donnell Show!* Several thousand bags have been sent out so far, and right now I have 5,000 more ready to go, sitting in my den. Those bags will go to kids in Maryland, Washington, D.C., and Virginia.

I have had a lot of help from a lot of people, but most importantly from my parents and my brothers. My brother Brock came up with the name for my project. He said I should call it "Children to Children" since it was all about kids knowing what other kids want and helping them get it. My brothers have also given me good advice about always sending thank-you notes to the people who help me. They told me I had to work hard, call tons of people and to never give up… and I haven't.

I know that this is just the beginning. There are 530,000 foster-care kids in the United States. My dream is for all the foster-care kids in the entire United States to receive a duffel bag and a cuddly friend. I know it can be done if everyone helps out. It is a lot of work but I never get tired of it. I remember the girl in the movie that I saw. If she had been given one of my duffel bags, she would have known that someone out there cared about what happened to her. I don't want any kid, anywhere, to go through what she or the two boys did. Kid to kid, children to children — that's what it's all about.

— Makenzie Snyder, 9 —

Run with It

Do what you can, with what you have, where you are.
~Theodore Roosevelt

The first time I saw Jeff was when my best friend, Brian, and I were in the fourth grade. When our teacher introduced Jeff to the class she explained that he was sick and that he might not be able to be in class all of the time.

Jeff was completely bald from cancer treatments, and he wore a hat. That was one reason that he and I bonded right away. Being the tomboy that I was, I liked wearing a hat — only I wasn't allowed to wear one in class. Jeff was allowed to wear his hat all of the time. Other than that, he was a normal friend to both Brian and me. Some things he couldn't do as well as the other kids because he had tubes in his chest for his treatments, but we never thought of him as sick because he didn't act that way.

The only time that we would realize that Jeff was sick was when he went for his chemotherapy treatments. We'd notice the difference, but we'd just sort of think, *Yeah, Jeff's not feeling really well now,* and then it would pass and things would be back to normal. Jeff, Brian and I were really sports-oriented, and we became best buds. We would swim, run and jump on the trampoline. As fourth grade progressed, Jeff got better and better. By the end of the school year he went into remission; the cancer was all gone.

Brian, Jeff and I spent tons of time together during the summer between fourth and fifth grades. We loved being outdoors, running everywhere and staying over at each other's houses. Before school started, Jeff went away on vacation with his family for a few weeks.

Then came the night that I will always remember. We were eating dinner when the phone rang. It was Jeff's mom, calling to say that Jeff was in the hospital. The cancer had come back. My reaction was, *Wait a minute. What's going on?*

Jeff and I talked on the phone the next day and he sounded like his normal self. I couldn't really imagine him being back in the hospital. Then, a few days later, my mom took me to visit him. When I walked into his room, Jeff looked really weak. His mom was talking about a trip to California for a bone marrow transplant operation, and how important it would be for Jeff. Even though everyone looked very serious and sad, the thought of losing Jeff never crossed my mind. I just thought he would get better.

During the next few weeks, before the operation, Jeff was allowed to play with Brian and me but he had to wear a surgical mask because he had to be careful of infections. I realize now that his parents wanted him to experience as much of life as possible while he could. One night, they took Jeff and me to this really fancy restaurant up in the mountains, and it felt sort of like a date. We both dressed up — which was weird for me, because I never wore anything but shorts and hats.

When Jeff left for California to have his operation I told him, "Bye, see you in a month or so," as if nothing much was happening. I wrote to him while he was there, and the letters that he sent to me talked about the things that we would do together when he returned home. It didn't even cross my mind that I might never see him again.

Then, one night, I went to a skating party. Brian was supposed to be there but I couldn't find him. When I got home, my dad was out in the garage working on a project. When Dad spotted me, he opened the door to the house to let my mom know that I had arrived. I walked into the house, and Mom said, "I need to talk to you alone in your bedroom, Susie." I grabbed some chocolate chips off the counter and bounded off to my room. "Jeff's mom called…" was all she had to say. I knew. The chocolate chips turned sour in my mouth, and I cried as my mom held me tightly. I've never been an emotional person, but my heart just sank and I felt empty. It was too hard to believe. Brian had heard about it just before the skating party, and that's why he hadn't been there.

That evening, Brian and I talked for hours. We had never talked much on the phone before, because we had always been doing things, but that night we talked and talked, reminiscing about Jeff. We started worrying about Jeff's parents and if they could handle the medical expenses. And that was the beginning of our idea. We wanted to do something, but we didn't know what.

When we figured out that Jeff's parents didn't need the money, we started thinking instead about something that would help everybody remember Jeff, something to honor him. Brian and I thought about the time the three of us did a run together. Jeff had loved running, but it had been hard for him to finish the run. He was really happy when he was able to cross the finish line, and so were we. Why not do a run for Jeff?

It seemed like a good idea. We knew that we would have to advertise in order to have enough runners, and that we'd have to get sponsors for food and drinks. We even thought we knew what the forms needed to look like for sign-ups.

I know now that all of this planning was part of our grieving process. All through it, we told each other stories about Jeff. Right around that time, his parents donated a tree to the school and we all planted it in Jeff's memory. It was tough on his parents, but it really helped all the kids. Everyone got to shovel some dirt around the tree, and Jeff's parents held hands with each other and cried.

If we'd been old enough to know what was really involved, we probably wouldn't have started it. But we were just some kids with a great idea, so we went for it. We took the phone book and started calling Coors, Pepsi and Mile-High Yogurt — anything we could find. "We want to do a run, and we're looking for sponsorship," we would say to whoever answered the phone. "Who can we talk to?" I wonder if the people on the other end could tell that we were only fifth graders!

Then one day, Mom came to me all excited. "A man from Pepsi called and asked to talk to you. What's going on?" I guess we'd been persuasive enough! After I called him back and got his pledge of support, I told my parents about the run and they promised to help. The vice-principal got involved and he brought the plans for the run to the gym teacher, who was a runner. All of the adults in our lives were encouraging us.

We started writing letters to lots of companies, which was pretty funny because Brian has the worst handwriting in the world. I don't know how anyone ever read what he was trying to say. But somehow it worked because we started receiving all kinds of gifts. The yogurt place gave us 500 free yogurts, and other companies donated money.

The plans for the run were growing so big that we needed a professional organizer. Someone came along and donated this service for free, and that's when things really started to roll. The entire community became involved: stuffing packets, raising money, writing numbers on racing bibs, holding meetings. Pretty soon, the whole city knew what was going to happen.

The day of the run finally came, and it was huge! Tons of people ran, ReMax donated T-shirts and there were awards for anyone who could beat the gym teacher's time. The park where the run was held was near Jeff's house, which was where the processional had gone after his funeral. Because of where it was held, the run had even more of a special meaning to Brian and me. And, we raised ten thousand dollars! We donated the money to the Leukemia Society in Jeff's name.

Even now, I think about Jeff quite a lot. If something's going on in my life that feels bad, I tell myself, *Come on, get over it. Stop feeling sorry for yourself. If Jeff were still alive, he would be glad just to have the opportunity to deal with this.*

The run made such an impact on my life. The biggest thing was (and I credit the adults for this) that no one ever told us "No." We kept hearing, "If you want to do it, you can do it!" It has helped me in everything I've done since, and I've had a "Go for it!" attitude about things.

There's a big bike ride I've heard about that goes from Los Angeles to Orlando, and I'm thinking about riding in it. Some of my friends think I'm crazy and they ask me, "Is that even possible?" Of course it is! *You're alive, you're here — so run with it!*

— Susan Overton —

The Back of David's Head

Have a belief in yourself that is bigger
than anyone's disbelief.
~August Wilson

I couldn't stand fifth grade. I didn't like the milk that was warm by lunchtime from sitting near the radiator all morning. I didn't like recess because I could never get a turn on the swing. But most of all I didn't like my teacher, Mrs. Kelly, because I was sure that Mrs. Kelly didn't like me.

Mrs. Kelly never let me pass out books or collect papers. Mrs. Kelly made me sit in the last seat of the sixth row behind David Abbot, the biggest kid in the whole class. David was bigger than most of the eighth graders, and he never, ever took a bath. The only thing I could see all day was the back of David's head.

At the beginning of fifth grade, Mrs. Kelly had explained all the classroom rules including the one about being excused for the restroom. She told all the students that they had to raise their hand with one or two fingers when they wanted to be excused. Then she would know what they were going to do in the restroom, and how long they would be gone from the classroom. The whole class would laugh whenever anyone held up two fingers to be excused.

One Monday in October, Mrs. Kelly said, "Clear your desks and take out your composition books. Today I want you to write a composition called 'Something Interesting' about something you have personally seen. Do not repeat any topics."

"Can we write about Disneyland?" Maureen Murphy asked. Everyone in the class knew that Maureen had been to Disneyland more than anyone else in the whole school.

"That would be perfect, Maureen," Mrs. Kelly answered with a smile.

I opened my black and white composition book. I tried to ignore the huge red U for "unsatisfactory" that partly covered the title, "My Summer Vacation." I remembered Mrs. Kelly's comments without even looking at them.

It has been brought to my attention that this composition is about your last year's summer vacation, and you have already written about the same trip for a composition last year during the fourth grade. Therefore, this assignment is unsatisfactory. Your penmanship is also unsatisfactory.

I didn't care about the penmanship comment. That was on every assignment I turned in. What bothered me was that Mrs. Kelly would not accept my composition about my train trip to Denver. The only trip I had ever gone on in my whole life had been the trip to Denver. In the fourth grade, my composition had been about all the things I had seen from the train windows on the way to Denver. For the fifth grade, I wrote a whole new composition about the hotel in Denver with the glass elevators.

Mrs. Kelly wrote an outline on the blackboard. One paragraph for an introduction, then three paragraphs to describe the topic in detail. A final paragraph for a conclusion. I knew that Maureen Murphy had a composition book filled with E's for excellent and even S's for superior while my best grade had been an F. In spite of Mrs. Kelly's red marks, I really liked to fill the pages of my composition book with words and ideas. I frowned and stared at the back of David's head.

That's when I noticed that the back of David's head looked like a brown forest with a long, brown, hairy trail that ran down his neck. He had three big brown freckles peeking out from the forest. The top of his head looked like a cartoon porcupine with brown hairs sticking up all over. David's ears were reddish tan with pudgy lobes that flapped against his neck when he raised his hand with only one finger. Looking at the back of David's head, I decided this composition could be different. It could be full of imagination instead of boring and embarrassing because I had never had the chance to see anything interesting, outside of the trip to Denver.

I opened my composition book and began to write. I wrote and wrote until Mrs. Kelly said, "Mary Ellyn, this is the third time I've called your name. It is time to line up to go home. However, you will stay after and write 'I will pay attention in class' one hundred times before you are excused."

On Wednesday, Maureen tiptoed around the room in her fancy shoes passing back everyone's composition notebooks. I ignored her snotty smile and opened my book, paging past all the F's and U's. I couldn't wait to see a beautiful letter at the top of my composition, entitled "The Back of David's Head."

By the time I found the page, my whole body was so tense with excitement I almost fell off my seat. But what I saw made my breath stop in a gasp. Across the whole composition Mrs. Kelly had scrawled a huge red U. It was the biggest and reddest U I had ever seen. The red words in the margin swam in a blur from the tears that filled my eyes. A huge tear plopped onto the page, splashing over the comment about penmanship. I slapped the book shut and raised my hand with two fingers. I didn't care who laughed.

In the bathroom, I sat on the edge of a toilet and cried for a long time. After a while I heard the restroom door swish open.

"I know you're in here, Mary Ellyn," Maureen Murphy's voice oozed under the green painted metal door. "Mrs. Kelly says you'd better get back in class, right now."

I waited for the sound of the door swishing closed. "You just wait and see, Mrs. Kelly," I said in a low scary voice. "Someday I'll show you. Someday I'll write lots of stories and SELL them for lots of money. Someday my stories will be in books! Just you wait and see."

And when I grew up, that's *exactly* what I did.

SO THERE, MRS. KELLY!

— Mary Ellyn Sandford —

Editor's note: Mrs. Kelly and readers might be interested to know that Mary Ellyn's work has been published in several magazines as well as *Chicken Soup for the Kid's Soul*.

Going to the Dogs

If we all did the things we are capable of doing,
we would literally astound ourselves.
~Thomas Edison

One day my mom and I were sitting in her office looking at a magazine called *Humane Society News*. We read a very sad story about a New Jersey police dog named Solo that had been sent into a building to catch an armed suspect. The last thing Solo did before entering the building was to lick his owner's face. A few minutes later, Solo was shot and killed in the line of duty. I knew how sad that officer must have felt because my own dog, Kela, had recently died. I felt like my world had ended when I lost Kela. She had been my best friend since I could remember.

The article went on to tell about a fundraiser that was going on in New Jersey to help buy bulletproof vests for the police dogs there. I thought, *Every police dog should be protected just like the police. I may be a kid, but why can't I do a fundraiser to help save the dogs in our area?*

Then I found out that a bulletproof vest for a police dog costs $475. My mom thought it was a lot of money for an eleven-year-old girl to raise, but she told me to go ahead and try anyway.

We called our local Oceanside Police Department and found out that their dogs needed bulletproof vests. At that point, I realized that I needed a name for the fundraiser and thought since I was trying to protect just one dog's life, I would call my program Vest A Dog.

I decided that veterinarian offices and pet stores would be really good places to go with donation boxes and Vest A Dog flyers. I used little green Chinese take-out boxes, decorated with a picture of Tiko, the dog I chose to vest, and me. I wrote on each box "Help protect the life of a police dog by donating a dollar."

One afternoon, after all the boxes had been distributed throughout our community, I got a call from a local newspaper reporter who had seen one of my fliers. The reporter decided to do an article about Vest A Dog. *That ought to spread the word,* I thought. I asked K9 Officer Jim Wall, who is Tiko's partner, if they would have their picture taken with me for the article and they did.

After the article came out, I waited for a few days before checking to see if there were any donations. I was really nervous when I finally went to collect the money. *Would there be anything in the boxes?* I wondered. I really wasn't sure that I could raise enough to buy the vest. But when I collected the first box, I couldn't believe my eyes. I realized that there are many generous animal lovers out there. The box was practically overflowing with dollar bills! I kept checking back to collect the donations every few days. After about three weeks, I counted the money from all of the boxes. It totaled over three thousand dollars! I was so excited and totally amazed at the amount of money that I had raised. Not only was there enough money to buy Tiko's vest, but Vest A Dog had raised enough to buy vests for the other five unprotected dogs on the Oceanside Police Department. I couldn't believe it!

When the officers from the K9 unit found out that they were going to be able to protect all six of their dogs, they couldn't stop thanking me. They decided to put together a presentation ceremony where I would give the six vests I was donating to the department's dogs. That's where I got to meet all of the other police dogs and their handlers. I was actually a little scared of them, but the officers assured me that the dogs were very friendly. I learned that these were not just police dogs, but also the officers' family pet. Again, I thought of my dog Kela and also about Solo. I wanted even more to make sure that these police dogs didn't die while trying to protect people.

Once I began presenting the vests at the ceremony, I kept seeing television reporters come in and set up cameras. I never expected to see so many news stations there! I was excited to talk with them about what I was doing. When they asked me if I was going to continue my Vest A Dog program to help protect the other fifty dogs in San Diego County, where we live, I replied, "Yes! We need to protect these dogs because they protect us every day."

Soon the phone was ringing off the hook! Each day, reporters from newspapers and television stations called with interview requests. They wanted more information about my Vest A Dog program and also wanted to know where donations could be made. The media is so powerful! People began to mail donations to Vest A Dog!

Looking back, the success of Vest A Dog totally surprised me at first. Then I realized that it wasn't unusual that a lot of other people felt the same way I did about these dogs. They just didn't know how to help before Vest A Dog got started.

So far, Vest A Dog has raised more than twenty-five thousand dollars and has supplied *all* of the law enforcement dogs within San Diego County with a protective vest! Then, just when I had achieved what I thought was my highest goal, people from all over the country began to call me to find out how to raise funds to vest dogs in their areas. So now my fundraiser is continuing nationwide, and I have a web page to tell other people how to organize a fundraiser like the one that I did.

Knowing that more and more dogs are being protected is really rewarding. It has made all my efforts more than worth it.

Then, one day after school, my mom told me that the Society for the Prevention of Cruelty to Animals (SPCA) wanted to honor me for the work that I had done to protect police dogs. They invited my mom and me to New York so that I could receive an award and a check for five thousand dollars! That vested another ten dogs!

I'm so proud and happy that the money I have raised is all going to the dogs. I'm still amazed that I have vested so many dogs when I really wasn't sure if I could vest even one. Even though some days I was tired from schoolwork, I knew it was important to continue fundraising to help save these special dogs. It was a lot of hard work but I learned that if you just keep going, you can accomplish anything. Don't think that just because you are a kid that you can't make a difference. Even if you think something is impossible, it can be done.

— Stephanie Taylor, 11 —

If I Could Change the World for the Better, I Would...

Follow your dreams and use your natural born talents
and skills to make this a better world for tomorrow.
~Paul Watson

Eliminate every manmade weapon and all war. I would make sure that everyone treats each other equally.

Lance Bass, *NSYNC

Find one positive thing that everyone in the world could believe in. Prove to everyone there is a common ground in all people, no matter what race, color, sex, faith, rich or poor. Bring people a little closer together, and remind them we're all the same. Just try to make it through life as human beings, and remember that every life is just as important as the next.

J. C. Chasez, *NSYNC

Have free ice cream breaks for everybody. I would have children have more say-so in the world, and ban all guns and drugs.

Joey Fatone Jr., *NSYNC

Put a smile on everyone's face.

Chris Kirkpatrick, *NSYNC

End racism and make equality for men and women. I would teach life through music.

Justin Timberlake, *NSYNC

Melt every cold heart and mold them into new warm ones.

Scarlett Kotlarczyk, 11

Help people realize that people like me who learn and do things differently than them are still really the same underneath it all. We want to be liked and smiled at.

Wilson Cook, 9

Find another way to test drugs instead of using them on animals.

Brandon Barger, 13

Make it so every kid would have a warm meal, and no one would go starving.

Timothy Blevans, 11

Open a house for all of the orphans of the world. I would get lots of people to help me take care of them.

Stacey Bergman, 15

Stop kids from making fun of other kids. Prejudice is just what we don't need. Kids hate being ridiculed.

Rachel Force, 11

Make people realize that it's not what other people think of you, but what you think of yourself. You shouldn't put yourself down when people say cruel things about you or do things to you, because they're the ones that need a little chicken soup for their soul.

Sarah Hampton, 14

Travel back in time, and make sure the people who invented drugs and smoking never discovered or invented them.

Lisa Cline, 11

Find a cure for diabetes. My little brother's friend has juvenile diabetes. Every year my family "Walks for the Cure." I wish there wasn't such a disease because he has to take shots and stuff.

Kristin Boden, 13

Want everyone to keep an open mind about everything, because with an open mind, you can accomplish anything.

Annemarie Staley, 14

Make everything solar powered including factories, vehicles and all types of machinery. By doing this, there wouldn't be as much air pollution and people could breathe easier.

Tracye Paye, 13

Give every child a grandmother like mine. She may not be rich and famous, but she has enough love in her heart for her twenty-one grandchildren and great-grandchildren, and plenty more to spare. How many millionaires can say that?

Casey Singleton, 18

Make it so that kids don't have to go through child abuse.

Kristen Hamilton, 11

Make every capable person do one hour of community service per month. This would include cleaning up rubbish, bathing and feeding homeless people, and planting trees.

Trevor Burton, 19

Make sure that no one in the world is harmed because of their religion.

Pratima Neti, 11

Stop child labor, which is unfortunately still going on in this world. Children deserve the right to live, and working at a very young age will not give you that freedom.

Jessilyn Yoo, 12

Pay teachers more, because teachers are the foundation of all learning. Without teachers, the world would just be a useless space full of useless people.

Angela Rotchstein, 14

Make sure that everybody in the world is able to read. Reading is the world's greatest gift for the mind and imagination.

Jessica Behles, 14

Have everybody just agree to disagree instead of fighting. After all, we are all different, and have our own ways; this is the spice of life.

Jill Ananda, 14

Plant the rainforests back all over the world, so that the trees will grow and the rivers will flow. I would bring back the animals that have died out, but without the dinosaurs!

Kyla Cangemi, 10

Make the world a happier place with no bombings or school shootings.

Chap Arst, 13

Show everyone the love that my adoptive mother showed me. I was angry at the world because I thought no one loved me or could ever love me. No one wanted a thirteen-year-old girl, but she came along and showed me that people could and do care about me. I would definitely give that to any person in this world. Love is all the world needs.

Mia Sifford, 17

Give every child a blanket, not only to keep them warm, but to snuggle with. We each need something to hold onto, and a fuzzy blanket would help keep away the problems of the world, if only for a moment or two.

Steve Hayden, 13

Let all the kids in the whole world know that they can succeed in anything that they put their heart into. There is always a solution for problems; you just have to look in your heart to find them.

Alysia Escalante, 13

Fix that hole in the ozone layer so the heat of the sun won't kill us.

Nikole Pegues, 11

Ask everyone in school to say one nice thing to another person every day. Have every family tell each other they love one another.

William Baun, 12

Have people talk to each other and listen more, and make sure that everybody would have enough play time.

Neil Gogno, 9

Stop all the violence that is on TV, which is where people get the idea that it is okay to hurt or kill someone. When we were channel surfing, my stepmom and I saw seven guns and three acts of violence all in one minute; even my dog got scared!

Bethany Hicks, 12

Want everyone to have at least one best friend that they could count on.

Andrea Hawsey, 11

Create vehicles that would run on natural resource waste material to stop the pollution.

Rosie Huf, 11

Get more clubs and activities going so that people would stay away from gangs, drugs and crimes.

Stacy Luebbe, 14

Bring back all our lost loved ones for a day.

Rita Koch, 10

Make sure that all children in the world can go to school and have *Chicken Soup for the Soul* books so they know that they aren't alone.

Allison Opsitnick, 12

A Run to Remember

Thirteen was a challenging age for me. Not only did I have to adapt to my changing body but I also had to deal with my parents' bitter divorce, a new family and the upsetting move from my country home to a crowded suburb.

When we moved, my beloved companion, a small brown pony, had to be sold. I was trashed. Feeling helpless and alone, I couldn't eat or sleep, and I cried all the time. I missed my family, my home and my pony. Finally, my father, realizing how much I missed my pony, purchased an old red gelding for me at a local auction.

Cowboy was without a doubt the ugliest horse in the world. He was pigeon-toed and knock-kneed. But I didn't care about his faults. I loved him beyond all reason.

I joined a riding club and endured rude comments and mean snickers about Cowboy's looks. I never let on about how I felt, but deep down inside, my heart was breaking. The other members rode beautiful registered horses.

When Cowboy and I entered the events where the horse is judged on appearance, we were quickly "shown the gate." No amount of grooming, vitamins or unconditional love would turn Cowboy into a beauty. I finally realized that my only chance to compete would be in the timed-speed events. I chose barrel racing.

One girl named Becky rode a big brown thoroughbred mare in the race events. She always won the blue ribbons. Needless to say, she didn't feel threatened when I competed against her at the next show. She didn't need to. I came in next to last.

The stinging memory of Becky's smirks made me determined to

beat her. For the whole next month I woke up early every day and rode Cowboy five miles to the arena. We practiced for hours in the hot sun and then I would walk Cowboy home. On the way home I would be so tired, those five miles seemed twice as long.

All of our hard work didn't make me feel confident by the time the show came. I sat at the gate and sweated it out while I watched Becky and her horse charge through the pattern of barrels, acing the course with ease.

My turn finally came. As I nudged Cowboy forward he stumbled, and almost fell, much to the delight of the other riders. I jammed my hat down on my head, stroked Cowboy's big red neck and entered the arena. At the signal, we dashed toward the first barrel, quickly whipped around it and with perfect precision rounded the second and thundered on to the third. We tore around the final curve and shot for the finish line.

No cheers filled the air. The end of our run was met with surprised silence. With the sound of my heart pounding in my ears, I heard the announcer call our time. Cowboy and I had beaten Becky and her fancy thoroughbred by a full two seconds!

I gained much more than a blue ribbon that day. At thirteen, I realized that no matter what the odds, I'd always come out a winner if I wanted something badly enough to work for it. I can be the master of my own destiny.

—Barbara L. Glenn—

Shining Down

You must be the change you wish to see in the world.
~Gandhi

One dark morning while driving to work, my dad, Clayton Kavalinas, swerved to avoid a deer in the road. His car skidded on black ice, hit a guardrail, and spun into an oncoming truck. He died in the crash. He was only thirty-five years old. Streetlights could have helped prevent the accident, but there were no lights on that stretch of highway called the Marquis of Lorne Trail on the outskirts of Calgary, Canada.

I was only eleven when he died. I was devastated over the loss of my father, especially when I realized that his death could have been avoided. In a two-year period, my father and one other driver were killed, and twenty-nine accidents happened on that area of the highway. Time and again I thought, *How can I find a way to make my dad's short life really count?*

I felt triumphant when I figured out what I could do. I decided that I would try to get some lights put up in that area to help other drivers see better.

Once I figured out what I had to do, I fought as hard as I could to get new lights on that road. But I didn't realize what a big deal that would be! I was determined and very motivated. I didn't want what happened to my father to happen to anyone else.

I was studying government in school, and I tried to find a way to increase public pressure on city hall to install lights. With help from my classmates, I handed out flyers at homes and shopping malls, and obtained over three hundred signatures on the petition needed to grab the attention of the politicians in charge of road safety issues. I contacted them, too, and told them what I was trying to do. I was pretty amazed when some of the politicians actually listened to a kid! Finally, there was a meeting at city hall about the need for new lights.

Before the meeting, the local media found out what I was trying to do and reported on the problem. The reporters helped people in the area "see the light" and acknowledge the danger on Marquis of Lorne Trail.

With TV, radio stations and newspapers covering it, more people understood why lights were needed. They also learned what it was like for a child to lose a father. A lot of people told me they were touched and they decided to help. The public pressure began to grow and within four months from the morning my dad lost his life on that highway, the city council agreed to spend $290,000 for new lights.

Sometimes, going through the accident over and over, in order to make a point, was a hard thing to do emotionally. At times, I had hard nights and I cried. But at other times, I'd be really happy and proud that my dad's life was the one that made the difference in helping to save many other lives from fatal accidents.

I was never so proud in my life as I was one September day nearly a year after I lost my dad. Speaking through a walkie-talkie at the side of the road, I gave a city worker instructions to turn on the lights for the first time. During the same lighting ceremony, I was given a plaque from the City of Calgary honoring me for my public service efforts. Since then, the number of collisions on Marquis of Lorne Trail has been drastically reduced.

While helping many people I'll never even meet, I think I also helped my mother, my younger brother, Shaun, and my little sister, Kaitlin, become more determined to continue to enjoy life. I helped lift their spirits, and they were there to support me. We all cried together. We all laughed together. We all thought about life together. My dad's death brought us closer together as a family, making something positive come out of the situation and helping to ease our grief.

But it was really my dad who ended up teaching me a lot about determination, courage and faith. In his own way, through this project, he helped me grow up. I learned that if you're determined, if you put your heart into something, you can overcome any obstacle. You can accomplish anything.

Life goes on now. The cameras have stopped filming and the civic leaders focus on other problems. But the streetlights will always be there to help me get through difficult times.

I know that I'll always be reminded of the terrible accident and I'll still suffer grief from losing my dad, but I gain comfort knowing that area of the highway is now a safer place. I feel my dad's presence there. I'll always have the comfort of knowing that every night, a little bit of Dad is shining down.

— Michael Kavalinas, 16, as told by Monte Stewart —

Dreams

*They say a person needs just three things to be truly
happy in this world. Someone to love, something to do
and something to hope for.*
~Tom Bodett

When I was three years old, I slept on a very small bed in a large room with twenty-five other boys and girls in an orphanage in Hungary. Being the youngest boy in the building, I got picked on often because I was the smallest. My sister, Kristin, protected me when she could, but the older boys were really mean to me. Kristin and I had been taken from our birth mother when we were only babies because she couldn't take care of us.

When I was about one year old, Kristin and I were taken in by a lady who became our foster mom. We thought we'd found a home and had really grown to love her, when about a year and a half later, she decided she couldn't afford to keep us any longer. She told us that she was taking us to the orphanage for a visit, but she never came back to pick us up.

We had lived in the orphanage again for about six months by the time Christmas came. None of us got any presents at all. I had only a few clothes of my own and no toys. We got two meals a day but the bread was hard and the food was terrible. I had one good friend at the orphanage named Attila, and we used to talk a lot about what it would be like to have somebody come and take us away from there.

Our dream was to have a real family and do things that most other kids did. I had never even gone swimming or seen a movie in my life. Sometimes Attila, Kristin and I watched the only show they had on television, which was *Teenage Mutant Ninja Turtles*.

Two or three times, people came to the orphanage and talked to my sister Kristin and me, but they never came back to see us again.

One day, this pretty lady with big hair and a big man with glasses came to see Kristin and me. We couldn't understand what they were saying, but the Hungarian girl who was with them told us that they had come from a faraway place called America. We spent a lot of time with them that day, and I told Attila what a good time I had.

They came back to see us every day for a week and took us for ice cream and long walks. The Hungarian girl told us that the man and lady wanted to adopt us and take us back with them to America. We were so excited and happy.

When I told Attila what was going to happen, he was very sad and didn't want us to leave him there. I told him he should ask the big man if he would take him so that he could come to America and be my brother. The next time the man and lady came, he jumped up into the man's lap and asked him if he could come with us. But, since the man didn't speak Hungarian, he didn't know what Attila wanted and just smiled at him.

Kristin and I flew on a great big jet plane to America. Things look very different but wonderful here. All the food tastes great, and I have my own room with a big bed and lots of clothes. I got a stuffed animal of my very own: my first toy.

Everyone was really nice, and our neighbors even gave each of us something called a bicycle. It didn't take long for me to learn to ride. Christmas came and there were lots of boxes under the tree for Kristin and me. America is a great place and I am very happy here.

After a year, we went with a group of kids to a special ceremony where we were made citizens of the United States! After the ceremony, two men with a TV camera came and asked us questions about what life was like in Hungary. That night we were on television like the

Ninja Turtles!

I hope that Attila got to see us and I wonder if he knows that dreams really can come true.

—Ryan Kelly, 10—

Friendship

When you are sad I will dry your tears
When you are scared I will ease your fears

When you are worried I will give you hope
If you want to give up I'll help you cope

When you're lost and can't see the light
I'll be your beacon shining so bright

This is my oath that I pledge to the end
Why you may ask?

Because you're my friend.

—Nicole Ritchie, 15—

The Code Word

Friendship is a sheltering tree.
~Samuel Taylor Coleridge

I was talking to some friends while standing in line in the cafeteria at my middle school. As I started to share a funny story about my weekend, my friend Elizabeth interrupted me. "Coco! Coco!" She called out. All my friends laughed. Elizabeth said it again louder and looked around to see how many other kids had heard her. Everyone laughed again. This is so weird, I thought.

Elizabeth was one of the girls that everyone wanted to be friends with. She always had the nicest clothes and told the funniest jokes. She seemed to have everything. I felt lucky to be friends with her.

Later that day, as we waited for algebra class to start, I tried to finish telling the story I started sharing at lunch. Before I even said two sentences, Elizabeth interrupted again. "Coco," she said, grinning at our classmates. Everyone laughed again.

Over the next week, every time I opened my mouth around Elizabeth, she interrupted me with that same word. I never wanted to ask what "Coco" meant. I assumed it was a code word for a cute boy or a word she wasn't allowed to say. I didn't want to be left out, so I started using the word too. Elizabeth thought it was hilarious when I interrupted someone else's story with our new code word. And since I wanted her to like me, I did it even more. Even though I still wasn't sure what it meant.

In the school library, I heard two girls whispering to one another. I called out "Coco" and everyone laughed. It was fun having everyone laugh at my joke.

Although I felt lucky to be friends with Elizabeth, I noticed that she often said bad things about other kids. "Did you see Tara's hair today?" She'd say. Or "Jessica wore those jeans yesterday, and I'm pretty sure her shoes are from Walmart." I would've never said those things about someone, but I laughed when Elizabeth said them.

One day, Sara, a classmate since grade school, stopped by my locker. We'd never been that close, but we had a lot of mutual friends and she had always been nice to me. But now, Sara looked uncomfortable as she asked, "Julia, do you know why Elizabeth started saying 'Coco' all the time?"

I shook my head. "I don't know, but I really wish I did."

Sara sighed. "It means she thinks you're being annoying. A few days ago, when you left our lunch table early, she told the rest of us that you were bothering her when you told stories. She said she wanted a code word that she could use without you knowing she was talking about you. I know it's really mean, and the rest of us shouldn't have gone along with it. I'm really sorry."

My eyes filled with tears. I couldn't believe it. The girl who I was breaking my back to be friends with was talking about me behind mine. I remembered how many times I'd used the word myself just to fit in, and it made me feel even worse. I wondered if the whole school thought I was annoying, just like Elizabeth did. I was mortified.

I woke up the next day with a pit in my stomach. I'd decided not to speak if Elizabeth was around. That way, I couldn't annoy her. But she still used her code word multiple times. People laughed and then immediately looked at me. I tried to keep a neutral facial expression, so nobody would know how much it bothered me, but inside, I was crushed.

The next morning, I packed my lunch so I wouldn't have to wait in line with Elizabeth. But by lunch time, she'd used the word so many times that I knew I couldn't sit with her. I searched the cafeteria, looking for a friendly face. I saw Macy, a girl who used to be part of my friend group but had stopped hanging out with us a few weeks ago. She was sitting with two girls who were in my English class and had always seemed nice. Nervously, I walked to their table and asked if I could sit with them.

Immediately, all three of them smiled. "Of course," Macy said.

I sat down and opened my lunch bag, praying that Macy and the other girls didn't know about Coco.

"You know Elizabeth is a jerk, right?" Macy said.

My heart dropped. They knew. Did they think I was annoying too? Before I could respond, Macy said, "Elizabeth does things like that to a lot of people. She's a bully, and I got tired of it. That's why I stopped hanging out with you guys." She smiled. "You didn't deserve to be treated that way, and nobody else does either."

I thought of all the times I'd laughed when Elizabeth had made fun of someone else. It only bothered me when she turned her mean streak on me.

"You're right, Macy," I said. "I should have stood up to her a long time ago."

Moments later, I felt a tap on my shoulder. I turned around to see Sara holding her lunch tray. "Can I sit over here too?" She asked. "Because I'm sure Elizabeth would make fun of me next."

We welcomed Sara to the table. I smiled at my new friends and then told them the funny thing my little brother had done the night before. They all laughed, and no one interrupted with a mean code word. I felt better than I had in days.

Middle school is a tough time for almost everyone. Most kids are trying to figure out who they are and who they want to be. It's easy to go along with the crowd, even when you know it's not the right thing to do. It took a bully turning her sights on me to teach me that I wanted to be kind more than I wanted to be popular.

The word "Coco" will always serve as a reminder that I need to stay true to myself and never compromise my values to be friends with someone. Because with the right friends, I won't have to.

—Julia Sonntag—

School Blues

The best things in life aren't things...
they're your friends.
~Author Unknown

When I was in third grade, my mom and I would walk to school every morning. The walk was short because the school is right next to my house. Mom would say goodbye and my day would start.

First, I would talk to my friends. Then we would go into class and begin our school day. Throughout the day I would play football with my friends and do schoolwork. The teachers were nice. My friends were nice, playful, and funny. I loved school.

Then COVID-19 hit. We did Zoom meetings for the rest of the year. It was not fun because I could not see my friends in person. Zoom was hard because I'm not really good with computers. I had trouble logging in sometimes. Sometimes I would get kicked off. I did not learn a lot on Zoom. I felt like I was getting really bad at most of the school subjects. I felt angry and frustrated. I feel like my teachers felt bad, too.

When the new school year started and we learned it was going to be Zoom school again, my parents pulled me out of Zoom school and homeschooled me instead.

I was happy because I didn't like Zoom and I liked that the schedule would be more flexible. During homeschool, I could go to school in my pajamas. I had my puppies with me. We even went on fun field trips. One of my favorite field trips was going to Lotusland, an amazing botanic garden in Santa Barbara. I also got to go to Calico Ghost Town, where I learned about the largest silver mining town in California. But sometimes, my mom and I fought because it was weird having her as my teacher and my mom. It felt strange. I wished my mom could just be my mom.

Toward the end, I got mad and sad that school started part-time, in-person learning and I couldn't be with my friends. The rule was that if you had switched to homeschooling you couldn't switch back to part-time going to school. My house is right next to the school, so I could hear my friends laugh and play from the other side of the fence. Sometimes, I would go over to the fence and talk to them. My friends were sad that I wasn't there with them too.

Then things changed. My school would be going back to full-time, in person learning. I would be going back in one week!

I was happy but going back to school felt a little weird. At first it was hard waking up early again. It had been over a year since I'd been in real school. But my first day back was super fun! It was so nice to see my friends again. The schoolwork was different than home school. It felt easier.

I've been back in school for a while. In the end I feel like I learned more in home school than real school, but I like real school better because I can see my friends. And now, my mom can just be my mom.

— Elijah LoMonaco —

Just Trying to Fit In

You attract the right things when you
have a sense of who you are.
~Amy Poehler

I had just gotten out of elementary school and was about to enter middle school. I was so excited to become a big kid, but I also knew I would miss my old school on the first day. I wasn't going to be walking into the same school, with the same friends and same teachers.

I thought I was ready for the change, though. I had a couple of friends who would be at my new school — my best friend, and my neighbor. I would be fine.

When I walked into school that first day, I was nervous. The teachers seemed really busy all the time, nothing like my other teachers. The schedule was so hard to figure out, and it was a huge change.

A couple of days in, I noticed quickly that the movies were kind of true about the cliques. There were so many cliques. If you didn't belong to one, then you were by yourself, or you had a small group. Some cliques were mean. I would get dirty looks if I walked by.

I soon realized my neighbor was "popular." She was part of that clique. She had her friends from elementary school, and I sat with them. They were nice but I liked sitting with my best friend. My neighbor kept inviting me to sit with her and her friends, but I knew I would hurt my best friend's feelings if I left her.

A part of me didn't want to be popular, but the other half couldn't help it. So, I sat with my neighbor. I soon noticed that when you sit in "the group," everyone is so nice. I made so many friends that I felt accepted. But I felt guilty for leaving my best friend to sit with the popular clique, so I invited her to sit with me. She left all her other friends and joined me in my new group. Then she changed very quickly. She dressed differently, she acted differently, and she talked differently. She got popular fast.

We slowly started to separate, and I stopped sitting with those girls. I couldn't go back to my old group because they were mad at me, and so I was forced to be alone. I tried making friends, but I felt it was impossible. I would be judged no matter what I did. I held back my tears walking around school. I would go without eating just so I didn't have to sit alone and look weird.

My neighbor had taught me the "rules" of being popular: how I should get a boyfriend, where I should shop, what I should say, and what I should stop doing. I just couldn't take it anymore. I talked to my mom about it and she told me "just be you." I thought that I was but I think she knew better. She knew how hard it was. One day after school, she gave me this tiny turtle charm. She told me, "Whenever you feel lonely, and you need a hug and I'm not there, you can look at your turtle and know that I love you and I am with you." It helped me a lot.

I did meet some new friends, but I wasn't myself around them. I changed myself. I'm in high school now and I'm not friends with half of those people. Now I do the opposite of what my neighbor told me to do to be "popular" because who cares? I'm the happiest I've been in a long time. I have amazing friends now who I met in eighth grade. I know they won't leave me because I'm my own person again.

I try hard to be the opposite of who I started to be in middle school. I was so mean to people when I was popular. I would strive to make people feel bad about themselves for walking alone; now I realize that just made me an ugly person. I learned that it's better to just be yourself and not care about what everyone wants you to be. Being who you want to be is so much better.

— Frances-Amelia Spadoni —

Coming Back to Seattle

*A friend is someone who gives you total freedom
to be yourself.*
~Jim Morrison

I've moved more times than I can count. Well, I can count them, but the exact number doesn't matter so let's just say I've moved a lot. With all these different homes, I've also gone to plenty of schools. I've met thousands of people with thousands of personalities at the different schools I have attended, but I never thought I'd meet my best friend at a school with less than three hundred kids.

Now, that's not to say I was bad at making friends; I wasn't. I'd like to say it came with the territory of moving a lot, but I've come to think I have some natural ability to make people like me. If there was a friend-making league, I would probably be the best player who got all the deals and sponsorships. I was friendly with everybody. Having all these "friends" helped me realize what a real friend looks like and, so far, I've only had one.

I met Dallas in first grade. I remember that first day at our parochial school, I was so stressed because I had enrolled halfway through the year and I wasn't fully caught up with everything. I remember keeping to myself for the first day, but on the second day, it was game on. I was pulling out all the stops. The first interaction that I remember was in the cafeteria. I remember looking up and seeing him; he saw me looking and stared back. I immediately realized what was going on, this was the proving ground; either you win the staring contest, or you live in shame forever. The staring contest lasted about ten seconds, and Dallas blinked first. I'd like to say the whole cafeteria exploded in cheers, but it wasn't that dramatic. In reality, Dallas and I both started laughing. We talked a bit after that.

Over the next three and a half years, my classmates, Dallas, and I grew closer as friends. The school had only 300 kids at the time. This was good because the education was amazing and most of the students stayed at the school from kindergarten to eighth grade. This made the whole school a small little community because everybody knew each other. But sadly, all good things must come to an end, and in 2017 my family and I moved to California.

In California, I went to three schools from fifth to seventh grade. I played basketball, went vegan, and a bunch of other things, but, over those three and a half years I spent in California, Dallas was the only person to reach out to me from my old school. Now, over the years, I've learned a lesson about friendship that means a lot to me. The phone works both ways. Dallas proved himself with a single text asking me how I'd been. Now it wasn't just me texting him, but him caring enough to message me sometimes. Almost four years later, the best news came. My family and I were moving back to Washington State! I was so happy because I could go back to school with Dallas.

A few months after the announcement we moved back. It was during the summer, so I had time to prepare. I only told Dallas I was back because I wanted to surprise the rest of the class. The first month of school was online because of COVID-19, but since the school was so small, we were able to return to in class learning faster than most schools.

During the four years I was away the school had gone down to 150 kids and was planning to shut down the next year. This meant we would be the final graduating class. I felt like the chosen one! I was very hyped, and my expectations were high. I'd learned we would have only seven kids, all boys I knew, in our class. When I arrived, I expected that when everybody saw me, they would smile and gather around for a bunch of high fives or something. Sadly, this isn't what happened. When I got there only Dallas and a boy named Anthony acted like they cared.

It was as if I wasn't a long-lost friend who came back after four years away in a different state. I thought maybe they were just tired, and they would be better the next day. I was half right. The next day they had better attitudes, but they were completely different people than I remembered. Over time I realized some of them were homophobic, transphobic, used racial slurs, and did a bunch of other bad things.

Lately, I've been hanging out with Dallas and playing basketball with Anthony, and when they hang out with the others I just chill alone. Next year I am going to high school, so I will have more choices of friends. I look forward to the hundreds of new experiences I will have and the many new friends I will make.

— Kobe Williams —

A Bossy Friend

Never dull your shine for somebody else.
~Tyra Banks

I first met Claire in second grade. We were best friends and we'd get in trouble for talking to each other during class.

Once we moved to third grade things started to change. We were no longer in the same class and I almost never got in trouble. At lunch I still saw Claire across the room, but we did not talk as much.

In fourth grade I was in Claire's class and once again we talked and got in trouble but not as much. At lunch Claire and I would talk with some other friends but if I started a conversation that Claire didn't like she would slap me. If I didn't go and get her something she wanted like a fork or spoon she would slap me. Eventually I got used to her slapping me; we both just laughed about it.

During the summer after fourth grade I had playdates with Claire. As per usual if I said something she didn't like she would say, "Kenedi! We are not doing that." And then she would slap me.

I am in fifth grade now and am homeschooled. I still see Claire on occasion. The week before my November birthday I was on my iPad talking to Claire on Facetime and I told her that I was going to have a Baby Yoda party. I thought she would have loved the idea but I was completely wrong. She screamed at me that I stole her idea and that she wanted to have a Baby Yoda party. I wanted so badly to tell her she wasn't the only one who could have a Baby Yoda party but as usual I kept my mouth shut.

I still have not stuck up for myself, but I plan on doing it next time I see her. I finally have the guts to stick up for myself.

— Kenedi Morgado —

The Forgotten Friend

*Friendship without self-interest is one of the rare
and beautiful things of life.*
~James Francis Byrnes

I t was my tenth birthday — double digits — and I would have the biggest party ever. The guest list, which I kept at the back of my homework assignment folder, began with a few close friends. But in the two weeks before that special Friday night, it had quickly grown from seven girls to a whopping total of seventeen. Nearly every girl in my fifth-grade class had been invited to sleep over at my house for a big celebration. I was especially happy when each guest I invited excitedly accepted the invitation. It would be a night of scary stories, pizza and lots of presents. But as I later realized, I would truly treasure only one gift I received that night.

The family room was a flurry of shouts and bursts of laughter. We had just finished a game of *Twister* and were lining up for the limbo when the doorbell rang. I hardly paid attention to who might be at the door. What did it matter, really? Everyone I liked from school was there, in my family room, preparing to lean under the stick held by my two sisters.

"Judy, come here for a minute," Mom called from the front door.

I rolled my eyes and shrugged to my friends as if to say, *Now who would dare bother me at a time like this?* What I really wanted to say was, *It's tough being popular!*

I rounded the bend toward the front door, then stopped. I know my mouth dropped open and I could feel my face turning red, for there on the front porch stood Sarah Westly — the quiet girl who sat next to me in music class — and she was holding a gift.

I thought about the growing list in the back of my assignment folder. *How had I forgotten to invite Sarah?*

I remembered that I only added a name to the list when someone had shown an interest in me (like kids do when they know someone is having a party and they don't want to be left out). But Sarah had never done that. Never once had she asked me about my birthday party. Never once did she squeeze into the circle of kids surrounding me at lunch time. And once she even helped me carry my backpack while I lugged my science project to our third-floor classroom.

I guess I had forgotten to invite her simply because she wasn't pushing to be invited. I accepted the gift from Sarah and asked her to join the party.

"I can't stay," she said, looking down. "My dad's waiting in the car."

"Can you come in for a little while?" I nearly begged. By now I felt pretty bad about forgetting to invite her and really did want her to stay.

"Thanks, but I have to go," she said, turning toward the door. "See you Monday."

I stood in the foyer with Sarah's gift in my hands and an empty feeling in my heart.

I didn't open the gift until hours after the party had ended. Hours after the games, the food, the ghost stories, the pillow fights, the pranks on those first to fall asleep and the snores.

Inside the small box was a ceramic tabby cat about three inches tall with its tail in the air. In my mind, it was the best gift I had received, even though I was never really into cats. I later found out that the figurine looked exactly like Sarah's cat, Seymour.

I didn't know it then, but now I realize that Sarah was my one true childhood friend. While the other girls drifted away, Sarah was always there for me, ever loyal and supportive. She was an unconditional friend who stood by me, always encouraging and understanding me.

Although I'll always feel bad about forgetting her, I also realize that I might not have discovered Sarah as a friend had I remembered to invite her to that unforgettable tenth birthday party.

—Judith Burnett Schneider—

Backfire!

*Actions, not words, are the true criterion
of the attachment of friends.*
~George Washington

I t was spring at last. The sun was high in a cloudless sky. Birds sang. Flowers bloomed. Best of all, it was Saturday — a perfect day to be out playing with friends. The problem was, we'd only been in town two months so I hadn't made any friends. My family moved a lot. It's hard when you're always the new kid on the block.

So, here I was, stuck with my baby brother John and Mary, the new sitter, while Mom and Dad were out of town on business. It was not going to be a fun day!

Just as we started lunch, the phone rang. I hopped up to answer it. "Hello, Morrells' residence. Lou speaking."

"Hi, Lou. It's Alicia."

My heart did a rapid pit-a-pat-pat. "Alicia Whitman?"

She giggled. "You know another Alicia?"

"No." There was only one Alicia: the most popular, prettiest, richest girl in my class.

"I called to invite you over to my house this afternoon. We can ride my horse."

"Hang on. I'll ask." Heart racing, I ran to the kitchen. "Mary, can I go play with my friend Alicia this afternoon?"

Mary was trying to scoop peas off the floor faster than my brother dropped them. "Where does she live?"

"Only a few blocks from here," I said, picturing the fancy brick house that we passed on our way home from school. I held my breath.

"Would your mom let you go?"

"Sure, she would. Please, Mary. Please, please, please."

John dumped the whole dish from his highchair.

"Oh, all right," Mary said with a sigh.

I rushed back to the phone. "Alicia, I can come. What time?"

"One o'clock?"

"Great. See ya then."

I was so excited I could hardly breathe. I was going to hang out with Alicia Whitman! Ride her horse. Every girl in class wanted to be Alicia's friend.

"Come eat your lunch," Mary called.

"I'm not hungry. I have to get ready."

I chose my outfit very carefully: my best shorts, clean T-shirt and brand-new shoes. I even washed my face and combed the tangles out of my hair. When I was satisfied, I called, "I'm going now, Mary."

I set off. The sun beat down on my back and bounced off the sidewalk. Cars and trucks swished by on the highway. I didn't care about the heat or the noise. I was too busy daydreaming about the possibility of becoming good friends with Alicia. I'd liked Alicia from the first day. We were a lot alike. We both loved to read. Our hands were the first up to answer questions. We mostly got A's. We both liked to play sports, although Alicia was always picked first and me last. And we both were horse-crazy. I just knew we could be best friends — if we had a chance.

The sidewalk stretched on forever and ever. It hadn't seemed this far in the car! My shirt was getting sweaty and one heel in my new shoes hurt like crazy. I stopped and pulled down my sock. A big, fat blister had bubbled up. *Youch!* I kept going, walking on my tippytoes. *It couldn't be that much farther now, could it?*

Several blocks later, across the highway, I saw the meadow with Alicia's horse, Buttercup, in it. Now all I had to do was cross four lanes of traffic. I sure hoped I wasn't late!

Cars and trucks whizzed past me. I waited the longest time for a break. When it came, I made a mad dash to the other side. *Whew!*

I was there.

The Whitman house was surrounded by big, old trees. The cool shade felt wonderful. I smoothed my hair and my shorts. My mouth was dry. I hoped Alicia would offer me a cold drink right away. I walked up to the front door and rang the bell.

No one answered.

I rang again, then knocked. No one came to the door.

Maybe they were out back? I walked around on the brick walk. There were no cars in the driveway. No one on the fancy rock terrace either. I knocked on the back door.

Nobody came.

Alicia's tree house was empty, too. I climbed up to check. Except for Buttercup, the whole place was deserted!

I couldn't believe it. *Had I heard Alicia wrong? Didn't she say today? Why would she invite me and leave? Maybe she'd gone to pick me up?* That was it! Alicia didn't walk to school or ride the bus. A shiny black car brought her and was waiting when school was out. She wouldn't expect me to walk all the way out here. We'd just missed each other.

Happily, I went back and sat on the front steps. I waited and waited and waited. It got later and later. No Alicia. No Whitmans. Nobody came.

I sat there with my head in my hands, growing more disappointed and confused by the minute. I finally decided that Alicia wasn't coming, so I got up and trudged home. I was ashamed of myself. I'd been so hungry for a friend that I'd fallen for her mean trick.

By Monday morning my shame had turned to anger. Being pretty and popular didn't give someone the right to trick people! I spotted Alicia on the playground, surrounded by the usual group of girls. I pushed my way into the circle. "What you did was mean, Alicia Whitman. I don't want to be your friend, now or ever!" I stomped away.

"Wait!" Alicia cried. "What did I do?"

Right there, in front of God and all her friends, I told her.

Alicia was shaking her head. "I didn't call you, Lou. It wasn't me. We were out of town all weekend."

Someone giggled and said, "Miss Brainiac got fooled."

I ignored the name-caller. "Then who called me, Alicia? Who played that dirty trick?"

Alicia looked around the group. Her gaze stopped on Morgan, who was trying to hide the fact that she was laughing to herself. "It was a dirty trick, Lou. I don't know who did it — for sure. But that person's no friend of mine."

Morgan turned bright red. "It was just a joke. Can't you take a joke, Lou?"

"Some jokes aren't funny. Right, you guys?" Alicia said, taking my arm.

Everyone nodded and closed in behind Alicia and me. Morgan's hurtful joke backfired. We all walked away, leaving *her* standing alone on the playground.

— Lou Kassem —

Best Friends

I thought she was my best friend
The best one I've ever had
Instead I found out the truth
And what I learned was sad.

We still call each other friends
But I feel we're far apart
Though we see each other every day
I have a broken heart.

She has made new friends
And I have made some, too.
We are talking less and less
And inside I'm cold and blue.

Each and every night I pray
That she will finally see
How much I want our friendship back
And how much she means to me.

—Whitney M. Baldwin, 12 —

My Big Solo

The day had finally arrived: the day of my big solo. Everyone was there; my mom and dad and my little brother. Uncle Scott and Auntie Tammy had even picked up my grandma from the nursing home so she wouldn't miss the big event.

And it was a big event: the Spring Fling Choir Concert. The whole class was dressed up and I had on a new dress that went on sale just in time for the event.

My name was on the cover of the program in bright yellow with a daisy chain drawn around it. "Cindy Hamond… Soloist."

I couldn't believe it when I saw my name. Not that it was my name, but that it wasn't Renee Swanson's.

Renee and I had been classmates since kindergarten. She was always wherever I was and she was always ahead of me.

Dance-class recital needs a big finish? Renee was picked.

Selling Girl Scout cookies? "Oh, I'm sorry," the lady at the front door would say. "I just bought twenty boxes from Renee Swanson. Such a nice girl." *Yeah, whatever.*

Softball? She played first base while I watched her from my position in the outfield.

And the school plays? Renee would have the leads while I was cast as her mother or sister or neighbor. I even played her dog once.

The only time I ever came in ahead of Renee was at roll call. Hamond comes before Swanson. Every time! Believe me, I count that as a victory!

The day of the choir concert tryouts was nerve-wracking. We waited in the library while Ms. Jenkins called us one at a time into the choir room.

When Ms. Jenkins got to the H's, my heart sped up each time she came to the door. By the time she actually called my name, my whole body was shaking.

When I came back to the library, Renee smiled at me. Ms. Jenkins called her name and Renee calmly followed her. She was still calm and smiling when her tryout was over.

When Ms. Jenkins made the announcement at the end of the week of who had made the special choral group, I wasn't surprised when Renee's name was on her list and mine wasn't. "So," I said under my breath, "what else is new?"

Sudden clapping brought me out of my sulking. Everyone was looking at me. *I've missed something here,* I thought.

Ms. Jenkins beamed down at me and said, "Cindy, you will have to start practicing with me during your study halls. The solos take extra preparation."

Solo? I got the solo? I glanced over at Renee. She grinned and gave me the thumbs-up sign. Oh, that's another thing. She is always *so* nice.

Now the day had come. We filed onto the stage and took our places. I was front and center. Ms. Jenkins raised her baton and we began to sing. I could see my mother leaning forward in her seat, her camera already flashing for pictures. My dad was smiling and winking at me.

My big moment was here. The spotlight flicked over me and then circled me in its bright light. Ms. Jenkins nodded and pointed her baton at me. That baton must have shot out a secret stun ray because I froze right there on the spot.

I couldn't breathe. I couldn't think. Most of all, I couldn't sing. The note started up and then stuck right there in my throat. The choir kept singing softly behind me. Ms. Jenkins began to look a little frazzled.

"You can do it, Cindy," Renee whispered from behind me. "I know you can." I wasn't as sure as she was.

My turn came again. I took a deep breath, opened my mouth and sang out as loudly as I could. All that came out was a rusty-sounding squeak. But in that same moment, from behind me, came the pure tone of the right note. Renee gave me a gentle poke. My voice lifted and matched hers. When the next note came, it was all me.

The rest of the solo went well. And when the concert was over, the applause was thunderous. We even received a standing ovation. Well, okay, it was our parents and they are easily pleased, but a standing ovation is a standing ovation.

When we filed off the stage my family met me with praise and hugs. Renee was next to hug me. It felt awkward.

"Thanks, Renee," was all I could get myself to say.

Renee flashed me her usual sunny smile. "It was nothing. You've always been there for me. All these years and all the things we've done together!" Renee gave me another hug. "What are friends for?"

Friends? Did she say friends?

"You're right," I said slowly, beginning to like the feeling of being her friend. This time I hugged her. "That's what friends are for."

— Cynthia Marie Hamond —

Now You See It, Now You Don't

One is taught by experience to put a premium on those
few people who can appreciate you for what you are.
~Gail Godwin

•

I could hardly wait to get to school and see my friends. What would their reactions be when they saw me? I didn't know, but I was sure it wouldn't be like it was the day when I had started school there three years before.

On that terrible day my stepfather, Buddy, had to take me to school early so that he wouldn't be late for work. When he stopped in front of the school, I didn't want to get out of the car. I looked out at the small group of students standing outside the building and suddenly felt sick, but it was too late to back out now. Swallowing hard and trying not to cry, I slowly opened the car door and pushed myself around to get out. I felt awkward and ugly. The body brace I wore held me so stiffly that I couldn't move very easily, but at last I was out of the car. Buddy said goodbye, then drove off leaving me standing there alone.

I felt abandoned. I didn't know anyone there. I wished I were still in my old school with all my friends. My old friends knew all about my brace. They had also known me before I got the brace, so they knew I wasn't really this... this... monster that I felt like now.

Some of the kids had gathered near the front doors, which were still locked. I didn't have to look at them to know they were staring at me. I could feel it. And who could blame them? I was sure I had to be the ugliest, strangest thing they had ever seen. *So let them stare,* I thought defiantly. *I'll just ignore them.* I turned my back to them and sat down stiffly on the steps that led from the sidewalk up to the school. Hot, angry tears fell on my new dress, but I quickly wiped them away.

I looked down at my dress. It would be a pretty dress — on someone else. The brace ruined everything. I felt like a freak. I wanted to cry, to run and hide so no one could ever stare at me again. But I was trapped. Trapped inside this hideous contraption made of leather and steel. The leather wrapped around my middle and rested on my hips. Two narrow metal bars ran up my back. A wider bar came up the front to support the neckpiece, which held my head in place. The only way I could turn my head was by turning my whole body.

That morning though, I didn't try to turn my head. I didn't want to see the curious stares of strangers. I should have been used to it. People were always staring at me, or worse, asking me what was wrong with me. I hated being different. And the brace made it even worse. There was no way to hide the ugly thing. It just stuck out there, inviting everyone to gawk.

As I sat there on the steps, I didn't think I could be more miserable. I was wrong. Even though it was September, the weather was still warm and as the sun rose higher, the shade disappeared. I could feel the sweat begin to trickle down my back and under my arms. *Great! Now I would smell sweaty on top of looking weird.* I wanted the earth to swallow me up right then and there.

But, of course, the earth didn't oblige by swallowing me up. I managed to get through that day, and the next, and all the days for the following three years. In spite of the horrid brace, I managed to make friends, once everyone got used to seeing it. I still felt awkward and ugly most of the time though, and I could hardly wait to get the brace removed for good.

That day finally arrived, one rainy Thursday in spring. I remember being so thrilled when the doctor said I could leave the brace off that I threw my arms around him and gave him a big hug. I told him I would always love rain from that day on. I was free at last!

At first I was going to call my best friend and tell her what happened, but then I decided just to surprise her at school the next day. I could hardly wait for the oohs and ahs that I expected to hear from everyone when they saw me without that dreadful brace. I danced up the stairs to the school building that morning. *Just wait until they see me,* I thought. *Just wait!*

And so I waited. In my first class, no one said a word. What was the matter with them? Couldn't they see how much I had changed? Maybe they were just too surprised to say anything. Probably in the next class, they would notice. Again, I waited. Still nothing. I was beginning to feel awful. Maybe I was just as ugly without the brace! Or maybe my friends just didn't care as much about me as I thought. Then on to the next class, where I waited again.

By the end of the day, I was feeling hurt and confused. Even Danielle, my very best friend, hadn't said anything, and she knew how much I had hated wearing the brace. I didn't know what to think. I at least had to know what Danielle thought. I was spending the night at her house, so I decided to bring it up if she didn't say anything about it by then.

After a few hours at her house, she still hadn't said a word. At that point, I chickened out and asked Danielle's younger sister, Ann. "Ann, don't you notice anything different about me?" I asked her cautiously.

"Did you do something to your hair?" she asked.

"No. Not my hair," I said impatiently. "It's the brace. The brace is gone!" I turned in a circle and nodded my head up and down to show her. "See? It's gone!"

Ann just looked at me and shrugged her shoulders. "Well, I kinda thought something was different, but I just didn't know what it was!"

It wasn't until later that I realized my friends had long since accepted me for who I was, and they simply didn't notice the brace anymore. With or without the brace, what they saw when they looked at me was their friend.

— Anne McCourtie —

Family

When monsters lurked beneath my bed,
And scary dreams ran through my head,
When thunder growled those sounds I dread,
There you were, my father.
When scuffed-up knees made me cry,
Soft hankies wiped my sad eyes dry,
Coaxing me each time I tried,
There you were, my mother.
Who held my hand when I was scared,
Ate candy that he should have shared,
The things I did because you dared!
There you were, my brother.
In times of trouble, times of need,
I feel such strength surrounding me,
Without whose love I can't succeed,
I love you all, my family.

—Lisa-Dawn Bertolla—

Browbeaten

Anyone who has never made a mistake
has never tried anything new.
~Albert Einstein

n fifth grade a group of girls in my class had a nasty debate titled "who has the biggest unibrow," a list of names on a sheet of paper that drifted from desk to desk along with a red pen to mark your vote. I was near the top of the list and I was beyond embarrassed.

The next morning, I was getting ready for school and couldn't forget the list that was passed around the class. I couldn't forget the giggles and hurtful comments. So, eleven-year-old me took a small compact mirror from my mom's make-up bag along with her pink razor.

I shut my bedroom door and propped up the mirror on my art easel. Then I began to shave between my brows. Unfortunately, I made a mistake and shaved the front of my right eyebrow, so I went to the left side and did the same. I kept going back and forth trying my best to get them to match each other.

I took a step back and looked in the tiny mirror. All that was left was a third of each eyebrow. There was a big space between them. I began to cry. I ran downstairs to my mother and cried "Momma, please help me."

My mother stared at me for a good fifteen seconds with her mouth open and then she giggled and got a little teary-eyed, too. She finally said, "Key, what on earth happened?"

After I told her, she phoned my gram and explained what happened. She then took out a black eyeliner from her make-up bag and a box of hair dye from the cabinet under the sink. I looked at her and shook my head no. She then phoned her hairdresser and asked for advice. Her hairdresser suggested I come into the salon so she could see the damage… or "project" as she called it.

I waited outside with a tuque pulled all the way down past my eyebrows for my dad to pick me up and take me to the salon. When we arrived, the hairdresser asked what happened. I was far too embarrassed to explain the truth so eleven-year-old me said, "I slipped with scissors, and my eyebrows came off."

She giggled and said, "Good thing they didn't poke out your eye." She put some brown tint over the places with missing eyebrow hair… pretty much the whole area. She explained it was semi-permanent and I'd have to wait for my brows to grow back, which could take months. And that's exactly what happened!

I definitely learned a couple of good lessons. When a challenge occurs, confide in someone. It doesn't have to be your parents; it could be someone you trust and feel comfortable talking to. If I had told my mom what happened at school, she would have helped me. Secondly, a kind heart is much more beautiful than a pretty face.

— Kyahna Hammond —

Accepting Change

No matter what happens in life, be good to people.
Being good to people is a wonderful legacy
to leave behind.
~Taylor Swift

"**M**OM! MOM!" I yelled, banging on the bathroom door with one hand and the home phone in the other.

My mom opened the door slightly and poked her head out.

"It's Grandma Katie! It sounds urgent. Here!" I told her as I handed her the phone.

The day had started out like any other summer day. I was in my room reading when suddenly the home phone rang. It went to the machine because we never answer that line anymore. But then, I heard Grandma Katie say in an urgent voice, "Please, someone pick up the phone!" I knew that something bad had happened because Grandma Katie rarely called and never talks like that. I rushed down the hallway and into the living room, grabbed the phone and ran to the bathroom where my mom was taking a shower.

My mom listened and then froze. She said, "Okay, I'm on my way right now. Don't worry."

"Papa Laci had a stroke," she told us, then burst into tears.

It felt as if the whole world stopped spinning. Questions flooded my mind. *Why? He didn't deserve this! How did this happen? Is he okay?* I started crying.

"Is he still…" my voice quivered. I just couldn't get myself to say it. What if he wasn't? "A… a… alive?"

"Yes." She paused. "But he might not be for long. I'm going to the hospital to be with him while you guys are at your cousins' house."

Before I knew it, my mom was driving my little sister and me to my auntie and uncle's house.

When we arrived, my cousins welcomed my sister Sierra and me. A little while later, my dad came to drop off some clothes, our pillows, and our sleeping bags. We would stay the night while my mom and dad stayed at the hospital.

When Sierra and I got home the next afternoon, our parents were waiting with some news.

"Girls," my mom paused. "Papa Laci…"

No. This couldn't be happening. He couldn't be dead. Could he? My heart started pounding. I wasn't sure I wanted to hear it, but I braced myself for what might come.

"Papa Laci is alive." my mom finally said.

A wave of relief washed over me and I felt my heart slow back to normal. He was still alive. It was a miracle.

"He won't be the same though." my mom added. "He can't use his left hand, and the left side of his face doesn't have any expression because of the stroke," my mom said sadly. "His voice is muffled, so it might be difficult to understand what he's trying to say. And it is really hard for him to walk."

A couple of weeks later, I went to the hospital to see my grandpa for the first time since his stroke. I wanted to get out of the room as fast as I could when I saw him, but I stayed. He didn't look at all like my grandpa.

"Auuhh Auh Eblesne Pasht." My grandpa's attempts to talk were useless. I felt bad for him. That's when I realized that I would never again enjoy the grandpa I had before the stroke, but he was still the lovable Hungarian grandfather I loved.

I wanted to walk right out of that hospital room but I decided to make a deal with myself that I would stay there — for him. I needed to be there — for him.

Weeks passed. I continued to visit my grandpa. After almost a month, he was allowed to leave the hospital. By then, I was almost used to the fact that my grandpa had forever changed.

The day that my grandpa left the hospital, Sierra and I decorated the whole house with streamers, cards, and pictures for his "Welcome Home" party at our house. He and my grandma were going to live in my room for a while before moving back to his house with Grandma Katie. So, in the meantime, I had to share a room with my eight-year-old sister. And I was *not* looking forward to it.

About two months later, my grandpa had to take a test to see if he could walk up the stairs of his four-story condo. Let me tell you, that day, I found out that the results from a test would change my life drastically.

My grandpa didn't pass the test, which meant he couldn't go back and live at his condo ever again. It also meant that he and my grandma needed a new place to live. About a month went by and my parents finally made up their minds. They would build a tiny 900-square-foot house in our backyard.

At first, I was disappointed. I didn't want to give up half our backyard to them. But I quickly realized that this was our only option. So, I accepted it. It would take about five months to build, and then I would get my room back. That made me feel a bit better.

Little did I know that COVID was beginning to spread throughout the U.S. and it would actually take nearly two years until the little house was even close to finished. As the months passed, my sister and I felt like we weren't getting much attention, so I decided to talk with my mom.

"Mom, I feel like Sierra and I aren't getting a lot of attention and nothing is going right," I told her.

My mom stopped what she was doing and sat down to talk. "I'm sorry, sweetie. I have been so busy with work and Papa Laci. It has been hard on all of us so don't take it personally. Just remember, there are many people in worse situations than you." she replied.

"I just miss having my own room," I told her.

I didn't realize I had started crying until my mom wrapped me in a tight, welcoming hug and said, "I know. A lot has changed, but everything will be okay. Eventually, it will all be over. I don't know how long it will take, but it will be over. I promise."

Hearing those words made me realize that no matter what, everything would be okay, as long as I stayed positive. It might be rough at first, but it would turn out in the end. Life will always change, but you have to accept the new reality. If you don't at first, you will learn to.

— Emma Kaefer —

A New Way to Learn

Life is either a daring adventure or nothing at all.
~Helen Keller

When the pandemic first started, I was living in Barbados, a small island in the Caribbean. My mother, younger sister and I had been there for three years and were preparing to move back to Canada in May. In March 2020, COVID-19 was only small talk at school until the day the first two cases were detected in Barbados. I still remember that day While we were eating lunch, we noticed that many of the younger kids were being picked up early and all the teachers were on their phones looking worried. Eventually the kids eleven and older pieced it together and the teachers had no choice but to tell us the unfortunate news.

When the cases started to rise, we had to switch to online class because we were going into lockdown. Luckily, we had our Easter break so our teachers had time to organize online classes. We had a full month off, which was fun for about a week. Then my sister and I got restless, especially since Barbados was in full lockdown — we couldn't even go to the beach or any of our other favourite spots! So my mum wrote up a schedule that included sorting our stuff for moving (even though we didn't know when that would happen anymore), doing arts and crafts, playing chess online with our grandfather, taking online painting classes with a friend in Canada, and doing math and grammar worksheets. We spent weekends sewing masks, mostly to keep us occupied. We didn't know that we would end up needing to wear them for months.

We spent the last couple days of our break setting up online school. We collected our books and pencils from school, and we borrowed a computer from a friend because my mum had to use hers for work and my sister was doing online school as well. We spent most of the rest of the school year exploring Google Classroom, but doing our work in our books and on paper and then sending photos to our teachers.

We returned to Canada in August and had to quickly decide between in-person school or virtual school. As a family, we chose the online option. Since my online schooling so far was mostly just sending photos of my work, online schooling in Canada was a bigger learning experience. I had to use Google Docs and Slides to show my work. I didn't hate it but tech issues and distractions around the house made it difficult.

Even though online schooling was frustrating, my teachers tried to make it fun. We did group assignments on Google Slides and then quizzed our class on what we presented to them using Kahoot. We solved math questions in groups using breakout rooms on Google Meet. We displayed our work using Jamboards. We also learned how to code on Scratch, which was interesting but challenging. The best thing was that every week someone joined our Meet to talk or demonstrate a topic. We had artists, people from First Nations communities, and other visitors to keep school fun and interactive.

Since I chose to go to virtual school I could bubble with my grandparents. Unfortunately, my friends didn't choose the same as me and I couldn't see them often. When I did see them it was outside, with a mask and socially distanced. Sometimes we would go hiking or walk around the neighbourhood, but that was nothing like having a sleepover or a playdate. Still, I think it was worth it because I got to spend time with my family, and I could even bring my computer to my grandparents' house and do school from there.

— Hazel Gonzalez —

Families That Care, Care About Families

We didn't have much, but we sure had plenty.
~Sherry Thomas

My tenth Christmas was one I was not looking forward to. Money was scarce. Dad was a preacher, and preachers for our church don't make much. Mom said we were old enough now to be brave and not count on gifts. Just being together would be enough.

We weren't the only family in our small community who would have a meager Christmas. But the knowledge that others were going through the same thing didn't help much. One night, as my sister and I huddled together in our shared bed, we had a small pity party for each other.

"How can I even wear that same old dress one more time?" I complained.

"I know," said my sister. "I think I might as well give up asking for a horse, too. I've asked for one forever but it just never happens."

"Yeah, and even if we got one where would we keep it?" I said, destroying her last hope.

I couldn't stop thinking about my sister's long-held dream to own a horse and decided I was willing to give up every gift for ten Christmases if only her dream could come true.

The next day, Mom added salt to my wounds by telling us that she had been saving up and shopping around so that we could give the Walters family a Christmas basket.

"If anyone needs some cheer, it's the Walters," Mom reminded us.

"But the Walters, Mom. I wouldn't be caught dead at their front door."

Mom gave me a dirty look.

But I knew she would have to agree that the Walters were the strangest people we knew. Looking a lot like a family of hobos, they could have at least washed their hair once in a while. After all, water is free. I always felt embarrassed for them.

Mom was determined. And it was our duty to load up our little sled and pull the basket full of flour and sugar, a small turkey, potatoes, and bottled peaches over to the Walters, leave it on the doorstep and run.

On the way we noticed that Mom had tucked a small gift for each of the children in among the food. I was distraught. How could Mom be so generous with someone else's kids when our own family didn't have enough?

We delivered the package, knocked hard on the door and ran fast to hide behind a nearby bush. Safely hidden, I looked back the way we had come and realized my sister was standing in plain view. I was so mad. I didn't want them to know our family had anything to do with this.

After the Walters gathered up their basket of goodies and had closed the door, I said in a loud whisper, "What are you doing? I know they saw you!"

"I wanted to see their faces when they saw the gifts," my sister said innocently. "That's the best part."

"Whatever," I said, relenting to the unchangeable. "Did they look happy?"

"Well, yeah, happy, but mostly they looked like, well, like they were thinking, *Maybe we do belong.*"

Christmas morning arrived just a couple of days later. To my surprise, I unwrapped a fabulous-looking dress. I smiled at my parents as if to say, "I can't believe you actually got this for me." Then I glanced at my sister's face, which was full of anticipation. There was only one small package under the tree. She unwrapped it and found a currycomb. *A currycomb? Had my parents totally lost it?* My sister's face was blank and

I was thinking, *Is this some kind of a mean joke?*

We hadn't realized that Dad had slipped outside. Just as I was about to speak, he rode up in front of the big picture window atop my sister's new horse!

My sister was so excited that she jumped up and down, then stopped and put her head in her hands, shook her head back and forth in disbelief and screamed, "Oh, my gosh... oh, my gosh!" With tears rolling down her cheeks, she ran out to meet her new friend.

"Mom, how did you do all this?" I asked. "We were ready for a no-present Christmas."

"Oh, everybody pitched in. Not necessarily trading but just helping each other. Mrs. Olsen at the dress shop let me bring your gift home now, even though I'll be paying for a while. Dad did some marriage counseling for the Millets's son. I hung up Mrs. Marshall's tree lights since her arthritis is getting her down. We were thrilled that Mr. Jones had a horse that needed some TLC, and he was thrilled we had someone to love it. And then for a moment we thought all was lost because we couldn't figure out where to house the horse. Then the Larsens, down the way, offered some of their pasture to keep the horse penned and well fed."

"I thought since you were giving away food to the Walters that we would never have enough. They really don't have anything to give in return."

"They will some day. But there is enough and more to share. Everything's God's anyway. Doesn't matter who can or can't give. If we just listen to our hearts, the right gifts will end up with the right families."

Mom always knew truth.

I glanced out the window at my sister now sitting on her horse, and thought about how she had described the expression on the Walters's faces when they discovered the Christmas basket. That "belonging" feeling was more precious than any of the gifts. And I thought, *Families that care, care about families. All families.*

That was the Christmas that I learned about the magic of giving.

— Rachelle P. Castor —

Forever Garrett

We shared so much laughter, shared so many tears.
We had a special friendship that grew stronger each year.
We were not siblings by birth but we knew from the start,
We were put together, to be siblings of the heart.
~Megan Youpa, 13

I followed Garrett into the kitchen to find Mom. Garrett had been with our family for about a month, and even though I was only five and he was eight, we had been getting along pretty great. Like me, he had a lot of energy and liked to run and play ball. Up until Garrett came to live with us I had played with three boys who lived on our street that were around my age. They liked Garrett right away, and the five of us had been playing together every day. Now, Garrett and I had argued and he was mad at me.

"I want to go back! I don't want to be here anymore," Garrett announced to Mom.

Garrett's face was set with determination and his eyes were shiny with unshed tears. I looked at Garrett and my face crumpled. I started to cry.

"I hurt him, Mommy, I hurt him. I didn't mean to!" I liked Garrett, and I didn't want him to go back to the adoption agency where he had lived before he came to us.

"You two wait until your father comes home tonight," Mom said as she cleaned both of our faces. Then she made me blow my nose as she said, "He'll have something to say about this."

When my dad got home that night, he sat us down and said that when he and my mom married they had a dream. They wanted to have a big family with both biological children and adopted children. He and Mom had been involved in the civil rights movement and wanted to adopt kids of mixed racial background because they knew how hard it was for these kids to get adopted. He told me that we were lucky to have Martin, my little brother who was a baby, and Garrett come to us.

Then Dad explained to Garrett that sometimes in families there are arguments and disagreements, but that didn't mean that we didn't care about each other. I knew all about that — I had had plenty of disagreements with my sisters and we always got over it. Dad said that Garrett belonged with us now and that was the way it was going to be; we were a family and families stick together forever.

I don't know who felt better after Dad's lecture, Garrett or me, but I do know that I really can't remember having another bad argument with Garrett after that day.

When I was in the third grade, our family moved from Wichita Falls to San Antonio. When I was younger, we had moved a lot because of my dad's job in the Air Force. In fact, my first words were in Italian because we lived in Italy when I learned to talk. But this was the first time that we had moved since Garrett and Martin had become a part of the family.

I didn't like moving. I was pretty shy anyway, and trying to make new friends wasn't the easiest thing for me. There was one exception: when I got on the playing field, whatever it was — soccer, football or volleyball — I felt like I was at my best and I was myself, 100 percent. On the playing field I could make friends. Garrett and I had that in common. We both loved sports.

I used to watch him play soccer and baseball and be amazed at how well he could play and how fast he could run. Not only was he fast, but he was also so competitive that what he lacked because of his size he made up for with his speed and aggressive actions.

Garrett would take me to play ball with the other kids, and when he got to pick his team, he always picked me first. I was his secret weapon. He liked to see the surprised looks on the faces of the boys on the team when I ran circles around them. Even though I was younger than most of the kids and I was a girl, I was a better player. With both Garrett and me on the same team, we couldn't lose.

Pretty soon, our whole family felt settled in our new home and started to love living in San Antonio. We lived right on the base and had tons of freedom to come and go without my mom or dad having to worry about us.

When we were finally all perfectly happy in San Antonio, we moved again. I was in the sixth grade, and for me it was the hardest move I had ever experienced. I had to leave behind the friends I had made and start all over again. Although our move was back to Wichita Falls, I didn't remember very much about living there before and missed my life in San Antonio. I told myself that the moving didn't matter, because my true home was the playing field. I threw myself into every sport that was offered, and I started to feel better.

We had been back in Wichita Falls for about two and a half years, and I was in the eighth grade, when we found out something terrible about Garrett. It was the beginning of his fight for life.

Garrett had chosen to attend a small Catholic high school instead of the larger public school, and he went out for football. During one of the first games, Garrett was tackled and had a hard time getting back up again. One of the dads attending the game was a doctor, and he went over to take a look at Garrett to see if he could help. He noticed that my brother had several large bruises on his back. He knew these bruises were not normal, and the doctor told my parents that Garrett shouldn't play again until he was checked out.

When my parents took Garrett to the doctors they did several tests on him to find out what the problem was. He was eventually diagnosed with aplastic anemia, a disease that happens when a person's bone marrow is either destroyed or not able to function correctly. People with aplastic anemia can bleed to death from internal hemorrhaging. The doctors told my mom and dad that all they could do for Garrett was to put him on steroids, and that might help. Then, they told Garrett that he couldn't play contact sports anymore at all.

I was shocked. My brother, Garrett, not play sports? That was impossible. But it was true. For months, all he could do was watch. I felt horrible for him and couldn't even imagine how I would feel if the doctors had told me the same thing. I think I even felt a little guilty that I could still do everything that we had once done together, and he couldn't.

Then, to the amazement of us all, Garrett went into remission. He was back to his old self, and the doctors gave him the go-ahead to play ball again. Garrett went out for baseball and I was so glad to see him on the field again. We all were. Life became normal again.

Garrett was fine for several years until he had a relapse when I was eighteen. During the next six years he moved to California to live with our grandmother and to go to college. While on a trip home to Texas to visit our mom, he met the woman who was to become his wife. They had a son, Dillon. Garrett also spent those years fighting for his life. He had to have several series of very painful treatments, but he never gave up. During that time, whenever I would think that I had it rough during training, I would remember what Garrett was going through. I thought if Garrett could go through what he was experiencing, I could tough it out, too. His determination gave me the strength to excel during my games. Garrett was able to come to Atlanta in 1996 and see me play in the Olympics where we won the Gold Medal.

In February 1997, the doctors attempted a bone marrow transplant on Garrett. The transplant itself was successful, but Garrett had many complications. In April 1997, my brother Garrett died at the age of twenty-eight.

In honor of my brother, Garrett, I started a foundation. Once a year, the foundation stages the Garrett Game, an all-star soccer game that raises money for bone marrow research. In 1999, during the half-time celebration, we brought together bone marrow recipients with their donors. It was the first time any of them had met each other and everyone was crying and laughing. It was one of the most rewarding experiences of my whole life and one of my best memories.

Although Garrett didn't live to see us play the World Cup in 1999, I felt his spirit with me every step of the way. I know that he is with me during all of my games, encouraging me to do my best. In my heart, my brother will always live on. In my mind, I can still see him playing—running hard, with that look of determination on his face. With him as my example, I have been inspired to never give up, to always play to win, to work hard with my teammates and to have my heart in the game. Garrett was one of the best athletes that I have ever known, but he was much more. He was my hero, my friend, my inspiration and my brother… forever.

—Mia Hamm—

Supper David

David is the baby. Ginny is the oldest, then Johnny, and then me. Sometimes, we have to help watch David. He plays quietly for Ginny and Johnny but not for me, even when I try to get him to watch cartoons. He will sit still for a little while, but then he'll drag out a book and ask me to read it to him.

David always smells like mustard. His favorite sandwich is mustard on plain hard bread. The smell makes it hard for me to concentrate on reading a book to him. And David sucks his thumb. His thumb is in his mouth for so long that it stays wrinkled, shriveled and wet all the time. It sticks to the paper when he tries to help me turn the pages of a book. When I can't read the words, I make up stories to match the pictures. David doesn't know because he is too little to read.

David loves costumes — he will wear anything. Ginny and Johnny dressed him up in Ginny's fancy green flower-girl dress. They put a yellow dust mop on his head to make him look like a princess. David became "Davaleena" as he twirled around the kitchen and sang in a squeaky voice.

My mother made a costume for David out of a pair of blue long underwear, a blue undershirt, a red dishtowel and red underpants. With his arms straight out in front and the dishtowel flapping behind, David becomes Superman. I made a sign for his chest that reads "Supper David." Johnny told me that I spelled "super" wrong, but I don't care. David can't spell either.

David never keeps his clothes on. He runs around the house naked. My mother says that David is going through a stage and that children have to learn how to take their clothes off before they can learn how to put their clothes back on. I don't remember that I learned to get dressed that way.

David likes to show off. In the middle of one of my parents' dinner parties, David took off his clothes and ran out the back door. When we caught up with his naked little self, David was busy jumping up and down on top of the car, waving goodbye to the company. My father laughed so hard that he snorted and tears streamed down his face. When the grown-ups were done laughing they went inside. I stayed outside to watch David.

My mom yelled, "Grandma's on the phone!"

"Vroom, vrroom!" said David.

"Mo-om! David is jumping up and down on the front seat of the car!"

"Barbara, please! Not now! Yes, Grandma, the children eat their vegetables."

"Honk, honk," said David.

"Mom, David is pretending to honk the horn in the car."

"Barbara, I've told you that I'm talking to Grandma. I can't talk to you right now. Yes, Grandma, the children are always in bed by eight."

"Wrr, wrr," said David.

"Mom, David is turning the steering wheel in the car!"

"Barbara! Yes, Grandma, the children are always polite."

"Ert, ert," said David.

"Mom, David is moving the handles next to the steering wheel!"

"BARBARA! Yes, Grandma, the children are healthy. Thank you."

Then I noticed that our car was moving. David was backing the car down the hill of our driveway!

"MO-OM, DAVID IS DRIVING THE CAR!"

I have never seen my mother run so quickly. She leaned into the car as it was moving down the hill — picking up speed as it went — pulled David out through the car window, smacked his bottom, and then hugged him tightly. The car hit a tree and stopped halfway down the hill. They both started to cry. So did I.

My mother turned toward me, and gave me a hug, too. We all stood like that for a while, and I thought how much I really loved

David even though he is a pain sometimes, and how I would have missed him if anything had happened to him. I made up my mind that Mom was a hero.

I decided to go to my room and pull out my construction paper and crayons. Then I made another sign. It said, "Supper Mom." Somehow, I didn't think my mother would care if I didn't spell it right.

— Barbara Lage —

Mom

I was only two and a half when my real mom died. One morning, my brothers and I went to wake her up, but she wouldn't answer us. When she didn't respond to our calls, my older brother, Shane, got my dad. The last thing I remember about my real mom was watching the ambulance taking her away from us. Although I was too young to really understand what was going on, somehow I knew that she was gone forever.

After my mom died, my dad started abusing my brothers and me. We were sent away to live with relatives. My brothers were sent to live with their real dad, but their dad didn't want me. I was sent to live with one relative after another. I was miserable almost all of the time. I thought that no one would ever want me. Finally, when I was four and a half, my mom's sister, Bonnie, and her husband, Jesse, said that they would take me, and they became my legal guardians.

From then on, they became my family. I called Aunt Bonnie "Mom" and Uncle Jesse "Dad." I felt really lucky because they also had two older kids that became my older brother and sister, and I didn't miss my brothers as much. I finally felt at home, with a family again.

Then, when I was six, my Uncle Jesse was diagnosed with cancer. He was sick for a whole year, and finally died shortly after my seventh birthday. I missed him so much. I cried for days after losing him. I still cling to the present he gave me on my sixth birthday.

Shortly after Uncle Jesse died we all moved to a new house in a new town. My mom told us we moved because of a job opportunity she had there that she didn't have in our old town. Now that it was up to her to support us, the move was important.

In our new house, I always felt kind of lonely and so did my brother and sister. We were in a new place and had to try to make new friends. It wasn't all that easy, and we all still missed Uncle Jesse. We kids spent a lot of time alone in our new house because Mom was always working. But we all felt like we could make it if we stuck together as a family.

Then one summer, the beginning of a miracle happened. My mom took us camping, and we took our grandma along with us. My grandma met the man that was staying in the cabin next to ours, and she introduced him to the rest of us. We all ended up becoming friends with this guy, David. He was so funny. He would bring flowers to my mom and also to my grandma at the same time. Maybe he thought we didn't know what he was up to, but we all knew. We didn't mind because he was really a great guy.

After we came back from our camping trip, my mom and David kept in contact with phone calls and by writing to each other. Eventually, they started seeing each other even though he lived in another city and it was a long drive for him. David would visit my mom and take us all out. He even remembered my birthday, and sent a birthday present to me! We all really liked him.

Then, two years after they met, David proposed to my mom. They got married three days before my twelfth birthday. Even though they were gone on their honeymoon for my birthday, David and my mom made sure that I still had a birthday party.

After my mom married David, our family moved in with his family, and our two smaller families became one big family. I gained two more brothers and another sister. I guess we are kind of like the Brady Bunch! Our family now consists of my parents, David and Bonnie, six kids plus a son-in-law and a daughter-in-law, and two grandbabies — with another one on the way!

When I look back on it now, I have come a long way from being a sad and lonely little girl passed from relative to relative to being the person I am today — part of a big, happy family. I can't imagine what my life would have been like if my Aunt Bonnie hadn't taken me in. She promised me that she would love me and take care of me — no matter what — and she has done exactly that. Without her in my life, I would have been a motherless child, but because of her I have a great family and the best mom in the world.

With my mom as my shining example, I have learned about strength, dedication and love. Even though I wasn't born to her, she has been my mother in every way. She has been there to hold me when I've been sick, to help me with my homework, to support me when I've needed her and to work hard to take care of all of us. In return, I love her more than she'll ever know. I don't know what I would have done without her. These words are few, but they are from the bottom of my heart....

Thanks, Mom. I love you!

— Apryl Anderson, 15 —

Love

True treasure is not found in pirate ships,
in chests of silver and gold.
True treasure isn't ruby rings
and jewels from long ago.
You don't need to use a treasure map
and find chests beneath the sea.
True treasure is simply the love
and joy found in you and me.

—Leigha Dickens, 11—

Bobby Lee

Love and kindness are never wasted. They always
make a difference. They bless the one who
receives them, and they bless you, the giver.
~Barbara De Angelis

I walked home with my little brother every day the same way, past an oil refinery. Mom always told us to walk together and never to talk to strangers. One day, that walk home changed forever. As my brother and I passed the oil refinery, I heard an old man's voice.

"Hey there, children."

I turned and saw a very old man standing there with a sweet smile on his face.

"Hi," I answered, still keeping my distance.

"Would you like a soda pop? I know you walk by here every day. I don't mean you any harm."

I was already hot from walking and carrying my heavy backpack, but I knew what my mother would do once my little brother ratted on me for talking to strangers.

"No thanks. I'm not allowed to talk to strangers," I replied.

"Oh, I understand. And your mama's right. My name's Bobby. Now run along," he said as he disappeared behind the gate of the refinery.

What a strange man, I thought. But I also felt bad, thinking I might have insulted him by calling him a stranger.

I went home and reported to my mom what had happened. My mother told me that I was right not to talk to strangers, so I tried avoiding this stranger for the following few days, but it was impossible.

Other streets were not as safe to walk on, and every time we passed the refinery, a familiar voice would say, "Hello there, children."

Then one day, my family was taking a walk around the neighborhood. We were just about to pass the refinery when I noticed the gate was ajar. I remember silently praying that Bobby would appear and prove once and for all that he was a "good" stranger. And there he was.

He smiled as he approached my mother, "Well, you must be Little Miss Pretty's mama! And you must be her daddy! It is so nice to meet you."

The genuine smile and surprise on my parents' faces were all I needed to see. They spoke for a few minutes and then, walking home, my parents said it would be safe for us to visit Bobby after school.

My brother and I would stop to visit Bobby after school every day after that. He would invite us into his tiny office to talk about my schoolwork, my friends and sports.

It wasn't long before I started getting a few friends to walk home with me just to meet Bobby. Before long, a group of about fourteen kids went daily to visit Bobby and receive our sodas and gum. Thinking back, I now realize that Bobby bought all those treats just for us... and there were a lot of us to treat!

We visited Bobby every day after school for about three years! My mother finally decided it was time to do something nice for Bobby. So, with some thought and a lot of effort, she arranged for a plaque-giving ceremony to be held at the refinery on Father's Day. All of the children who visited Bobby, and even some of their parents, were invited. And you know what? Most of them came.

On the plaque, my mother had engraved "To the Neighborhood Grandfather," and all of our names were engraved below that. I remember that Bobby cried when he received it. I don't think he'd ever been surrounded with so much adoration in his long life.

The following holiday, my mother gave Bobby an enlarged photograph of the "Neighborhood Grandfather Ceremony" with all of us kids standing around him.

One cold afternoon in February, we stopped by as usual, only to be told that Bobby had died. I remember crying for days after hearing the news. He really had been like another grandfather to me.

My mother went with two other mothers to the funeral service. There, right on the coffin, were three items: the American flag folded into a triangle shape (as is customary for war veterans), the plaque we gave him and the photograph of that memorable Father's Day ceremony with all of us kids standing around him. Bobby had no children. I guess *we* were his children.

To this day I think about him — an old man with no responsibilities to family, taking in a group of "strange" little kids who ended up meaning so much to him. I know now there was a reason why I met Bobby and why a group of us went to see him every day. He was able to die knowing that somebody loved him.

— Daphne M. Orenshein —

Love Lives On

Whatever happens inside of you that makes you fall in love with horses happened to me. I devoured every horse book I could get my hands on, checking them out of our library again and again. *Man O' War,* the true story about the greatest thoroughbred racehorse of all time, was my favorite. I must have read that book ten times. I pictured myself owning the huge red horse, loving him with all my heart, but knowing I could never ride him because he was a champion racehorse, not a pet.

I asked my parents if I could take riding lessons and they agreed. I learned to ride well, made many friends at the stable, and my love of horses and the sport of riding grew.

After a year of lessons, I decided that what I wanted more than anything on Earth was a horse of my own. I asked my parents, and they agreed — *if* I earned half of the money to buy the horse. I worked all summer and saved one hundred dollars, a fortune in those days. At last, my dad said, "Find your horse, girl!"

Two hundred dollars wasn't much to buy a horse, and the one I had my eye on was going for five hundred dollars. "A deal is a deal," said my dad, so I could only watch as the beautiful black mare was sold to someone else. Disappointed, but still determined, I was introduced to a woman who told me that she had a horse she would sell me for two hundred dollars, but she doubted that I would want him, explaining that she had rescued him from an abusive owner and that he hadn't been ridden in years.

As we walked to the back of the stables, I was so excited that my heart was pounding. The woman explained that she thought I was a good horsewoman and that when she heard that I was looking for a horse — on a limited budget, no less — she had thought that perhaps it was time for this horse to come back to the world.

We walked up to the stall and she opened the door, cautioning me "not to expect too much." I was trembling with excitement as the sunlight spilled into the stall. There he was, an old giant of a thoroughbred, with gray sprinkled through his shiny, flame-colored coat. He turned and looked cautiously at us, and as I stepped into the stall he flattened his ears and bared his teeth. The woman explained that he had been beaten and had a mistrust of strangers, but that he wasn't mean, just afraid.

"What's his name?" I asked.

"We call him Rusty," she said.

"Rusty," I called gently, and his ears came up at the sound of his name. The woman handed me a carrot, and I held it out to him. He stepped forward slowly, but before he took the treat, he turned his head slightly and looked into my eyes. We held the gaze for just a moment, and then he took it from my hand.

When he was done munching his carrot, we led him out into the sunlight. What I saw was the most beautiful horse I had ever laid my eyes on. What most others saw was a twenty-year-old, swaybacked horse, sporting a potbelly.

"I'll take him!" I cried, startling him so that he jerked his head back and snorted all over me. I laughed and reached up to pet the long, white blaze that ran down the front of his nose, and he lowered his head and begged for more.

That summer we were inseparable, and I spent all my free time riding him. He grew strong and energetic for his age. I often saw the woman who had sold him to me, and she would tell me how good he looked.

That fall, we moved Rusty to a small stable near our home, so I could ride him as often as possible during the school year. I began getting involved in the world of competitive horse showing. Rusty thrived on all the attention and competition, and even though he usually was twice the age of the other horses, the judges loved him, and we took home many blue ribbons during the next two years.

But one morning, as I arrived at the stables to go riding, something was different. Instead of standing, ears pricked forward and bellowing a hello, Rusty was still lying down in his stall when I walked up. He rose when he saw me, nickering softly, and I figured maybe it was just his age getting to him. After all, he was twenty-two years old. We rode quietly that day, stopping for lunch to share the same sandwich and chips. How he loved potato chips! But he was not hungry, and when I told my dad about it, he decided to call the vet.

The vet came to see him, and what he said was a shock to us. He believed that Rusty had cancer, and he referred us to a specialist for further tests. My parents and I had talked about the situation, and we decided that due to his advanced age, if the specialist told us that he was suffering, that we would elect to have him humanely put to sleep. I understood this on one level; on my heart level I was crushed.

That morning we loaded Rusty into the trailer and I waved good-bye to him, pretty sure it was for the last time. My parents had thought it would be best if I didn't go with Rusty to the vet. I had spent the entire night before with him, crying and laughing, remembering all the things we'd done together and the lessons we'd learned. I'd thanked him for being there for me during a tough time in my life when I didn't think anybody cared, but I knew he did. Unconditional love, that's what he had given me.

Later that day, I was lying on my bed at home, all cried out, when my dad came in. He told me, "There is a guy out front who wants to see you." I was fifteen years old, and I figured it was just one of my school friends coming by to talk. I asked my dad to explain that I couldn't come out now, but he said, "Honey, you'll want to see this boy."

I rose up from my bed and looked out the window. There, backed up into our driveway, was the horse trailer, and inside was Rusty! I tore outside and jumped up next to him, hugging his neck and crying with happiness. He stood quietly and took in my love, and when I stepped back, he turned his head and looked into my eyes, as he had done years before, and winked.

Rusty stayed with me for another happy year before the cancer took him. By then, we were a little more prepared.

All these years later, I still miss him. But, even though he isn't here physically, I realize that love lives on, and that Rusty will live in my heart forever.

—Laurie Hartman—

The Teacher Who Cared

A teacher affects eternity; no one can tell
where his influence stops.
~Henry Adams

Mrs. Barrow, room 501, room 501, I repeated to myself as I scanned the hallways looking for the room number. It was my first day of fifth grade and I was really scared.

I came to the end of the hall and found an open door. Stepping into the room, I suddenly felt out of place. I tried to act normal, but Mrs. Barrow saw right through me.

"Good morning, Courtni. You may pick your seat."

I glanced about the room and took an empty seat near a girl named Wendy Barber. As the year slowly progressed, Wendy and I became good friends. I felt no closeness to Mrs. Barrow, though. I saw her as "just another teacher."

Mrs. Barrow had us write a paper on what we wanted to be when we grew up. Some kids asked why. She explained that when her former students graduated, she liked them to come back and share their fifth-grade dreams together, as a memento of their childhood. I decided right then and there that I liked Mrs. Barrow.

Then, my grandmother, who lived with us, was diagnosed with pancreatic cancer. About a month later, Grandma slipped into a coma and died. Losing her was unbearable for me. I missed some school because I was so sad.

At the funeral, I was sitting there feeling sorry for myself when I looked up and saw Mrs. Barrow standing there. She sat down next to me and held my hand. She comforted me by reminding me that now Grandma had no more pain or suffering. It had never occurred to me that it was better for my grandma this way. All I thought about was how sad it was for me.

After the funeral, we went to my aunt's house to see the flowers that had been sent. My mom handed me a pretty ivy plant in a pink pot. The attached card read:

> *Courtni,*
> *I'm sorry about your grandmother. Never forget, I love you.*
> *You are like one of my children.*
> *With love,*
> *Mrs. Barrow*

I wanted to cry. I took the plant home, watered it and put it in my grandma's old room. I am in eighth grade now and I *still* have that plant. I never thought a teacher could care that much about her students: now I know.

I say this with all my heart: Anyone who is lucky enough to have a teacher like Mrs. Barrow in their life, even for a short while, is privileged beyond words. She may not know it, but she means more to me than she'll *ever* know. I can only hope this gives her inspiration and repays to her a tiny portion of what she has done for me.

To Mrs. Barrow — I love you very much. You're much more than a teacher — you are like a mother to me.

— Courtni Calhoun, 13 —

The Act of Love

hate pulling weeds! I thought. *It's hot. It's sticky. And it's Saturday!*

Still, I made sure to pull every stinking weed out of that flower garden. My dad was Mr. Perfecto Lawnman. He could detect a single weed a mile away. And if he spotted so much as one little clover, I'd be back pulling weeds for the rest of the day.

"Dad, I'm done," I shouted from the garden, feeling sure that I had done a good job.

Dad stormed out of the house. "Don't be yelling outside, Kathy," he grumbled. "Use those two feet of yours and come get me."

Suddenly, a sick feeling came over me. It was the kind of feeling I had when my dad was going to find that one stinking little clover.

"Geez," Dad said, waving an irritated finger, "you missed a spot."

I sighed, went to the spot and pulled the weeds. Afterward, I looked back at Dad, still standing there with a scowl on his face.

"Okay," he said, turning away, "I guess you're done."

As Dad walked back to the house, I wondered if I'd ever done anything good enough or right enough for him. Sometimes, I wondered if he even liked me.

Like the night I had taken out the trash without being told. That was a big deal for me. But Dad didn't see it that way. He was mad because I didn't put the trash can lid on tight enough to keep our dog out.

Well, I'm sorry, I thought, *but I can't help it if Sugar's a trash picker.*

The other day, when I was in a rush to get to school, Dad stopped me at the door. In his hand was a topless tube of toothpaste, the same one that I'd used just moments before.

"Where's the cap to the toothpaste?" he asked, his eyebrows

bunching in the middle. "And how many times do I have to tell you? Squeeze from the bottom!" *At least I brushed my teeth,* I thought.

Just then, a sloppy, wet tongue washed over my face, breaking me from my thoughts.

"Sugar!" I said, hugging her tightly. "Where did you come from?"

Sugar looked at me, her big sloppy tongue hanging to the side. I smiled.

"At least you like me." Then standing up, I brushed the dirt from my knees and headed for the house.

Two weeks later, on the morning of another weed picking weekend, I was sick. I was sweaty and feverish and I ached all over.

"Let's go," Dad said, lifting me from the bed. "You need to see a doctor."

"Please, no," I said, in a shallow, sickly voice, "I'd rather pull weeds."

He took me anyway, and the doctor said I had pneumonia. The only nice thing about it was that I didn't have to pull weeds. I didn't have to take out the trash. And since I had to stay in bed, I didn't have to brush my teeth. If having pneumonia was ever good, it was good then. And as I rested, Sugar stayed with me, lying down beside my bed. She liked me.

That night a noise woke me from my sleep. I opened my eyes just a sliver, and I saw a tall, slender form. Enough moonlight shined through my window so that I could see it was my dad. But why was he there? I didn't say, "Hi, Dad," or anything like that, I don't know why. He came up to me and put his hand against my forehead. When he took his hand away, I saw him lay something on my nightstand. He looked at me again, then left.

When he was gone, I reached over to the nightstand and picked up a necklace. It wasn't like any I'd ever seen before. Dangling from a golden chain was a puppy in a basket, and the puppy looked just like Sugar. With shaking hands, I held that necklace to my heart and cried. My dad, who never gave hugs and never said, "I love you…" had just said it all.

— Kathy Kemmer Pyron —

Cry When You Are Sad

Never apologize for showing feelings. Remember that
when you do, you apologize for the truth.
~Benjamin Disraeli

On a sunny Monday in April, I had two loving grandmothers near me, but when Tuesday came, only one was left. One of my grandmothers who was dear to me, had died. I had a feeling that this awful day was going to come soon, but now that it was here, all I wanted to do was cry. But I wasn't brave enough to shed a tear, for I was always taught that boys should never cry.

Later, as the time came for the funeral activities, I had the hardest time keeping my sadness inside.

My relatives soon arrived from all over the country. I really had to hold back my tears now that my relatives were here, because I did not want to look like a crybaby in front of them. I figured out that my parents, my sister and myself were the only ones that had lived in the same town as my grandma. That explained why her death was hitting me the hardest, while my cousins seemed as though they were here just to get away from home. They really hadn't known her like I had.

Soon, all of my relatives gathered at the funeral home, waiting for the viewing to begin. What I thought was going to be the easiest part of my grieving turned into the hardest.

The moment I walked into the room where my grandma was lying in a coffin, my heart dropped. This was going to be the last time that I would ever see her. At first I was afraid to proceed with the rest of my family up to her coffin, but then I realized that I would have to sooner or later. I grabbed hold of my mother's hand and kept my mind on remembering not to cry.

When I came up to the kneeler, in front of where she was lying, my mother made me do something that almost brought me to tears. She told me to touch Grandma's hand, for that was going to be the last time that I would get a chance to touch her. I reached over to her hand very slowly, afraid of what she might feel like. When my hand touched hers, I was relieved for a moment. She felt the same way she always had, except a little cooler than usual.

When I looked up at my mom, she began crying uncontrollably. I knew this was the time that I really had to be strong. I reached my arms around her and slowly walked with her back to our seats.

During the next few hours, I met many different people. All of them were telling me that they were sorry about my grandma passing away. I just smiled and reminded myself not to cry, because I had so often been told, "Boys should be strong and not cry." I kept reminding myself that soon this night would be over, but the next day would be the actual funeral... the last goodbye.

My mother woke me early the next morning, making sure that I looked my best. I promised myself when I was getting dressed that I would hold back my tears no matter what. I had to be strong and help my grieving parents.

When we arrived at the church, we all waited as they took my grandma's coffin out of the big black hearse. We had to follow it in so everyone knew that we were family. Once inside, we took our seats. My family sat in the very front because we were the closest to my grandma. I was surprised to see that even before the service began, my parents were crying. I was trying to hold back my tears, but as the priest began talking about my grandma, it seemed as though not crying was going to be an impossible task.

About halfway through the mass, he began telling the people about how much my grandma was loved by her family and friends. He then mentioned how every night I stayed with her while my parents were working. That reminded me of all the good times we had together throughout my life. In the summer, we would glide on her swing.

In the winter, we would always ride sleds down the big hill behind her house. There were so many good times that went through my mind that I almost forgot where I was. I began to realize that those good times were gone forever. At this exact thought, I began to cry uncontrollably. I didn't care anymore about what other people thought of me. It was something that I just had to do. I could not hold back my sadness anymore.

When my father noticed me sobbing, he leaned me up next to him and we cried together. My father, my mother, my sister and I sat next to each other, crying as if the world was going to end. At this point I promised myself that if I ever had a son, I would tell him: "Real boys show emotions. Cry when you are sad, and smile when you are happy." This was the last time I would say goodbye to my grandmother, but I was a better person for letting my tears show everyone just how much I loved her.

— Jonathan Piccirillo, 15 —

Only Love Lasts Forever

Yesterday, after telling my brother, Rhys, and me to stop playing like wild animals in the house for what she said was the thousandth time, Mom went to take a bath. That's when it happened. We were playing around, bopping each other with pillows, when one slipped from my brother's grasp and smashed the glass dome on the coffee table, shattering it into a zillion pieces!

With her supersonic hearing, my mom heard the tremendous crash and then the sound of glass hitting the tile. Wasting no time, she came flying into the room to find out what had happened. I was sure my brother and I were dead meat and she was going to start yelling at us, but instead she just knelt by the pieces and began to cry.

This made Rhys and me feel pretty awful. We went over and put our arms around her, and she explained to us why she was so upset. Under the shattered glass dome was a white porcelain rose. Dad had given it to her on their first wedding anniversary. He had said that if he ever forgot to bring flowers for an anniversary in the future, Mom was to look at that one. It was like their love — it would last a lifetime.

Now it lay chipped on the floor, one petal gone. We began crying, too, and offered to glue it for her. She said that wouldn't really fix it. Now that it had been broken, the value of the "limited edition" had lessened. We got our piggy banks out to pay for it, but Mom replied that to her the rose represented Dad's love and could never truly be restored.

As Mom slowly began to pick up the mess, we tried everything we could think of to cheer her up, but even our best funny faces didn't work. Mom just looked away. Rhys and I were even really nice to each other, which always makes her eyes twinkle, but she didn't seem to notice. The tears kept coming down her cheeks as she cleaned up the mess.

After everything was picked up and Mom was on her way back to the bath, I stopped her in the hall and said I had something important to tell her. She tried to go around me, replying "Not now," but I wouldn't let her by. I told her, "I want to say something very important; it's a rule of God."

I put both hands on her shoulders and told her, "All things can be broken, Mom; everything breaks sometime. The only thing that isn't like that is love. It's the only thing that can never be broken."

Mom hugged me very tightly then and finally smiled. She said that I was pretty wise and understood some things that even much older people didn't!

After dinner that night, we had a family meeting. We discussed mistakes and the importance of learning from them. Mom glued the petal back onto the rose. The tiny petal now had a thin, almost invisible line of glue. Then Mom softly said, "Even though other people have 'limited edition' roses, mine is truly unique. Its tiny flaw reminds me of something more important: the realization that only love lasts forever."

— Denise and Rett Ackart —

The Reason for Living

*Love cures people — both the ones who give it
and the ones who receive it.*
~Karl Menninger

'm only twelve years old, but I know sadness and the fear of death very well. My grandfather has been smoking since he was a young teenager, and now he has a terrible disease called emphysema that ruins the respiratory system.

Ever since my grandmother died, my grandfather has been depressed — mad at the world. He is a very ornery man and has said some hurtful things to nice people. But when he is around me, it's like a whole soft side of him becomes exposed.

Recently, my grandfather got very sick. He underwent surgery on his throat and had to use a machine called a respirator to help him breathe. The doctors thought that his days were numbered, but miraculously he recovered. He was taken off the respirator, but still he couldn't talk. It strained his voice badly to make the slightest noise.

While my grandfather was in the hospital, my mother and I flew to Pittsburgh to be with him. We were very fearful we wouldn't see him again.

When we reached my grandfather's hospital room, I was shocked by his condition. He looked so sickly. He was hardly able to even grunt. Somehow though, he managed to mumble, "I… you."

"You what, Grandpa?" I whispered. He didn't have the energy to answer me. He had exhausted all his strength with those two syllables, "I… you."

The next morning my mother and I had to leave. I kept wondering just what it was he had tried so desperately to tell me. It wasn't until I was back home in Georgia that I learned what he had tried to say.

A week after we returned home, my family received a phone call from one of the nurses in the hospital. She told us that my grandfather had said, "Call my granddaughter and tell her 'love.'" At first I was a little confused, thinking why he would just say, "love." Why not, "I love you?" Then it hit me. The day we were in the hospital he had been trying to say, "I love you." I was really touched. I felt as if I was going to cry, and I did.

After many painful weeks, my grandfather was finally able to talk. I called him every night. Normally he had to stop after about five minutes because he was too weak. No matter what, though, every time we hung up he would say, "I love you" and "I'd do anything for you." These, along with his moving words, "You're the only reason I live," are the best compliments I have ever received.

My grandfather is still very ill and I know our time is limited. I feel very honored that he has shared his feelings with me. I have learned a lot from this experience. But the most important thing I've learned is that a simple "I love you" is really not simple. It's a reason for living.

— Lauren Elizabeth Holden, 13 —

Death and Dying

She'll stay with you
As long as the wind blows
She'll always be in your heart
She didn't leave you all alone
She has eternal life
Her spirit is always within you
And if the sun shines in the sky
And rain should fill the air
And a rainbow lights up your day
Know that she is there.

—Karli McKinnon, 10—

Ryan's Story

The most daring, courageous and patient person I have ever known was my cousin. Ever since I can remember, my cousin Ryan and I seemed to have a special bond. I have two special memories of Ryan when we were very young.

The first one happened on a hot summer day, at Disneyland in California. I can still hear the laughter and voices from people around us. I remember looking up when Ryan pointed toward the sky. My Mickey Mouse balloon and his were tangled up together.

The second memory I have is when Ryan and I were playing with little cars in our grandparents' family room. He had a green car and I had a brown one. I smashed my car into his and broke it. I didn't mean to, and I felt bad. Looking back, I now realize how important and special memories are.

Then my Uncle Rick, Ryan's dad, moved his family to Pocatello, Idaho. I didn't get to play with Ryan anymore, but we kept in touch by phone.

It had been some years since I had heard from them, until one particular evening. Ryan was seven and I was six at the time. After my Uncle Rick and my mom had talked, my mom hung up the phone. That's when she told me that Ryan was sick.

Ryan had leukemia. It was in his bloodstream and eventually it went into his bone marrow. Can you imagine? A seven-year-old! I don't know how he had the courage to live, each day knowing that he was dying of cancer.

After that, we kept in touch a lot over the phone. Finally, when he was eleven, they came to California to visit us for two weeks. Ryan was able to come because he had wished for this, and the Make-A-Wish Foundation was paying for it. This special foundation tries to make terminally ill children's wishes come true. Ryan wanted to go to all of the nearby theme parks like Disneyland, Universal Studios and Sea World.

One day during this visit, Ryan and I went in-line skating together. We sat down on the curb, and we talked about when we had been little together. He told me his memories of us and I told him of mine. He remembered the balloons at Disneyland. It meant a lot to both of us that we remembered the same things.

Eventually, the two weeks came to an end, and Ryan and his family went back to Idaho. We kept in touch throughout the next year. When Ryan was twelve, he needed a bone marrow transplant, but the odds were against him. The chances of finding a matching donor were one in ten million people, so Ryan had to have an experimental transplant. It had been tried only once before, and the man had died. The doctors took Ryan's father's bone marrow and gave it to Ryan. Ryan lived through it.

About a month before he had this transplant, I talked to him on the phone. I felt embarrassed to tell him that I loved him, but I told him anyway, right before I hung up. Finally, Ryan died. He had so much medicine, and so many chemicals in his body, that his lungs couldn't help him breathe anymore, and they collapsed.

I was sad when he died, yet I felt peaceful about it. I was so glad that I had worked up the courage to tell him that I loved him. Now I'll never be ashamed to tell someone that I love them before it's too late.

Although I miss him, I think it's better that he isn't suffering anymore. Now Ryan walks with God in heaven.

— Kelli Frusher, 14 —

My Life

Sometimes life can be a pain
When your life stays the same
I've had cancer not once but twice
And it isn't very nice.

I hate cancer really a lot
It ties my life up in a knot
Sometimes I think the doctors lie
At times I think I'm going to die.

Before I end up in a coffin
I'll do my fun things soon and often
I had my transplant — it wasn't fun
It's hard to believe that I'm finally done.

Sometimes I wish I could roll over and die
Now I think I'm going to cry
When you're there you have to roll with the punches
Especially when it comes to their nasty lunches.

When I went to receive what my dad had to give
I was the second to do it, but the first to live
It was hard for us all — it could make you hysterical
But if you think about it... I'm a living miracle.

—Ryan Alexander—

I'll Never Forget Him

His name was Matthew. I always called him Matt. He had white-blond hair and blue eyes. He always had to do everything that annoyed me, but I guess that's what little brothers are for. Inside I still loved him. He was only four when he died of meningitis.

It was a beautiful winter day. I woke up, got ready for school and went to the bus stop. When I stepped on the bus that morning my brother, Matthew, was outside riding his bike. That's what he did every morning.

After a normal day of third grade, I rode the bus home looking forward to playing with my friend, Jessica. Two years ago she had moved next door to us with her parents, her little brother, T. J., and her sister, Brittany. They were all attached to Matt, like they had known him forever. When I got home I went straight to Jessica's house.

At three o'clock that afternoon, my grandmother, who I call Nana, and my other grandmother, who I call Grandma, took Matthew to the doctor. My grandfather said that Matthew was complaining about not being able to move his head or neck.

The doctor examined Matthew and diagnosed him with the flu. My grandmothers were told to give him something for his fever and that he would be fine in the morning.

When they came home from the doctor's office, they put Matthew in my room. I remember getting a sleeping bag and finding a cozy spot in front of our fireplace. I don't know all of the events that took place that night, but my Nana told me what she recalled. She said that Matthew woke up and had to use the bathroom. By then he was so weak he couldn't even walk on his own. His eyelids were stuck together, and he had little purple splotches on his face and arms. He had to be carried to the bathroom.

I woke up later and heard the ambulance driver in our kitchen. He was saying that he wouldn't take my brother to the hospital in the ambulance because "it's only the flu." Since the ambulance driver wouldn't take him, Nana and Grandma got ready and drove him themselves. When they were about halfway there, Matthew started to hallucinate. He said, "Sissy, my feet are burning." By the time they were at the hospital and the doctors diagnosed him, it was too late. They couldn't do any more for him.

My mom and dad woke me up at about 6:30 the next morning. I knew there was something wrong. It sounded like they were crying. Maybe they were. But when they told me what had happened, I wasn't sure if I was awake or still dreaming. I remember not crying, but inside I felt like it. Later that day, a lot of people we knew came to our house. They all asked if they could do anything for us. But they couldn't bring Matthew back.

Over the next few days, I tried not to think about what happened. I knew my brother was in heaven, but I wanted him back. A few of my teachers took off from work to come to his funeral. For a while, I couldn't concentrate at school, but eventually things got back to normal — as normal as they will ever be without Matthew.

A few years later, at a youth rally, we were asked to write advice on a piece of paper and throw it back into the air. I wrote, "It helps to cry when you lose someone." And today, I *know* it's true.

— Megan Weaver, 12 —

An Angel in Disguise

Love is the only force capable of transforming
an enemy into a friend.
~Dr. Martin Luther King, Jr.

hen I first met Damon, he was working on a fence that divided our property. My mom and I were in the field across from him. He seemed like a nice enough guy once we were acquainted, but since his kindness was being directed toward my mother, in my mind he became the devil in farmer's clothing.

I had just turned ten and the only man I had ever been around a lot was my father. So when Damon and my mom began to see more of each other, I didn't know how to handle it. My dad had not been a great example of the male species, so Damon didn't have a chance in my heart. To put it bluntly, I hated the man.

The only reason I could figure why Damon kept hanging around was so he could hurt our family and cause us all a lot of pain. Now I couldn't let that happen, could I?

For about six months, Damon tried every way imaginable to win my approval. He bought me things and was always taking my side in everything, no matter if I was right or not. He let me get away with everything. So, of course, I kept up my attitude even more. I was seeing this grown man begging for me to like him or at least accept him. So for just as long as he tried to win me over, I shot down every single attempt with a harsh word or a hatred-filled look. Sometimes I would do both.

But he never quit. Every time I hurt him, he just kept right on trying. Eventually it began to work and finally Damon and I became friends.

Surprising as it may seem, that crazy old man and I had a lot in common. He understood me more than I thought anyone could. Damon was a lot of fun to be around, and my friends and I loved going places with him. He liked to do all the things we did.

I remember him saying once, "I would rather you kids be with me having fun than be out on the streets getting into real trouble." He loved kids and he wanted all of my friends and me to be safe. He wanted to provide a place for us to call home.

Damon had two daughters. Mom had Nichole, Josh and me. All of our friends became part of the family. Whether we were working or eating dinner together, we always had fun and always found something to laugh about.

Although we didn't always get along, those times are nothing compared to the really good memories I have of Damon. For five years of my life, he was always there. Damon became the father I had never had. We had an unspoken bond between us that made us inseparable. I liked working with him and watching him work.

Right before my sixth-grade summer, Damon and I bought two bottle-fed bull calves. I called one Floppy, because of his ears, and the other Doofus (Doofus was named after Damon). We had fun with them because it was something we could do together. We built a pen in the barn for them and took turns feeding them about five to ten times a day. Usually Damon was the one taking turns.

He knew how I longed for a horse and, although he wasn't quite "cowboy" material, he made sure that I got one.

Damon not only gave me material things, he also taught me a lot of things about life and how to live it. When I met Damon, I was going through tough times. I had just realized that my daddy wasn't the saint I had thought he was, and like I said, the male species wasn't on my list of things to like. I lived in an unhappy world, and Damon was the only one who was able to get the walls around my heart to fall. I had always kept my emotions bundled up inside, and he showed me that talking was a good thing. I was finally happy with myself and my life, thanks to him.

One day out of the blue, Damon had a cerebral aneurysm. Earlier in the year my Papa Troy had had an aneurysm and had died the first night. So, regardless of what anyone told me, I was thinking the worst. But Damon survived the first night and the next night, too, and we all became hopeful. He was in a room in the ICU wing of the medical center.

After the aneurysm, he also had a few strokes and because of them he could not speak. I did not like going to see him because Damon was not "Damon" without his voice. He also looked so weak and helpless, and it hurt me dearly to go see him. I always got a knot in my stomach when I went to the hospital. But I went with hopes that he would respond to me.

Each time I went, though, I could not make myself talk to him. Damon was in ICU for about two or three weeks, and for a while he seemed to be getting better.

Then we found out that Damon's insurance would not pay for the type of care he was getting. He would have to be moved out of the hospital. In July, we moved Damon to a rehabilitation hospital in a nearby town. It was the closest thing we could get to home.

After Damon was moved, I only went to see him three times. I hated seeing him in that environment. Around the middle of November, Damon developed some kind of disease in his bloodstream and his health began to gradually decline.

In December, I went to see Damon because my mom said he was a lot worse and that he might like to see me.

When we went into the room, Mom explained to me that if I was going to hold his hand or touch him in any way I had to have gloves on because he was really sick. I was standing beside him watching him struggle for every breath, watching him suffer, and I couldn't do anything to help him. I broke down. I had been holding it in for so long I just couldn't do it anymore.

That night at home I went to bed with a heavy heart. I prayed that Damon would quit suffering regardless of the cost to me. I prayed that

I could see him one more time. But I didn't want to see the man lying in that hospital bed. It wasn't Damon. I wanted to see the Damon that I remembered: the one that I hadn't seen in almost seven months. After I had prayed, I was afraid to go to sleep. I was afraid that if I dreamed about him, which I often did, I would wake up to find him gone.

But I didn't dream about him again until Tuesday, December 22. That night I woke up around eleven o'clock to my mother's crying. At that moment, I knew. My brother came and told me, and I went and sat with Mom for a while. But I went back to sleep shortly and I slept soundly the rest of the night.

In the dream I had that night, I saw Damon on his tractor. He was smiling and I knew it was him. I also realized that he was free from any pain.

On the day of the funeral, I was a wreck. I finally realized it was over. I was going to miss him so much, but then again, I had been missing him for seven whole months.

It is now just over a month since we laid him to rest. As I write this, I still get a little teary-eyed. Damon was the greatest man I have ever met but I never told him. I never even told him that I loved him. I always thought that there would be time for that later.

Now, in everything I see, I am reminded of him. I miss the sound of the tractor and the smell he had when he came in after a long day of work. I even miss the annoying way he laughed. I just wish that one more time Nichole and I would be able to laugh with him.

Life is such a precious thing. Every day is taken for granted. There is a song called "One Day Left to Live," and I think everyone should live by it. It says to live your life like you have one day left to live. Don't live for the future and don't live for the past. Live for right now. Because right now is the only time that matters.

— Megan Jennings, 15 —

Don't Forget to Say I Love You

Two summers ago my family took a vacation, but we stayed in town. We went to downtown Chicago to see museums and to the Navy Pier. I saved all the ticket stubs and pictures from our vacation. I didn't know then how important they would become to me.

A few weeks later, my family had just come home from a party. My dad wasn't feeling good at all. A little while later my mom decided to take my dad to the hospital.

He came home about two days later. It seemed like nothing was wrong, but I overheard a phone call and realized my dad had cancer.

A few weeks later, my dad went back to the hospital to have surgery on his lung where they had found the cancer. That week, I spent almost every night at a friend's house because my mom spent almost all her time with my dad.

When I finally got to go see my dad, we spent all day just being silent and watching TV together. I was uncomfortable with this, and my dad could tell. I was Daddy's princess and he always told me he'd be there for me forever. That's what he said.

Toward the close of the day, we had to leave because he was starting to feel weak. I forgot to say I love you when I left.

Some days later, I spent the night at my friend Melanie's house because we had camp the next day. We laughed and giggled until ten o'clock.

My mom came over the next day to see me. She seemed really sad.

She told me my dad wasn't doing so well. Although I was worried, I left to go swimming at camp. As soon as we pulled out of the driveway, I looked back at my mom and saw that she had started to cry.

When I got home she kept asking me if I wanted a snack before she talked to me. Then, she told me that my dad had died. The two of us cried together for hours. Suddenly nothing felt the same.

My dad said that he would always be there for me. Suddenly I realized something very important. *He would always be there for me, but not in the way that I had thought. He would be watching over me from heaven.*

Now when I'm lonely for my dad, I take out those ticket stubs and pictures, and pretty soon I feel happy. And I'll always remember what he told me: "Never go to bed mad at someone, because you never know what can happen and when you will get to see that person again. Always tell the people you care about that you love them, when you have the chance."

— Nicole Fortuna, 10 —

Grandma's Cloud Game

I worked hard picking that bouquet of dandelions from the field in back of Grandma's house. When I presented my gift to Grandma she smiled and hugged me.

"Oh, child," she'd said, "you warm the cockles of my heart."

"You have cockles in your heart, Grandma?"

She laughed. The best part of Grandma was her laugh. It wasn't exactly the sound so much as the way it filled her whole face, and the way her belly made her white apron wiggle.

Grandma placed the dandelions in a glass jar filled with water. They stayed on her kitchen windowsill until every last one of them was as brown as the wood it was sitting on.

Grandma smelled like vanilla and coffee. I remember the first time we made cookies from scratch. I thought one of the cups of stuff she put into the bowl was "scratch." She explained, "There are two kinds of cookies; store bought and scratch."

She had a secret recipe and it was magical because it didn't matter if we put raisins or nuts or even chocolate chips in the batter, the cookies always tasted like heaven. Grandma gave me her secret scratch recipe and I keep it in my wooden treasure box under my bed.

I also have a four-leaf clover in my box. Grandma taped it to a piece of cardboard for me. We spent two hours crawling around on our hands and knees in her backyard looking for that four-leaf clover. We held hands and danced in a circle when I finally found one.

I loved spending the night with Grandma. She taught me how to play rummy. I always added up the points because she said I was such a good counter.

The smell of coffee was usually what woke me up in the morning. Breakfast always tasted great. Breakfast started with a big kiss on my forehead followed by orange juice. Sometimes we had eggs, but Grandma knew pancakes were my favorite. She always made more pancakes than we could eat. We crumbled the leftovers and scattered them in the backyard for the birds. I think the birds came from miles around to visit her backyard when I spent the night.

Grandma had what she called a "bottomless" candy dish. We could eat candy in the afternoon and after dinner in the evening. The next morning the candy dish was full again. It always held my favorite kind — white buttery mints. Grandma taught me to hold them on my tongue and feel them magically melt. We held contests to see who could keep their mint on their tongue the longest. Most of the time Grandma won that game.

Grandma's porch swing was my favorite place in the whole world. She sat on one side. I sat beside her and leaned against her, my feet and legs taking up the rest of the swing. I could smell Grandma's cookies in her cotton apron and coffee on her breath as she hugged me. We found pictures in the clouds as Grandma gave the swing a nudge once in a while with her foot.

Mostly, we talked. We talked about the neighbor's good corn crop. We talked about Dad's job and Mom's charity work. I told her my most important secrets and she crossed her heart she would never tell.

"Someday," she told me, "when I'm living with the angels, you look up into those clouds and say hi to your old grandma, okay?"

"Okay, Grandma, I will." I never worried about that day because I knew it would never come.

That was two months ago. Mom and Dad are in the house now packing Grandma's belongings. I am sitting on Grandma's porch swing, giving it an occasional push with my foot. The backyard is quiet. There is no laughter. I don't know if I will ever laugh again.

Grandma is here. I feel her presence everywhere. Her kitchen still smells like vanilla and cinnamon and coffee. Maybe she's just playing our game of hide-and-seek and she's out of sight just beyond that old lilac bush she loved so much. I know better, but I sure wish that was true.

A white, fluffy cloud moves across the sky, directly overhead. I look up, remembering our "pictures in the cloud" game. The wind shuffles the cloud as I watch. I see Grandma! There she is, sure as the world! Her wings are spread wide and her white dress is falling in folds around her feet. She has a happy smile on her face!

"Hi, Grandma," I call out, "I love you!" I knew she was there! She just doesn't need this old house and all the stuff in it anymore. I see her gently wave. Smiling, I spread out on the porch swing to watch her as she floats across the sky.

—Nadine Rogers—

Mr. Oberley's Star

I was nine years old the last summer that we lived next to Mr. Oberley. By then, he was retired and living alone — if you could call sharing a house with about twenty-five cats living alone. Early in the morning, I often heard shouts from his porch.

"Where did you come from?" His voice shattered the morning quiet. "Go away, Kitty! The hotel is booked!"

I smiled, knowing it was another stray. Mr. Oberley grumbled and complained, but never once did he turn away a needy cat. Their happy mewing often drifted out his open windows. Mom and Dad called it "The Cat Chorus."

Mom told me Mr. Oberley used to be a veterinarian. Once, just for fun, he wrote a cookbook for cats. But now he spent his days in the garden, among the daffodils, his arthritic back as stiff as a board. He joked that he was too old to be good for anything but conducting The Cat Chorus.

Sometimes my parents would let me stay up late. One night Mr. Oberley and I sat together, watching the night unfold. We breathed in the sweet perfume of lilacs as lightning bugs flickered like stardust strewn across the lawn. A parade of cats trampled over my stomach before scurrying into the purple dusk.

As the first star appeared, Mr. Oberley squinted into the sky.

"Life is so much larger than we can imagine," he said. He chuckled softly, rustling my hair. "Usually we think it's our problems that are so vast. Look, Cindy, sweetheart, look over there." He pointed to the largest and brightest star.

"One of these days, I'm going to climb that star and make it my swing," he said. "I'll ride it across the whole wide galaxy and see everything there is to see."

My first worry was, "But what if you fall?"

"I won't fall," he told me. "And just think, from the vantage point of my star I'll be able to watch you grow up. I'll even be able to hear the cats sing."

I thought long and hard about that. The following day, I told Mr. Oberley, in a most somber voice, that I did not want him to go off chasing stars.

"I'll miss you too much," I said. "And what about The Cat Chorus? The cats only sing when you're here."

It was true. Last year, when Mr. Oberley visited his sister, the cats had refused to sing at all. I bribed them with their favorite shrimp-flavored treats, but they didn't give one lousy meow… not until Mr. Oberley came back.

"I don't know," he said, tiredly. "Having a star to ride sounds pretty good when you have a body as old as mine."

Later that summer, Mr. Oberley became ill. His niece, Sarah, came to take care of him. The long, hot days passed slowly as I waited for him to get well again.

One day Mom and I brought him some chicken soup. I was shocked to see how thin he had become. He was almost too weak to lift his spoon. The worried cats serenaded him tirelessly, day and night.

The daffodils and lilac blossoms had wilted, but the roses were in full bloom the day Sarah knocked on our door.

"How is Mr. Oberley?" I asked right away.

His niece took a long, slow breath. "He told me to give you a message," she said finally. "He said you would know what it means."

"He found his star, didn't he?" I said, watching her eyes fill with tears. "Mr. Oberley went to ride on that great big old star."

Sarah nodded yes.

"And the cats?" I asked. "Who will take care of them?"

"I will," said Sarah. She planned to move into Mr. Oberley's house with her husband and young daughter, who was my age.

"Now you'll have a friend," she said.

"But Mr. Oberley is my friend," I insisted.

"Forever and always," said Sarah, wiping her eyes.

After Mr. Oberley's death, his cats refused to sing — except at night, after the first star lit the sky. And when that great big old star appeared, they sang until their hearts nearly burst. I knew then that it had to be true: Mr. Oberley was up on his star, just as he'd wanted.

— Cynthia Ross Cravit —

In Every Thought

Some people come into our lives and quickly go.
Some stay for a while and leave footprints on our
hearts. And we are never, ever the same.
~Author Unknown

I don't remember exactly when he came into my life. He was just always there. My grandfather was the most incredible person in the world.

Some days, Papa and I would go down to a little creek that flowed into the river and go fishing. He taught me how to cast, reel, and the scariest of all, bait a hook. I remember what it was like to catch my first fish, which Papa called a blue gill. For the first time in my life, I felt I had accomplished something useful. I was proud of myself.

Other days we'd sit on the front porch in the rocking chairs he had made and talk.

But the thing I most loved was when we'd go out to the barn and he'd make things out of wood. He made me my first rocking horse when I was four. It wasn't anything fancy, but like me, Papa believed if it came from the heart, then that alone made it beautiful.

Above all, anything that could bother a seven-year-old was something that I could always talk to him about. Papa would set me on his knee and listen to me cry. He made the world go away with one hug.

Whenever I needed punishment, he always talked to me about what I had done. He'd ask me why I made that mistake, while every other authority figure I knew went straight to physical punishment. He was the one person who had my respect, and who actually treated me with respect in return.

Something else I admired was that he didn't treat me like a girl who only related to pink ribbons and Barbies. He treated me like a person.

When I turned eight, a horrifying fact changed my life forever. That fact was death.

In September, they discovered that Papa had cancer. It never sank in, even at his funeral the next February, that I'd never see him alive again.

The agonizing six months of his sickness were long and cruel, especially to my grandmother, who could not talk without crying. I didn't know what death was.

Everything was a big, rushing blur. It was too much for an eight-year-old, so I blocked it out. Whatever death was, it wasn't real to me.

Slowly, I learned I couldn't block it out. There were no more rodeos, no more fishing, no more horses and no one left to talk to. When I walked into my grandmother's house, there was no longer the smell of smoke mixed with coffee and sawdust, which was what Papa always smelled like. Everyone around me was sad, and I was learning what it was like to be sad.

It finally hit me that he was gone. Things started getting rough with guys and friends. I knew if Papa had been alive, he could've helped. Instead I faced the world alone, and believe me, there are many pressures from sixth grade to high school. The world had become very cruel to me, or so it seemed, and I missed Papa. Night after night, I would go to bed crying.

In seventh grade, I hung out with the wrong crowd. One morning, in the bathroom, a girl offered me a cigarette. All of a sudden, something clicked in my mind. Cigarettes are what had killed Papa.

"No," was my simple but strong reply. Regardless of their comments like "good girl" and "too-good," I stuck with my no smoking policy. Since then, I have been offered cigarettes many times, and I have always replied with a simple "no." I wouldn't want my grandchildren feeling the way I did if they lost me to smoking.

I was too young to figure out what a great role model I had around me when he was alive. But I realize it now. Papa is in every thought I have today. I still have all our special memories in my heart. He always made me believe in myself. Anything I do, he has influenced in some way. No one has ever or will ever have the patience he had with me.

His death taught me many lessons, but the one so harshly instilled in me is that no one, even someone as great as him, is invincible.

—Leslie Miller, 14—

Attitude and Perspective

Each morning, when I open my eyes, I say to myself: "I, not events, have the power to make me happy or unhappy today. I can choose which it shall be. Yesterday is dead, tomorrow hasn't arrived yet. I have just one day, today, and I'm going to be happy in it."

—Groucho Marx—

An Odd Name

*What I want young women and girls to know is: You
are powerful and your voice matters.*
~Kamala Harris

I vividly remember the sixth grade, not because it was a great start to junior high, but because it was plain awful. The slow walk to the bus stop in the morning left me with a pit in my stomach. It was a dreadful feeling every single day. The bullying was constant.

I'm Indian American, born in the USA to first generation immigrant parents. I was going to a school that wasn't very diverse and I certainly stuck out.

"Your name is not real. Who made that up?"

"You smell like curry, so gross."

"I guess you can't help what your parents feed you."

"Why do you have that greasy oil in your hair?"

If I was lucky enough to find someone who'd let me sit next to them, I'd do my best to shrink. Shrink small enough to hopefully go unnoticed. To call zero attention to myself. There were three girls who used me as a target every morning and three more that would try to change the subject but never stood up for me.

This was the year that shaped the type of young adult I would become. Self-confidence didn't come easily, and I was constantly struggling to fit in. One day, after a boy in class made a joke about my religion, the teacher, Mrs. Langley, asked me to stay behind in class. What she said will forever stick with me. "You don't have to be like them to be a part of them."

I didn't have to change myself, my culture or who I was to fit in. I was a part of the story of this country and that mattered. Going forward, I stopped hiding the culture that made up half my life. I didn't agree with jokes that were made, and I would correct kids who made mean comments. It took years for me to understand that their bullying came from a place of fear: a fear of someone who didn't look like them or who had an odd name.

Later in my life, one of those girls from the sixth grade found and added me as a friend on social media. She had definitely changed her opinion of Indian culture by that time. Her posts were filled with chai tea lattes, yoga classes, turmeric foods and coconut hair oils — the same things she had hurtfully mocked me about years before. I decided to mention it to her and explain how much her words had impacted me. I didn't expect any kind of response but was blown away by the one I got. She apologized and said, "I had no idea how much it affected you. I saw someone different and lashed out about what was unfamiliar to me." In her small twelve-year-old world, there had never been a person that looked like me.

The way we grow up and the stories of our families shape who we are. We can't forget that every person we come across has a different journey. Meeting new people and learning their stories at a young age will forever shape the person you become. Inevitably, that shapes the future of the world we live in.

— Seema Patel-Trivedi —

A Healthy Mindset

I have insecurities of course, but I don't hang out with
anyone who points them out to me.
~Adele

Dear Preteens,

My name is Abigail and as I sit at my desk in my dorm room at my university, I am currently nineteen, 5'4", and weigh around 160 lbs. Although my BMI says I am still overweight for my age and height, I am no longer considered obese.

Rewind ten to twelve years: I am sitting at the dinner table eating snacks twenty-four-seven. I am statistically considered obese. I sneak snacks and hide the wrappers from my family. I take Klondike Bars into the bathroom and hide from my family. I bring extra snacks to school with me to hide from my family. I enjoy eating.

I am sitting at my squeaky desk at my middle school in New Jersey. A navy-blue plastic chair connects to my wooden desk by a metal rod. If the chair moves, the desk moves. If the desk moves the metal rod moves into my side and causes discomfort as it presses into my plus-size body.

My teacher stands at the front of the room to teach us about the fifty states. He is very tall and very thin. He is wearing black dress pants and a white button-down shirt. To my left is the smartest boy in sixth grade. He is one of the smallest kids in our grade. To my right is the class clown. As my teacher is going through each state, we come across the topic of government. Of course, the smart kid raises his hand and knows the three branches of the government. The clown, not knowing anything about the government, raises his hand to tell the teacher that he is going to be President one day. Our teacher smiles and says on that day he will move to Canada. The smart kid smiles, stands up, and says that one day he will become President too. I smile and admit when that happens, I will move to Canada with our teacher. I think we are all joking and having fun, but little do I know that was not the case. Next thing you know, the smart kid looks at me and says, "Well by the time I am President, you will still need liposuction to be skinny."

I never viewed myself as overweight until the day he mentioned liposuction to me. I don't know if I was oblivious or simply too young to know about health, but I do know that once he said that to me, I found myself looking in the mirror every day. I began to suck in my stomach as much as possible. I began to compare my body type to my friends. I began to have negative thoughts about being overweight and ugly.

That one sentence from the really-not-so-smart kid created a chain reaction of negative thoughts in my mind—whether my friends or family knew it or not. For that entire year, I didn't eat much. I stopped sneaking snacks and hiding the wrappers. I stopped sneaking the Klondike Bars into the bathroom. I stopped packing extra snacks for school. Now, you might say it was a good thing that I stopped eating junk food; however, the problem is I went cold-turkey and let the words of a sixth-grade boy get the best of me and dictate my life and control my thoughts for over a year. That is not okay.

Fast forward to the present. I sit at my desk typing this letter. I can tell you I was an eleven-season varsity athlete in high school, and I am now a collegiate field hockey player. Yes, I am still considered overweight, but I am healthy. I eat fruits and vegetables every day. I work out and play field hockey every day. I have positive thoughts about my body every day. Yes, those cruel words from long ago will always be in the back of my mind, and yes, I admit I compare my body to my teammates', but I have accepted that this is the body God gave me and I worked for. I should be proud of myself. I run. I eat. I laugh. What else could a healthy body need?

I wish I learned at a younger age that the only person who needs to love and accept my body is myself. For years I was jealous of my friends who wore size 0 jeans because that's what was portrayed in the media as the desired body type. I would look in the mirror and be saddened by my lower roll and thick thighs. However, as society progresses, females are being empowered by spreading body positivity. More people are accepting plus-size models and looking to embrace curves and chub. Today, I look in the mirror and love my lower roll and thick thighs because they are a part of me.

We weren't talking about bullying and body image when I was in sixth grade. We should have. Bullying is an awful thing that should not exist. It tears people down and causes a lack of confidence in individuals who are destined for great things. As you walk away after reading this letter, I hope my experiences have taught you to never let anyone bring you down. I want you to love yourself and accept your beautiful body and work hard for what you want. I wanted to be a healthy athlete with loving friends and family, to prove to my classmates and myself that a healthy mindset is a healthy lifestyle and a healthy body. I am currently on track and I hope you will be too.

Good Luck!
All the Best,
Abigail

— Abigail Williams —

Big at Heart

*Every man stamps his value on himself... Man is
made great or small by his own will.*
~Friedrich Schiller

My best friend's exceptionally small. We're in the fifth grade,
but Larry's as short as a first grader. Although his body's
small, Larry's big at heart. He has a sharp mind, too. All the
kids who know Larry like him a lot.

Sometimes he gets his share of teasing, but Larry knows how to
handle it. When some smart mouth calls him Dopey, Sleepy or Bashful,
Larry just laughs and starts humming, "Hi, Ho!"

Larry loves sports, but he can't play some, like football. One
tackle and he would be wiped out. But one sport seems to be made for
Larry — baseball. He's our star player. The legs that are too short for
track and hurdles can pump up and down, carrying him around those
bases faster than you can see. He can slide to safety under a baseman
before he's noticed. And when he's in the field, he catches and throws
that ball like the biggest of us.

I remember when he first came to try out for our Little League
team. The coach took one look and shook his head.

"No, I'm sorry, but we need big, strong players. Tell you what — we
could use a batboy!"

Larry just grinned and said, "Give me a chance to try out. If you
still think I'm a weak player, I'll be the best batboy you ever had!"

The coach looked at him with respect, handed him a bat, and
said, "Okay, it's a deal."

Well, obviously no pitcher could aim the ball inside Larry's ten-inch strike zone! He would be a sure walk to first base every time, and the coach knew how to take advantage of that. And when he saw how fast Larry's legs could travel and how well he handled the ball, he bent over, patted Larry on the back, and said, "I'm proud to have you on the team."

We had a winning season, and yesterday was our final game. We were tied with the Comets for the championship. Their pitcher, Matt Crenshaw, was a mean kid who never liked Larry — probably because he could never strike him out.

Somehow we held the Comets through the top of the ninth inning, and we were tied when it was our turn at bat. As Matt passed our bench on the way to the pitcher's mound, he snarled at Larry, "Why don't you go back to Snow White where you belong?"

I heard him and jumped up, ready to give Matt a punch, when Larry stepped between us. "Cut it out!" he yelled, pushing me away from Matt. "I can fight for myself."

Matt looked as if he was going to clobber Larry, but my friend held out his hand and said, "Let's play baseball, okay? I know you want your team to win and it must be tough to pitch to a shrimp like me."

"Chicken, you mean. You won't even swing at the ball!" Then he stamped off to the mound as Larry slowly dropped his outstretched hand.

We had two outs when it was Larry's turn at bat. The bases weren't loaded, but the coach told Larry to wait for a walk, as usual. Larry held his ground for three balls. One more and he would walk to first.

Then, for some reason — maybe because Matt had called him "chicken" — Larry reached out for the next pitch. It wasn't anywhere near his strike zone, but he swung the bat up and around. He connected. We heard a loud crack and saw the ball sail over all the outfielders. They had to chase after it, and Larry's legs started churning. Like locomotive wheels, they went faster and faster, rounding second and third and heading for home. The Comets finally retrieved the ball and passed it to the catcher. Larry slid safely under him as he caught it.

We had our winning run, the game was over, and we were the

champs. After we were presented with our winner's trophy, we gave it to Larry and took turns putting him on our shoulders and marching around the field.

I was carrying him when we passed Matt. "Put me down for a minute," Larry said. He walked over to Matt with his hand extended again for the handshake Matt had refused earlier.

"It was a good game," Larry said, "and you came close to winning it…."

Matt looked at Larry for what seemed like a long time, but finally Matt took Larry's hand and shook it.

"You may be a shrimp," he said, "but you're no chicken. You deserved to win."

Then Larry and I ran back to the rest of our team. We were all going to the pizza place for a victory celebration. I sure was proud to have Larry as a friend. Like I said, he's big in the ways that really count.

— Mark Schulle as told by Bunny Schulle —

The Best Christmas I Never Had

*To gain that which is worth having, it may be
necessary to lose everything.*
~Bernadette Devlin

My sister, Yvonne, was fourteen the year our home and everything in it was destroyed. I was seventeen. Our home was heated by a wood-burning stove, and every fall, my family and I would mark dead trees, cut them down, haul the wood and stack it in the basement. The week before Christmas, the basement was half full of dry wood.

Yvonne and I were home from school, and she did as either of us had done a thousand times before: checked the furnace, tossed a few more logs on the fire and slammed the door shut.

At the time, I was upstairs sulking. I had a sink full of dishes to wash, homework to tackle and my grandfather, after a lonely day at home, wouldn't leave me alone. Stomping around the kitchen, listening to him chatter, I thought about how I couldn't wait to get out of this house, this town. *Lightning could strike this very spot and I wouldn't care.* Or so I thought.

The house seemed a little smoky, but that wasn't unusual. It often became that way after the furnace had a few new logs to chew up. I simply waved the smoke away and kept doing dishes and daydreaming of getting away from my family. My sister's cats were no help; they were as starved for affection as Grandpa, and kept twining around my ankles.

My sister wandered in and said, "Don't you think it's a little too smoky in here?"

I shrugged sullenly and kept washing dishes. But after another minute, we knew something was wrong. The smoke was much too thick. My sister and I looked at each other, then at our grandfather. He was the adult, but he lived with us because he couldn't take care of himself. If there were decisions to be made, my sister and I — high school students — would make them. The thought was daunting, to say the least.

Without a word to each other, we went outside and opened the garage door (foolish in retrospect) and stared in disbelief as smoke and flames came out.

We had no time for tears or hysterics. That would come later. Instead, we both turned and ran up the hill. My sister shot through the kitchen door and raced for Grandpa's coat while I searched frantically for my keys. "There's a fire, Grandpa," I said abruptly. *Where in the world had I put my purse?* "We have to get out."

"Oh. Okay," he agreed. Amiable as a child, Grandpa stood still while my sister jerked him into his coat. She made sure he was warm and tightly bundled, forced warm slippers on his feet and hustled him out the door. I was so busy wondering where my keys were and trying the phone, which was dead, I never noticed that in her great care to make sure our grandfather was protected from the elements, she had neglected her own coat and boots.

I glanced out the window, blinking from the smoke. December in Minnesota was no joke... and no place for two teenagers and an old man to await help. If I could find my keys, I could get back down to the garage and probably, if the flames hadn't spread that far, back the van out of the garage. We could wait for help in relative comfort, and at least my mom's van could be saved.

Memory flashed; I had tossed my purse in my room when I'd come home. My room was at the end of a long hallway, far from the kitchen. Daughter and granddaughter of professional firefighters, I should have known better. But things were happening so quickly — my little sister and my grandfather were standing in the snow, shivering — I had to get the van. So I started for my room, the worst decision I've ever made.

The smoke was gag-inducing, a thick gray-black. It smelled like a thousand campfires and I tried not to think about what was being destroyed: my family's pictures, their clothes, furniture. I'd gone three steps and couldn't see, couldn't hear, couldn't breathe. How was I going to make it all the way to my room?

I wasn't, of course. I instantly knew two things: if I went down that hallway, I would die. Number two, what was I still doing in this inferno? Ten-year-olds were taught better. My sister was probably terrified, and in another moment, she'd come after me. How stupid could I be?

I stumbled back to the kitchen, took one last glance around my home, then went out into the snow.

Yvonne was sobbing, watching our house burn to the foundation. Grandpa was patting her absently. "That's what insurance is for," he said. A veteran of the New York City Fire Department, I couldn't imagine how many house fires he had fought. For the first time, I could see him as a real person and not my aged, feeble grandfather who took up entirely too much of my time with his endless pleas for me to sit down and talk to him.

"I'm going to the neighbors' to call for help," Yvonne said abruptly. She was wearing a sweater, jeans and slippers. I was in sweatpants, a T-shirt and socks. The closest neighbor was down the length of our driveway and across the highway, about a mile.

"Okay," I said. "Be careful crossing the…" But she was gone, already running through the snow and down the driveway.

Then I remembered Yvonne's three cats, which were, I guessed, trapped in the house. When she remembered them, I thought, she would go right out of her mind.

It seemed she was only gone for a moment before I saw her puffing up the driveway. "I called," she gasped, "they're on their way."

"You should have stayed with the neighbors and gotten warm," I said, mad at myself because I hadn't told her to stay put.

She gave me a look. "I couldn't leave you out here in the cold."

"Actually, I'm not that…," I began, when suddenly Yvonne clapped her hands to her face and screamed.

"Oh my God, the cats!" she shrieked, then burst into hoarse sobs.

"It's okay, Yvonne, it's okay, I saw them get out," I said frantically, reaching for her. I could tell she didn't believe me, but she didn't say anything more, just wept steadily and ignored my fervent assurances — my lies.

As it swiftly grew dark, our burning house lit up the sky. It was as beautiful as it was awful. And the smell... to this day, whenever someone lights a fire in a fireplace, I have to leave the room briefly. A lot of people find fireplaces soothing, but to me the smell of burning wood brings back the sense of desolation and the sound of my sister's sobs.

We could hear sirens in the distance and moved out of the way as two fire trucks and the sheriff pulled in. The sheriff screeched to a halt and beckoned to us. In another minute he was talking to my grandfather while Yvonne and I sat in the back of the police car, getting warm.

After a long moment, Yvonne sighed. "I just finished my Christmas shopping yesterday."

I snorted... and the snort became a giggle, and the giggle bloomed into a laugh. That got my sister going, and we laughed until we cried and then laughed some more.

"I got you the CD you wanted," I told her.

"Really?" she said. "I bought you a new Walkman."

We listed all the things we had bought for friends and family that were now burning to cinders. Instead of being depressing, it was probably the highlight of the evening. The sheriff interrupted our spiritual gift-giving to open the door and say, "Your parents are here."

We scrambled out and raced down the driveway. If I live to be one thousand, I'll never forget my mother's face at that moment: bloodless and terrified. She saw us and opened her arms. We hurled ourselves at her, though we were both considerably taller than she was and nearly toppled her back into the snow. Dad looked us over, satisfied too that we weren't hurt, and some of the tension went out of his shoulders. "What are you crying about?" he asked, pretending annoyance. "We've got insurance. And now we'll get a new house for Christmas."

"Dad... for Christmas... I got you those fishing lures you wanted but..."

He grinned. "That reminds me. I picked up your presents on the way home." He stepped to the truck and pulled out two garment bags. Inside were the gorgeous jackets Yvonne and I had been longing for since we'd fallen in love with them at the mall.

We shrugged into them, ankle-deep in snow, while the house crackled and burned in front of us. It was a strange way to receive a Christmas present, but neither of us were complaining.

"We'll have to come back here tomorrow," Dad said. "It's going to be depressing and stinky and muddy and frozen and disgusting and sad. Most of our stuff will be destroyed. But they're only things. They can't love you back. The important thing is that we're all okay. The house could burn down a thousand times and I wouldn't care, as long as you guys were all right." He looked at us again and walked away, head down, hands in his pockets. Mom told us later he had driven ninety miles an hour once he'd seen the smoke, that they both gripped the other's hand while he raced to the house. Not knowing if we were out safe was the worst moment of her life.

Later we found out the pipe leading from the furnace to the wall had collapsed, spilling flaming coals all over our basement. If it had happened at 2:00 a.m., we all would have died of smoke inhalation. In less than half an hour, our house transformed from a safe haven to a death trap. Asleep, we would have had no chance.

We lived in a motel for more than a month, and we spent Christmas Day in my grandmother's crowded apartment eating take-out because she was too tired to cook. For Christmas, Yvonne and I got our jackets and nothing else. My parents got nothing except the headache of dealing with insurance companies. All the wonderful things my family had bought for me had been destroyed in less time than it takes to do a sink full of dishes. But through it all I had gained long-overdue appreciation for my family. We were together. That was really all that mattered.

I'll always remember it as the best Christmas I never had.

— MaryJanice Davidson —

The Hidden Treasure

Old Man Donovan was a mean man who hated children. He threw rocks at them and even shot at them with a shotgun. At least that's what we had heard.

His small farm bordered our neighborhood where my younger sister, Leigh Ann, and I lived when we were growing up. His farm was long, narrow and quaint. It held two treasures. One was his beautiful fruit.

There were many varieties of fruit: pears, apples and lots more I just can't think of. The fruit naturally drew the children to his land. It made them into thieves. But my sister and I didn't dare to take his fruit because of the horrible rumors we had heard about Old Man Donovan.

One summer day, we were playing in a nearby field. It was time to head back home. My sister and I were feeling very daring that day. There was a short cut to our house that went through the Donovan farm. We thought he wouldn't be able to see us run across his property around the luscious fruit trees. We were almost through the farm when we heard, "Hey, girls!" in a gruff, low voice. We stopped dead in our tracks! There we were, face to face, with Old Man Donovan. Our knees were shaking. We had visions of rocks pounding our bodies and bullets piercing our hearts.

"Come here," he said, reaching up to one of his apple trees. Still shaking, we went over to him. He held out several ripe, juicy, red apples. "Take these home," he commanded. We took the apples with surprised hearts and ran all the way home. Of course, Leigh Ann and I ate the apples.

As time went on, we often went through Old Man Donovan's farm, and he kept on giving us more luscious fruit. One day, we stopped by to see him when he was on his front porch. We talked to him for hours. While he was talking, we realized that we had found the other hidden treasure: the sweet, kind heart hidden behind his gruff voice. Soon, he was one of our favorite people to talk to. Unfortunately, his family never seemed to enjoy our company. They never smiled or welcomed us in.

Every summer, we would visit Mr. Donovan and talk to him. He told us all kinds of stories we loved to hear. But one summer, we heard that he was sick. When we found out that he had come home from the hospital, we visited him right away. His voice box had been removed. When he placed his fingers on his throat, his voice came out as a whisper. We couldn't understand him, but through his eyes we could tell what he meant.

The next winter, word got around that Old Man Donovan had died. Leigh Ann and I were heartbroken and decided to go to the funeral. We were scared because we didn't know if the family would welcome us.

When we got to the funeral, the family kindly greeted us and said they were so glad we had come. We all wept mournfully, but our wonderful memories of Old Man Donovan comforted us.

During those summers with Mr. Donovan, my sister and I learned not to judge a heart until you know it. One may just find a hidden treasure.

—Debbie King, as told by Ashley King, 11 —

The Snow Angel

Love the moment, and the energy of that moment will
spread beyond all boundaries.
~Corita Kent

E ver since I was little, my favorite season was winter. I loved to play in the snow and enjoy the hot chocolate.

Unfortunately, winter never gave me the special gift of snow on my birthday. The snow disappeared before my birthday and started after it.

I would ask my grandmother why it didn't snow on my birthday. She would laugh and tell me I asked too many questions. But one day, she promised that she would make it snow when I was enjoying life to the fullest. I thanked her and asked for snow on my next birthday.

That year, before my birthday, my grandmother died. I was at an emotional loss, but angry because she had promised me to make it snow. The day of my sixth birthday, I woke up and ran to my window, hoping to see just one snowflake.

Unfortunately, there was no snow. I cried and cried all day because my grandmother had let me down.

Before my birthday every year, I would pray for snow but it never came. I felt mad at my grandmother; she had broken a promise.

By my sixteenth birthday, I had lost all hope of getting my snow, even though I still wished for it. During my party, I had the best time ever! I enjoyed the company of my friends and family, and I was truly happy.

I was outside with a friend when she asked me if I was having a good time. I told her I was having the best time ever! I was enjoying life to the fullest. Then I saw the white snow falling all around. I became like a little child on Christmas morning as I ran around screaming and laughing. I was so excited that my friends looked at me as if I were crazy, and I think I was. They asked me if I had ever seen snow before, and I laughed and said that I had, but that this was special snow. They all laughed at me, but I didn't care.

When I got home, my grandpa told me he had a gift for me. I was confused because he had already given me my gift. He gave me a small white box that had snowflake wrapping on it. The box looked old, and it was turning a little yellow. I asked him what it was and he told me to stop asking so many questions and just open it. I did, and nestled in white paper was a crystal snowflake with a card that said, "Happy Birthday."

I asked my grandfather how this could be. He told me that it was my grandmother's final wish to give me this on my "sweet sixteenth." I cried and hugged him, although he didn't understand. I said a silent prayer to my smiling grandmother angel who I was certain was, and always had been, watching over me.

— Christine Fishlinger, 16 —

You'll Be Good for Him

I heard the rhythmic clatter of metal crutches coming down the hallway. I looked up to see ten-year-old Brian smiling at me in the doorway, his blond hair tousled. Every day, Brian arrived at school cheerful and ready to work.

Brian had a great sense of humor and loved his own jokes. He was my first "handicapped" student. Everyone who worked with Brian told me, "You'll be good for him."

Brian worked with the adaptive physical education teacher and swam three mornings a week. He kept a busy school-day schedule. Everything he did required more effort than it did for the other students.

One day, Brian agreed to talk to the class about his handicap. The students liked Brian and wondered what he did after school. He told them that he watched a lot of TV or played with his dog. Brian felt proud to be a Cub Scout and enjoyed being a member.

The students then asked him why he used different paper and a special magnifying lens and lamp when he read. Brian explained that he had a tracking problem, and that he could see better out of one eye than the other. "I'm going to have another eye operation," he said casually. "I'm used to it. I've already had six operations." He laughed nervously, adjusting his thick-lens glasses. Brian had already had two hip surgeries, two ankle surgeries and two eye surgeries.

Brian explained how he'd been trained to fall when he lost his balance, so that he wouldn't hurt himself. I felt bad when he fell, but he didn't fuss. I admired his fortitude.

He said he often felt left out; then somebody asked if people ever made fun of him. He replied that he'd been called every name you could think of, but that he usually tried to ignore it.

I asked Brian if he ever became discouraged.

"Well, to tell you the truth," he said, "I do. Sometimes I get really mad if I can't do something. Sometimes I even cry."

At this point I ended the discussion. I felt the important questions had been answered. The students applauded.

"Can you walk at all without your crutches?" one of the boys shouted.

"Yeah," he said shyly.

"Would you like to walk for us?" I asked him gently.

"Yeah! Come on, Brian. You can do it!" several students shouted.

"Well—I guess," he answered reluctantly.

Brian removed his crutches and balanced himself. He proceeded to walk awkwardly across the room. "I look like a drunk," he muttered. It wasn't smooth, but Brian walked on his own. Everyone clapped and shouted.

"That's great, Brian!" I placed my hand on his shoulder.

Brian laughed nervously while I had to hold back tears. His honesty and courage touched me. I then realized that maybe I wasn't as good for Brian as he was good for me—for all of us.

—Eugene Gagliano—

Scott

I t was time for the ice cream social fundraiser that my small youth group had awaited for many months. The group consisted of five boys; one of them was Scott.

Scott always had a positive attitude. He looked on the bright side of things and never criticized anyone. But Scott was different from the rest of us. He was disabled. Oftentimes, he was unable to participate in activities. No one ever made fun of him to his face, but at times, people would snicker or stare in his presence. But Scott never worried; he just kept his head up high and ignored them.

Finally, the night of the ice cream social came. We rushed to the church basement and waited with scoopers in hand for the guests to arrive. One by one, people filed in, all hoping to get a nice, creamy glob of ice cream. But what they ended up getting was a hard, frozen mass. We waited for a while for the ice cream to thaw, and eventually it did.

Once the ice cream thawed, we had another problem. It had melted into three pools of vanilla, chocolate and strawberry. But we persisted in serving it. We all had our chance to serve, except for Scott. So, being as kind as possible, we gave Scott a chance to scoop and serve.

As soon as Scott gripped the scooper, our ice cream troubles turned into the World's Greatest Ice Cream Massacre. Milky ice cream was flung in every direction. Scott wouldn't stop. He kept scooping and scooping and scooping. Then, suddenly, in the thick of the chaos, Scott stopped. We looked at Scott. Scott looked at us. And that's when I realized why he had stopped.

Scott was looking at a small, cute girl who entered the basement. Scott stated, "That's m-m-my friend." Our jaws fell open. The most beautiful girl we had seen all night was Scott's friend.

We pushed Scott out of the way, hoping that we could get to serve her. But Scott just looked at us and said, "I-II want to scoop the ice cream for her." We backed off.

The girl slowly approached him. Scott stood poised, ready to scoop again. The girl said, "Hi, Scott."

"H-h-hi," stuttered Scott.

She began to make conversation with him by saying, "Look. I got my new braces today." She looked up and gave a wide, bright smile to show off her gleaming braces.

"Th-th-they're neat," responded Scott. The two carried on a short conversation; then the girl sat down.

That night I realized that somebody had overlooked Scott's problems and had seen him as a friendly, normal human being.

I realized something else, too. It was time for all of us to see Scott the same way.

— David Ferino, 12 —

Adam's Apples

After all, there is but one race — humanity.
~George Moore

One afternoon, my son came home from school with a puzzled look on his face. After asking him what was on his mind he said, "Are all people the same even if their skin color is different?"

I thought for a moment, then I said, "I'll explain, if you can just wait until we make a quick stop at the grocery store. I have something interesting to show you."

At the grocery store, I told him that we needed to buy apples. We went to the produce section where we bought some red apples, green apples and yellow apples.

At home, while we were putting all the groceries away, I told Adam, "It's time to answer your question." I put one of each type of apple on the countertop: first a red apple, followed by a green apple and then a yellow apple. Then I looked at Adam, who was sitting on the other side of the counter.

"Adam, people are just like apples. They come in all different colors, shapes and sizes. See, some of the apples have been bumped around and are bruised. On the outside, they may not even look as delicious as the others." As I was talking, Adam was examining each one carefully.

Then, I took each of the apples and peeled them, placing them back on the countertop, but in a different place.

"Okay, Adam, tell me which one is the red apple, the green apple and the yellow apple."

He said, "I can't tell. They all look the same now."

"Take a bite of each one. See if that helps you figure out which one is which."

He took big bites, and then a huge smile came across his face. "People are just like apples! They are all different, but once you take off the outside, they're pretty much the same on the inside."

"Right," I agreed. "Just like how everyone has their own personality but are still basically the same."

He totally got it. I didn't need to say or do anything else.

Now, when I bite into an apple, it tastes a little sweeter than before. What perfect food for thought.

— Kim Aaron —

Who Said There's No Crying in Softball?

Character building begins in our infancy
and continues until death.
~Eleanor Roosevelt

Our team was playing softball against a team that we were tied with for third place. I was toughing out the position of catcher, and we were winning. However, my knees started to not feel so tough. In the bottom of the second inning, they had started to hurt.

I've had bad tendonitis in my knees, and I just couldn't take any more abuse to them that day. So I limped over to the manager, who is also my dad, and told him that my knees were hurting. I asked if he could have the back-up catcher, Jill, catch for the rest of the game. He called Jill into the dugout and told her to put on the catcher's gear.

One of the other coaches overheard this conversation and came running over. I could tell that he was mad at my dad's decision because he was steaming like a whistling teapot.

He yelled at my dad, "Are you crazy? Jill can't catch — she has a huge cut on her finger!"

My dad explained to the coach about my knees.

"So what!" The coach rudely yelled at my dad.

Then he furiously walked over to me. His face was red, and I could feel my heart pounding in my chest.

"You'd better get that gear back on and get back out there right now. If you don't, I swear this will be the worst softball season of your life! Every game! Every game you complain about your stupid knees! If your knees keep hurting so much, I don't understand why you even play! You certainly aren't even good enough!" he screamed at me.

I couldn't believe what he said to me. Amazingly, I was able to choke through my tears, "I'm sorry! My knees hurt so bad! If I catch any more I'll collapse!"

"So what! Do you think I care?" he yelled.

By that time I was sobbing hard. The coach stormed off grumbling something over and over, leaving me in tears.

Later that night, I was lying in my bed thinking. Then a very important question came to my mind.

Why should I continue my softball season if I don't even have any respect? I asked myself.

Then, from somewhere deep inside my heart, I found the answer.

It doesn't matter what the coach thinks about me, it only matters what I think about myself. I love softball and I have a right to play, even though I may not be the best catcher in the world. That doesn't make me a loser. But I would be a loser if I believed what he said instead of believing in myself. I would lose my self-respect. No one, even the coach, can make me quit. All I have to do to be a winner is to keep showing up, sore knees and all. And I will.

— Amy Severns, 12 —

The Yellow Piece of Paper

When you're a young teen, it can seem like your parents have no feelings whatsoever. They don't understand when you just HAVE to get that new CD, even though you don't like the music that much. And that you HAVE to buy the new swimsuit, even though it costs sixty dollars for just two inches of material. Or, that you MUST impress the object of your affection by showing up at the movies, even though you'll dump him after two weeks of boredom. And then you have a huge zit and you need a dermatologist RIGHT AWAY, even though no one else can even see the zit.

These were my sentiments exactly. I never cared about my parents' feelings. I thought they weren't like me and had no idea what emotions were. I didn't believe that they could ever feel the same things I could. How could they? In my mind, they were old and cranky and that was that.

Then all that changed.

Snooping through my mom's purse was sort of a pastime of mine. It was usually for money, which — with my mom's permission to retrieve — allowed me to go to the movies or wherever the hot spot of the evening was. It was like an art form to dig through my mom's purse. Messy was one word for it, but I can think of others! I never found anything too interesting, so I tried to keep my digs quick and to the point, which was getting my money.

One Friday night, while I was looking for ten dollars, I pulled out my mom's black wallet. A piece of yellow paper fell out.

Curiosity killed the cat... Right?

Naturally, I hesitated.

Satisfaction brought him back.

I opened the piece of paper. It looked like a diary entry of some sort. Maybe it wasn't my mom's? That was highly doubtful, considering it was her sloppy cursive. I read it. It hit me; it was about my brother and his friend who died of leukemia. I didn't remember ever meeting the boy, who died when I was barely three.

I was overcome with shock as I read the contents of the letter. I quickly folded up the piece of paper and put it back where I had found it.

The next day, my curiosity overcame me again. Making sure my mom was out of the room, I got out the piece of yellow paper and read it again. It said:

June 3, 1987

I saw grief on my son's face today. He is eight years old. His friend died from leukemia. I've seen hurt, anger and bewilderment on my son's face, but never before have I seen grief on the face of one so young. I wonder what he is thinking. I told him that his friend had become an angel. Even though I had tried to avoid the word "died," he immediately realized what I meant. I'll never forget his look. Somehow I didn't expect such an adult expression of anguish. My angel story could not remove the pain of the passing of his friend. We knew for several months the bone marrow transplants had failed and that my son's friend was on limited time. And yet when the call came, I felt shocked. I had just seen him a couple of weeks before and he looked so good. How could God let life rob us of him so soon?

I keep thinking of his mother's pain. Her son died in her arms on the way to the hospital. Where did he go? How will she survive the loss? The pain must be so great. I see her grasping, trying to find her son. As a mother, it pains me to think of her great agony. There can be no experience worse than the loss of one's child.

For all of us, things will now be different. Next year, in the third grade, there won't be a seat waiting for my son's friend to

come back. Our parish won't be praying anymore for that miracle.
And his mother will be forever grasping, trying to find her son.

I cried a little, thinking about what my brother had to go through at such a young age. At least he had my mom, dad, sister and a little baby — me — to love him and help him through it.

My mom actually did have more feelings than I thought. Maybe my small problems of needing to have a certain CD, of buying a swimsuit, the need to impress some guy or an invisible zit weren't as important as I thought.

I can't say that, after reading the letter, all of those things still don't cross my mind, but I have a new respect for my mom. I don't ask her for things *as much,* and I don't yell and cry *as much* when she says, "No."

What did change was that I can tell her more about my own feelings, because now I feel that she will understand. I'm glad I found out early enough, before I grew up and left home. I have my mom to talk to, when I need to.

I don't know what would have happened if I had never read that letter. I don't think I want to know. I'm just glad that I did.

— Lauren Thorbjornsen, 14 —

Hard Work Pays Off

*Find out what it is that interests you and that you can
do well, and when you find it, put your whole soul
into it — every bit of energy and ambition
and natural ability you have.*
~John D. Rockefeller III

A s a young boy, I grew up with my eight siblings in a tin-roofed shack in Summerfield, Louisiana. I didn't see my circumstance as an obstacle, even though we didn't even have a real toilet in the house. I saw my life more as a card that had been dealt to me and I tried to make the most of it.

I was the youngest of five boys and also had four sisters who had to pull together and take care of each other. Dad wasn't around, so I never knew him well. He committed suicide when I was three years old, leaving Mom with the job of raising and providing for nine kids. She worked at a sawmill running a forklift for fifty dollars a week and had another job at a poultry plant. She was a very hard worker, and in order to make ends meet, she hardly ever rested.

My mom believed in doing all she could do to take care of her responsibilities, so no matter what, she never asked for a handout. You can imagine; we kids didn't get what we wanted, but we always got the things we needed. With my mom as my example, I learned that hard work is the best way to get what you want.

While growing up, I was surrounded with temptations to do negative things like drugs, alcohol and all that. I chose not to go there. Even as a little boy, I knew I was going to be successful. Some people take that to be cocky or conceited, but I wasn't going to let anybody tell me that I couldn't do whatever I set out to do.

Of course, I dreamed about what I wanted to be when I grew up. At first, I wanted be a state trooper, then I wanted to be in the Special Forces. After a while, I decided that I wanted to drive eighteen-wheelers. There was even a period of time that I wanted to be in construction. I wanted to play football in high school; in fact, I still do. But regardless of what I chose, I wanted to make my brothers, sisters and mom proud of me — not only by being successful in what I chose to do, but also as a person who could be looked up to for the right reasons.

Surprising as it might seem, basketball wasn't in my plans. One day, my mom cut a rim off an old water barrel and then held it up for me to throw an old rubber ball through. By junior high, I started playing basketball on a team. I loved to compete. There was a positive high I got by going out and playing against other people and working hard to win. For me, it paid off. I just let my success in basketball take its course but I always put the effort in, every day.

No matter what I've done, some people wait for my downfall, saying, "Karl Malone can't do it." Instead of letting people like that get to me, they are actually my motivation and I continue to prove them wrong every single day. I try to do the best job I can in a positive way on and off the court. I realize that no matter what I'm dealing with, there's somebody else out there who has it a little bit worse off. I've been there. And I know that without continued hard work, I could be there again.

I am grateful for the life I've enjoyed as a basketball star. But when I see these shirts that say "Basketball is life," I think *Yeah, right!* It is not life. It can be exciting. But the important thing about basketball is that it gives me a way to do good things for others as I move through this journey called life.

Success is really about choosing right from wrong, making a positive contribution to the world around you and valuing the things that are really important — like family and friends.

While everyone else was looking to popular athletes, actors and musicians as positive role models, my mom was my inspiration, and she continues to be all these years later. She taught me that hard work never killed anybody. My mom is my hero. She, my family and friends bring me more joy than anything else in life does.

At the end of my life, I don't want to be remembered as the kind of person who just sat on his rear end and said, "I've made it." I don't ever want to have to say that I didn't give it everything that I've got. Sure there are days that I don't feel like working hard... but I do it anyway, 'cause that's who I am.

— Karl Malone —

Overcoming Obstacles

Lost in dark depression
Not knowing where to turn
I opened the windows to my soul
To see what I could learn
I swept up the depression
Scrubbed the sadness and the hurt
I put it all in trash bags
And set them by the curb
I found stashed in a corner
Tucked high upon a shelf
A treasure chest of knowledge
That I could love myself
And wherever my future takes me
I know that I will win
Because I opened the windows to my soul
And let the light shine in

—Hope Saxton—

I Did It!

Impossible is just an opinion.
~Paulo Coelho

ow repeat after me!" Mom said in a kind but demanding voice, "I DID IT!" She paused as she waited for me to obey her.

When I tried to speak the only thing that escaped my mouth was a small sob. With one strong loving arm around me, my mom used the other hand to wipe the tears that I was no longer able to control.

Being a twelve-year-old girl is hard; being a twelve-year-old girl with dyslexia makes it even harder.

"It's okay sweetie, I understand it's hard. You know that I struggle with the same issue, but it doesn't have to define who you are or how smart you are!"

I was standing in my mom's bedroom with my unfinished math homework in my hand feeling like I was standing in front of a roadblock that was taller than my large imagination.

"I can't do it, Mom; I don't understand it!" Although I couldn't see clearly through my teary eyes, I could still sense my mom's face was filled with concern.

"Can I see your homework, hon?" As instructed, I slowly handed over the paper. After a short pause she excitedly announced, "You got the fifth question right!"

Shrugging my shoulders, I replied, "Yeah, but the rest are probably wrong."

Mom lifted my chin with a gentle hand and said, "Just because you got some answers wrong doesn't make the answer you got right any less impressive!"

I wanted to believe her, and in moments when it was just her and me it was almost easy to let her positive words affect me. But the confidence my mom gave me seemed to melt away when I was sitting next to kids my age and watching them complete work that I couldn't comprehend.

As we stood in silence, she lightly held my shoulders and slowly turned me so I could see myself in the large mirror that leaned against her dresser. Tears still streaked my face, but my vision was clear enough to see my mom's reflection as she stood behind me raising both her arms above her head in a champion pose.

"Now sweetie, I want you to stand like this, look at yourself in the mirror and repeat after me."

I halfheartedly adopted her pose, and because I was not new to this drill, I didn't have to wait for her guidance before saying in an unconvinced tone, "I did it." We both stood there, arms up in the air, staring at ourselves in the mirror.

My mom took a moment to pause and then before I had time to drop my arms she said, "Okay, now I want you to say it like you mean it! Like you truly believe that you just accomplished something!"

I was about to explain that getting one answer right was not an accomplishment but then thought better and in a more convincing, yet apprehensive, voice I said, "I did it!"

We dropped our stance and my mom immediately took me into her arms in a tight, protective embrace that reminded me I wasn't alone in the trials that we shared. Like so many times before, she held me close as my racing heart slowed and matched hers.

With a reassuring hand on my shoulder, Mom said, "Lucky for you, you have someone in your life who knows that your learning style is different and different is a beautiful gift! You know that I went through, and still go through, the same hardships. But I know I'm competent, smart and successful and it's so important that my daughter knows how intelligent she is. Now, let's take a look at your homework."

Together we looked through and completed the math homework. Mom took the time to dissect the concepts so my brain could soak in the material that seemed so easy for most people to get. After each problem we got right, we would high five as if I had just mastered something big. Although I didn't know it, each little problem I got right was a huge victory; by celebrating them as such, it taught me how to take challenges one at a time and to treat each success, no matter how big or small, as a great accomplishment.

"Now, tomorrow when you are doing your math, I want you to take the problems one at a time and say 'I DID IT!' after completing each one. Okay?" said my mom.

"Okay, I'll try."

I was feeling a little better about the situation and was ready to respect my mother's wishes whether she was there to witness it or not. So, the next day, as I sat at my desk in front of my dreaded math test, I took a deep breath and blocked out every problem except the one at the top of my sheet. After spending what seemed like an eternity on it, I felt confident in my answer. Before I had the chance to celebrate, I couldn't help but notice the many questions that came after the one I had just spent so much time on.

Instead of comparing myself to the people who were far ahead of my slow calculations, I took a deep breath and whispered to myself, "I DID IT!" Then I simply moved on to the next question, and the next, then the next, until eventually I had said "I DID IT!" so many times that I couldn't help but believe that I had actually done something great!

As I walked through the front door that night, I had a smile on my face. When Mom came to greet me with her usual hug, I raised my hands above my head in the champion's pose, and with a newfound confidence I announced, "I DID IT!" My mom and I both exchanged excited high fives.

Did I get all the questions on my math test right? No. Did I work as fast as the other kids my age? No. But that wasn't the point. The point was that I not only did my best, but I was able to congratulate myself for doing the best I could do!

Being a student is hard; being a student with dyslexia makes it even harder. After years of the same situation playing out, starting with tears and ending with a confidence boost from my mom, she has successfully instilled her "I DID IT!" trick into my everyday life. Whether I'm about to take a test, make a speech or walk into an interview, thanks to my mom, I now hold the knowledge that I CAN DO IT!

— M. Eliza Hryniewicz —

Finding My Voice

Never be bullied into silence. Never allow yourself to
be made a victim. Accept no one's definition
of your life; define yourself.
~Harvey Fierstein

The scratchy sound of ripping paper fills the room, and my stomach somersaults when I hear, "Up next we have Emily." I rise from my desk and walk to the front of the noisy classroom. As I turn to face my peers, they grab their pencils and get ready to compose their reviews of my performance.

I am on display before a mixture of preppy jocks and timid bookworms. Their stares challenge me and offer no comfort. I close my eyes and breathe deeply; my nervousness begins to fade. When I open my eyes, my public speech teacher gives me a bright, reassuring smile and nods her head. Calmness washes over me. I begin to speak.

Things were different five years earlier. I was ten years old and in the fifth grade. When it was time for recess, my classmates ran outside but I remained seated. My teacher would guide me through empty hallways until we reached the familiar wooden door with a big, yellow smiley face painted on it. Behind this door, the woman who was helping me fix my problem sat waiting. I slowly turned the doorknob, stepped inside, and sat down. Without delay, we got straight to business.

She held up an oversized flashcard, and on it was a picture of a spring daisy. "What is this, Emily?"

"That's a fwowa."

My speech impediment haunted me everywhere I went. Ready

to make me feel insecure when I had to answer a question in class. Ready to embarrass me when the cafeteria ladies couldn't understand my request for "fwench fwies" and "hambuwgews." And, worst of all, ready when my peers wanted someone to mock.

No matter how many special education speech classes I went to, no matter how hard I tried to move my mouth differently, I could not talk normally. My classmates were no help. They laughed and called me stupid, saying that I sounded "like a baby." My self-confidence began to diminish. I sat alone during lunchtime and avoided interaction with them altogether.

Over the next few years, my speech impediment began to fade, but my shyness persisted. I was too fearful of what my peers might think of me to speak up in class, during dance practice, and at yearbook meetings. Rather than make myself vulnerable, I would sit silently in the back of the room, hidden in a book.

Memories of their cruel, correctly pronounced words flooded my mind until my sophomore year when I transferred to another high school on the opposite side of the state. Nobody there knew me. Nobody there had ever heard me speak.

For the first time, I vowed to finally find my voice. I jumped at opportunities to put myself out of my comfort zone and speak: I introduced myself to all of my classmates, signed up for as many student clubs as I could handle, and volunteered to usher at the first school dance. I even found myself voicing my opinion in classroom discussions and excelling in, of all things, speech class.

Now, my speech is over. I pause, look into the sea of faces before me, and breathe a sigh of relief. I realize that I have overcome the fear my speech impediment caused. Now, not only can I say "flower," I can confidently speak in front of a group of people. I walk back to my seat, knowing I have done my best. After I sit down, I rip off a piece of paper, ready to write a review of the next student's performance. I look up and give him an encouraging smile.

— Emily Andrews —

From Freak to Friend

My solitary mornings on the corner of Hampshire Court and Eastbrook Lane had become almost unbearable. The other kids at my bus stop would chat in huddled bunches, carve their names into an unfortunate oak tree, and, occasionally, smoke cigarettes. Only once had a blond girl with pink lip gloss and unblemished skin invited me to join them and I had declined, instead continuing to read whatever thick book was my current library find. I'd given up on finding someone to sit with on the bus.

The summer prior, my family moved to Webster Groves, a small suburb of St. Louis. Before, we had lived in another suburb a few miles away, and I had attended a St. Louis Public Schools magnet program: the "international" school. I shared my classrooms with kids from all over the world — from Nigeria to Guatemala to Bosnia to Russia. I loved school; as a fifth grader I was well-known and admired for my spelling bee wins and oratory contest accomplishments, earning me the nickname "Matilda" after the precocious Roald Dahl character.

Now, I was just another white kid in a white suburb where being the teacher's pet marked you as dork of the century. I had expected culture shock, but I hadn't prepared for the loneliness.

Most of the first semester of sixth grade passed in a blur of awkwardness and solitude. I harbored a few massive crushes. I managed a daily exchange of pleasantries with the girl who shared my music stand in band class. The local YMCA hosted preteen nights monthly, and I bravely stood in line alone and wandered around the dance floor, trying to "make friends," a vague task from my parents that I never seemed to accomplish.

So, instead of socializing, I observed the socializing going on around me, anthropologically. I could label every friend group and detail the drama within and between them and identify whose crushes returned their interest. I kept copious notes about people in my journal, secret missives that I wrote backwards so no one could decipher my observations. After a mean boy who sat across from me in homeroom grabbed my notebook and teased me loudly to the rest of the class — "What a freak! What the hell are you writing?! You've got some weird freak language!" — I was certain my isolation would be permanent. I wished every night that my parents would send me away to boarding school.

Then, one day, Alyssa McFarlane sat next to me on the afternoon bus.

According to my notes, Alyssa was friends with Ali and Toni, cool girls who wore their hair in neat ponytails, kissed boys, and had impressive gel pen collections. But Alyssa was different — she wore her hair in pigtails high on top of her head adorned with cat ears and an accompanying tail. One day in gym class she removed the tail from her jeans and pinned it on her gym uniform; we did the rope climb that day, and her tail gracefully arched beneath her as she scaled the height with ease.

I don't remember what we talked about, because the surprise of not being alone made the whole conversation fuzzy, but she saved me a seat beside her the next morning, and again that afternoon, and then, suddenly, I had a friend.

Alyssa and I were both strange in our own ways, but where I hid my differences, she was outspoken about hers. This bravery inspired me: the next time that mean boy from homeroom called me "Fat Robin," I spat back an insult so mean he ran from the room crying. My teacher was stunned into inaction. This kind of behavior from Robin Lane, always on time and asking for extra homework, always raising her hand before she spoke? More than a friend, Alyssa became my protector, and no one ever called me a freak again.

Even when my new confidence occasionally failed me, Alyssa turned those moments into hilarious memories. Once, we spent an evening on her bedroom floor attempting to pluck our eyebrows. Alyssa insisted that we finish the job correctly, by brushing the hair of our eyebrows up, just so, and then evenly trimming the edges. When she pulled out a pair of large kitchen shears, I hesitated, but she assured me that her older sister did it this way. After one snip I saw the look on her face: disaster. I peeked at my reflection and then immediately shut myself in her closet, crying.

"How am I supposed to go to the dance on Friday looking like this? I look so stupid!"

From the other side of the door, Alyssa serenaded me.

"There's a hooole in your eyebrow," she crooned, convincing me to add the response: "Alyssa, Alyssaaaaaa."

The goofy song coaxed me into a laugh and out of the closet. I don't remember how we ended up repairing the damage to my eyebrow, but that mattered less than her ability to see the lighter side of things.

I didn't expect to stay friends with Alyssa, because the dominant narrative is that you grow up and grow out of childhood friends, that you change so much and move so beyond who you are as a child. It's true that many middle school friendships aren't authentic; they are based on convenience or happenstance or trying to fit in. But I think I was able to be the truest version of myself as Alyssa's friend, because she always loved me unconditionally, no matter what personality, style, or interests I tried on. Now, as we approach our twentieth year of friendship, at my core I am still optimistic, genuine, creative, and a bit dorky — just like that eleven-year-old girl hanging out with her best friend.

— Robin Lanehurst —

Annie Wiggle-Do

To live with fear and not be afraid
is the final test of maturity.
~Edward Weeks

"Look who's here to see you, Brenda," the nurse said.

She led a tired-looking woman to the girl's bedside.

Brenda huddled on her side, facing the wall. When her mother touched her shoulder, she pulled her head closer to her chest, as if making her body smaller would help her disappear altogether.

The nurse patted the mother's shoulder.

"Brenda's still not talking to us," she said in a low voice.

Brenda's mother bit her lip to keep from crying. She remembered exactly how bubbly and happy Brenda had been before the car accident that led to the amputation of her leg. She'd been one of the most popular girls in her sixth-grade class.

When Brenda first awakened from her surgery, she had raged at her mother. *Why had this happened?* Now, she felt like a freak. No one would ever want to be her friend. She would never date, never have a boyfriend. Then, Brenda had just stopped talking.

"I wish I could bring her friends to visit her," said Brenda's mother. "It's just too long a bus trip, though, about three hours each way."

The nurse smiled. "Don't worry. We have a plan."

Shortly after Brenda's mother left, two nurses wheeled in a stretcher.

"Moving day, Brenda!" one said cheerily. "We need this bed for someone who's really sick. We've picked out the best roommate in the hospital for you."

Before Brenda could protest, the nurses had rolled her onto the stretcher and whisked her down the hall. The room was awash with light, posters and music.

"Here's your new roomie, Annie Wiggle-Do," one nurse told a dark-haired teenager in the other bed. "She's just beginning to get better, so please don't kill her with your corny jokes."

Fourteen-year-old Annie grinned. As soon as the nurses left, she hopped out of her bed and sat on the end of Brenda's.

"I lost my leg from bone cancer," she announced. "What happened to yours?"

Brenda was so astounded she couldn't even form a word.

"You're lucky," Annie continued. "You've still got your knee. They had to take mine, hip and all, see?"

But Brenda's eyes had already found the raw scar and empty hip socket. Her gaze seemed frozen, like a magnet held it there.

Annie scooted back to her bed. "I'd like to socialize, but my boyfriend's due any time now, so I have to get ready."

As Brenda watched transfixed, Annie reached up and took off her hair! Her head was completely bald.

Annie giggled. "Oh, I forgot to warn you, the stuff they gave me to kill the cancer also killed my hair. But check this out! My parents, my grandma, my boyfriend and some kids from school all brought me wigs!"

From her bedside stand, Annie removed a tangle of wigs. Brown wigs and blond wigs, short-haired and longhaired wigs, curly wigs and straight wigs.

"That's when I thought up 'Annie Wiggle-Do,'" Annie said. "Get it? 'Any wig will do.' Annie Wiggle-Do?"

Laughing at her own joke, Annie chose a curly blond wig and arranged it on her head. She just managed to dab on some pink lip gloss before a group of boisterous teens burst into the room. Annie introduced Brenda to them all. Her boyfriend, Donald, winked at Brenda and asked her to keep Annie out of trouble.

Before long, Brenda began chatting with Annie and her friends.

They didn't make her feel like a freak at all! One girl even shared with Brenda that her cousin wore an artificial leg, played basketball and rode a motorcycle. By the time the nurses shooed all the visitors from the room, Brenda felt more like the old Brenda.

The girls talked into the night. Annie shared her dream of becoming a comedy writer. Brenda told Annie about her secret desire to act in live theater.

"Ladies!"

A night nurse came in and shined her flashlight on Annie and Brenda. "It's after midnight," the nurse scolded. "What do you have to say for yourselves?"

"Nothing, your honor," Annie said. "We don't have a leg to stand on!"

They all laughed, but Brenda laughed hardest of all.

As the nurse's footsteps faded down the hallway, Brenda snuggled under her blanket. "'Night, Annie Wiggle-Do," she whispered. "I can hardly wait 'til morning."

— Kathleen M. Muldoon —

Two Percent Is Enough

From the day I was born, I was a sickly, weak child who never had as much energy as a child my age should. When I turned four, everything seemed to go wrong. I had asthma and for the most part I was in constant pain. Every day, I had a nagging side pain that seemed to never go away, and I was in and out of doctors' offices many times, but they could never figure out what was wrong. "Simply growing pains," they told my parents.

One night, I had a fever, high blood pressure, nonstop vomiting and my feet were purple. My parents rushed me to the emergency room, where they were told that I needed my appendix taken out. I lay there that night, getting worse by the minute. Finally, purple feet became numb and my stomach was empty of everything. My parents lost control of their emotions. The next morning, my urine was brown. At that point, the doctors knew it was more than my appendix.

The next day, I was taken by ambulance to Children's Hospital under the care of Dr. Kohen, a kidney specialist. I was diagnosed with a rare form of kidney disease called glomerulonephritis. After two weeks of treatment, I was still not responding. My kidneys were only functioning two percent of the time and if something wasn't done, I would die.

My parents were faced with choices they never thought they would have to make: steroids, dialysis or a transplant. They were told that their only daughter was dying and without vast improvement would be put on a waiting list for a kidney transplant.

That night, my dad sat down by my bed and told me that I was going to have to fight harder than I had ever fought before. All of a sudden, I reached up and — mustering all the energy I had — I punched him in the nose! He knew then that I was not going to give up without a fight.

The next morning I was evaluated for a transplant. I was put on a steroid. Within a couple of days, I started showing steady signs of improvement, but my parents were told, "Krissy will never have as much energy as a normal kid, even if she pulls through."

Within four days I was strong enough to return home. For the next couple of months, I was under constant supervision. As a four-year-old little girl, I was taking fourteen pills a day and having my blood taken every other day. Gradually, I was taken off of the medicine and my doctors' visits grew further apart. But still, I was given no chance of a full recovery.

Well, ten years later, I can proudly say, "Look at me now!" I am fourteen years old; I play four sports, I am a member of the National Junior Honor Society at my school, vice president of Student Council, have a 3.5 grade point average, and I am a living miracle to my doctors, family and friends. I thank God every day for giving me my life. Even if you are only given a two percent chance of survival, that's all you really need.·

— Krissy Creager, 14 —

The First Day of Middle School

*The transition into middle school will be the hardest
change kids experience during their school years…
Compared to this, the first day of high school
is a piece of cake.*
~Allan Mucerino
Principal, Ensign Intermediate School

My stomach was tied in knots, and I could feel the sweat soaking through my T-shirt. My hands were clammy as I spun the face of my combination lock. I tried and tried to remember the numbers, and every time I thought I had it, the lock wouldn't open. Around and around went the numbers, left, right, right, left… *which way was it supposed to go?* I couldn't make it work. I gave up and started to run down the hallway. As I ran, the hall seemed to get longer and longer… the door I was trying to reach was farther away than when I had started. I began to sweat even worse, then I could feel the tears forming. I was late, late, late, late for my first class on my first day of middle school. As I ran, people were watching me and they were laughing… laughing… laughing… then the bell rang! In my dream, it was the school bell. But as I sat up in bed, I realized that it was my alarm clock jarring me awake.

I was having the dream again. I started having the dream around the end of sixth grade, and as the start of seventh grade drew closer, the more I had the dream. This time the dream was even more real, because today *was* the morning of the first day of seventh grade.

In my heart, I knew I would never make it. Everything was too different. School, friends — even my own body.

I was used to walking to school, and now I had to walk six blocks to the bus stop so that I could take the bus to and from school. I hated buses. They made me carsick from the jiggling and the smell of the fuel.

I had to get up for school earlier than in the past, partly because of having to be bussed to school and partly because I had to take better care of myself now that I was in my preteen years. My mom told me that I would have to shower every morning since my hormones were kicking in — that's why I perspired so easily.

I was totally uncomfortable with my body. My feet didn't want to respond to my own directions, and I tripped a lot. I constantly had a sprained ankle, wet armpits and things stuck in my braces. I felt awkward, smelly, insecure and like I had bad breath on a full-time basis.

In middle school, I would have to learn the rules and personalities of six different teachers instead of just one. There would be different kids in all my classes, kids I didn't even know. I had never made friends very easily, and now I would have to start all over again.

I would have to run to my locker between classes, remember my combination, open it, put in the books from the last class and take out different books . . . and make it to the next class all within *five minutes!*

I was also scared because of some stories I had heard about the first day of middle school, like being canned by the eighth graders. That's when a bunch of eighth graders pick you up and put you in a trash can. I had also heard that when eighth-grade girls catch a new seventh grader in the girls' bathroom alone, they smear her with lipstick. Neither one of these first-day activities sounded like something I wanted to take part in.

No one had ever told me that growing up was going to be so hard, so scary, so unwelcome, so... unexpected. I was the oldest kid in my family — in fact, in my entire neighborhood — and no one had been there before me, to help lead me through the challenges of middle school.

I was on my own.

The first day of school was *almost* everything I feared. I *didn't* remember my combination. I wrote the combination on my hand, but my hand was so sweaty it came off. I *was* late to every class. I didn't have enough time to finish my lunch; I had just sat down to eat when the bell rang to go back to class. I almost choked on my peanut butter and banana sandwich as I ran down the dreaded hallway. The classrooms and the teachers were a blur. I wasn't sure what teacher went with which subject and they had all assigned homework... on the very first day of school! I couldn't believe it.

But the first day wasn't like my dream in another way. In my dream, all of the other kids had it together and I was the only one who was the nerd. In real life, I wasn't the only one who was late for classes. Everyone else was late, too. No one could remember their combination either, except Ted Milliken, the kid who carried a briefcase to school. After most of the kids realized that everyone else was going through the same thing they were going through, we all started cracking up. We were bumping into each other in our rush to get to the next class, and books were flying everywhere. No one got canned or smeared — at least no one I knew. I still didn't go into the girls' bathroom alone, just in case. Yeah, there was laughter in the hallway, but most of it was the laughter of kids sharing a common experience: complete hysteria!

As the weeks went by, it became easier and easier. Pretty soon I could twirl my combination without even looking at it. I hung posters in my locker, and finally felt like I was at home. I learned all of my teachers' names and decided who I liked the best. Friendships from elementary school were renewed and made stronger, and new friends were made. I learned how to change in gym in front of other girls. It never felt comfortable, but I did it — just like everyone else did. I don't think any of us felt very comfortable.

I still didn't like the bus; it did make me carsick. I even threw up on the bus once. (At least it was on the way home, not on the way to school.) I went to dances and parties, and I started to wonder what it would feel like to be kissed by a boy. The school had track tryouts, and I made the team and learned how to jump the low hurdles. I got pretty good at it, too.

First trimester turned into second, and then third. Before I knew it, eighth grade was just around the corner. I had made it through.

Next year, on the first day of school, I would be watching the new seventh graders sweating it out just like I did — just like everyone does. I decided that I would feel sorry for them... but only for the FIRST day of seventh grade. After that, it's a breeze.

— Patty Hansen —

Perfect, I'm Not

"Owwww!" Robert yelled, backing away from me. "That hurt!"

"What do you mean? I just hit you with my jacket!" I said, laughing. Robert was the cutest boy in class, and I had a major crush on him. I hadn't meant to hurt him; I wanted him to like me. Besides, it was just a lightweight jacket.

But Robert didn't act like someone who had been hit with a lightweight jacket. He was crying and holding his left shoulder.

"What's going on?" our sixth-grade teacher, Mr. Mobley, asked.

"My shoulder... it hurts!" Robert groaned.

The next thing I knew, Robert was heading to the nurse's office. And I, bewildered, was marching back from recess and into our classroom with the other kids.

We started our spelling lesson, and I tried to pay attention as Mr. Mobley read the words for our weekly practice test.

Then someone knocked on our classroom door. When Mr. Mobley opened the door, a student volunteer from the office handed him a note. Every pair of eyes was riveted on Mr. Mobley. A note from the office usually signaled big trouble for somebody. This time, the somebody was me. Mr. Mobley looked up from the note and said, "Julie, Mr. Sinclair wants to see you in his office right away. He says you should take your belongings with you."

Oh, no! I was being sent to the principal's office. What would my parents say? With all eyes now turned in my direction, I dragged myself over to the coat hooks and grabbed the offending jacket. Embarrassment floated around me like a dirty cloud of dust.

How could a stupid jacket hurt anybody? I wondered as the door clicked shut behind me. I slid my arms through the jacket sleeves and slipped my hands into its pockets. *Huh?* My right hand closed over a hard, round object. I pulled it out. I had forgotten that my brand-new Duncan Imperial yo-yo was in my pocket. I felt my legs weaken. So I had hurt Robert not with my jacket, but with my yo-yo. As I crossed the courtyard to the principal's office, I prayed, *please don't let Robert be hurt too badly. And please don't let Mr. Sinclair call my mom.*

When I reached the office, the school secretary ushered me in to see the principal without making me wait — not exactly a good sign.

"What happened, Julie?" Mr. Sinclair asked. He came out from behind his big wooden desk and sat on a chair next to me.

"We were goofing around… and… I hit Robert on his shoulder with my jacket. I… um… I guess I had this in my pocket." I opened my palm to show him the shiny red yo-yo I'd bought with my allowance. "I'm sorry. I'm really sorry. I was only teasing. I didn't mean to hurt him." Little snorting sounds were coming out of my nose now, and my shoulders were heaving with barely suppressed sobs.

"I know you well enough to believe you. But Robert has a knot on his shoulder that's about the size of your yo-yo. His mother is very upset. She's taken him to the doctor."

My head hung so low, it nearly touched my knees. More than anything, I wanted to melt into a puddle and trickle away under the door.

"I'm sure you didn't mean to hurt anyone," Mr. Sinclair went on. "But because Robert was injured, I have to send you home for the rest of the day. Please wait in the outer office until your mother comes to pick you up."

My eyes widened. *Now I'm going to get it!* I thought.

I had plenty of time to think while I waited for my mother. I was always trying to be the "perfect student." Straight A's and praise from my teachers were rewarded with more praise and affection at home from my parents. *What will happen now?* I wondered. I had never been in trouble at school before.

Ten hopelessly long minutes later, my mother opened the door to the office. Her face looked serious. "Come on," she said. "You can tell me about it in the car."

During our short ride home, I told her the whole story. I'd been teasing Robert because I had a crush on him. I hadn't meant to hurt him. We pulled into our driveway. "I'm s-s-sorry, Mom," I said. My body tensed, ready for the punishment I knew I deserved.

Mom leaned toward me, and I sucked in my breath, waiting to see what would happen. Would she yell? Would she slap me? I really didn't know what to expect.

My mother put one arm behind me and reached across in front of me with the other. Then she wrapped me tightly in a hug.

"I never told any of you kids this," she said, "but I did something even worse when I was in elementary school. I bit a boy on the arm — on purpose. I got called to the principal's office, too." *What? My mother, who never did anything wrong, had bitten a boy at school?* The thought was too funny. I caught her eye. "I guess we're just a couple of troublemakers, aren't we, Honey?" Mom said with a smile.

"I guess so," I said. In spite of the tears streaming down my face, I started to laugh. Pretty soon, Mom was laughing, too.

The next day, Robert was back at school, recovered except for a little tenderness. As soon as I saw him, I apologized, and our lives went back to normal.

But something important had changed. I had learned that life goes on, even when you make a mistake, and that a child can grow up to become a wise adult even after doing something foolish or hurtful. And to my great surprise and relief, I learned that I didn't have to be perfect to be loved.

—Julia Wasson Render—

A Little Coaching

The two important things I did learn were that you are
as powerful and strong as you allow yourself to be,
and that the most difficult part of any endeavor is
taking the first step, making the first decision.
~Robyn Davidson

For me, it was normal to feel lost at the inter-camp track and swim meet. Four camps of kids were ready to lead their teams to a blue ribbon and win the day. Not me. I was too little to be a leader and too skinny to be an athlete. I knew this by the time I was twelve, because my camp counselors and the other kids reminded me of it every chance they got. So when our camp needed a fourth runner in the two-mile race around the lake, I knew I was no one's first choice.

I hid in the shade of a maple tree as they called the names of the runners. My body tensed as I heard a counselor call, "Noah! Where's Noah! He's in this race!"

It was Bronto. His name was really Alan Bronstein, but everyone called him Bronto. He spotted me under the tree and lifted me up by my elbows. It was more than just his name that qualified him for his "Brontoism."

"Noah, we need a twelve-year-old who hasn't been in other events to run the two-mile."

"But you've got three guys."

"We need four. You're in."

He gave me a push toward the starting line. Trying to save myself from the humiliation of taking last place as four camps watched, I pleaded with him.

"But I don't know the way around the lake!"

"You're in. Just follow Craig." Bronto smiled.

Craig was my friend and the fastest runner in our camp. And then Bronto said, "When you make it to the last stretch on the field, just throw your head back and run."

At the starting line, I stood next to Craig and trembled.

"On your mark… get set…" The gun cracked and sixteen of us took off. Kicking up dust on the dirt road leading to the lakeshore path, I was determined not to get lost. I stayed close on Craig's heels. A little too close for Craig, I guess, because he shouted at me, "Back off!"

I did. Two guys passed me but I kept my eye on Craig.

It was tiring. The distance was widening between Craig and me. We made the turn from the dusty road onto the muddy, wooded trail that wound around the lake back to the field. Through the trees I saw Craig slip and fall out of sight. A runner from another camp passed him.

In a moment, he was up again and running. He yelled to me, "Watch the roots. They're slimy!" Struggling to keep my legs moving, I looked down and saw the tree root stripped of its bark. I puffed over it. Fifty yards later I was out of breath, but I turned up the hill into the sunlight again, which shone on the open field. My energy was spent. I scrambled up, ready to see the rest of the pack crossing the finish line and was about to drop to my knees and quit, when I saw not the fifteen guys that I thought would be in front of me, but three. The crowd was roaring, but I could hear Bronto over the rest of them, yelling, "Run!"

I threw my head back and told my legs to go. I never looked ahead and I never looked back for those last hundred yards. I felt free. Nobody was telling me what I was, or what I wasn't. My legs were running a race against my brain and I was winning.

I didn't know when I crossed the finish line. Bronto caught me and I collapsed — winded, but happy that I finished. Then I realized Bronto wasn't just holding me up. He was hugging me!

"You flew! You flew, man! Second! You passed two guys!"

There was a crowd of kids around me patting me on the back,

giving me high-fives. I had come in second. Craig had finished first… by a step, they said.

They gave me a red second-place ribbon. Even with that and all the high-fives and cheers of the day, the best prize that I walked away with was my confidence. That year I discovered I could do a lot of things if I put my energy into them.

I never got to say thanks to Bronto right after the race. But during the next events, I spotted him over at the lake. He was coaching a reluctant kid who was going to swim in the freestyle relay. I ran over to cheer him on. With Bronto coaching, I had no doubt that this was going to be another good race.

— Noah Edelson —

The Power of the Pen

Woman must not accept; she must challenge.
She must not be awed by that which has been
built up around her; she must reverence that
within her which struggles for expression.
~Margaret Sanger

The very first speech I ever had to write changed my life more than I could ever have imagined. I was a third grader when I chose Susan B. Anthony to be the topic.

When I got the assignment, I went to the library and began researching the Women's Fight for the Right to Vote. I learned that Susan B. Anthony led the fight to give women a say in our society. She overcame a lot of obstacles in order to do that. I never really thought about a time when women had no voting rights and that their opinions didn't count.

It was sad that Susan fought so hard for women's rights and never got to vote. She died fourteen years before the passage of the 19th Amendment that gave women the right to vote. But she knew that her goal would be achieved. She said that "failure is impossible," and she was right.

About a week after giving my school speech, my mom read a newspaper article about "The Group Portrait Monument," a statue honoring Susan B. Anthony and other early women's rights leaders. The problem was that few people ever got to see the statue. It was dedicated in the U.S. Capitol Rotunda in 1921, but within twenty-four hours it was taken down to the Capitol basement and stored where it had remained for nearly eighty years.

When I read that article, I was furious! This statue belonged in a place of honor. I felt that it should be in the Rotunda, along with the statues of Abraham Lincoln, Martin Luther King Jr. and George Washington. There were *no* statues of women there?

The article asked for donations because it would take $74,000 to move the thirteen-ton statue out of the basement. I decided to write a letter with a self-addressed envelope asking my relatives and friends to send a Susan B. Anthony coin or a $1 bill to me to contribute to the Women's Suffrage Statue Campaign. I really wanted to help get that statue moved out of the basement.

Every day I ran to the mailbox after school. Every night, after my homework, I wrote more letters at the kitchen table. Pretty soon the whole family got involved in the project. My seven-year-old brother, David, licked stamps and envelopes. My mother and grandmother found addresses for people I wanted to contact and my dad drove me around and gave me tons of encouragement when I spoke to big groups. I passed around a piggy bank for donations at the end of each speech. I sent more than $500 to the fund in the first three months. Pretty soon, I had raised $2,000. I began visualizing that statue up in the Rotunda next to the greatest Americans in history.

I was discouraged when I heard that four other times, in 1928, 1932, 1950 and 1995, people had tried to get the statue out of the basement and had failed. I learned that the House and Senate would have to vote on relocating the statue. More determined than before, I spent three weeks writing to every representative and senator in the United States, urging them to vote yes on the bill to relocate the statue. This was not about politics. It was about respect and responsibility. Susan B. Anthony fought for my rights, and now I was fighting for hers!

The Senate unanimously voted to restore the statue to the Rotunda, but Newt Gingrich, the Speaker of the House, didn't want to use any tax money to pay for the cost of relocating the statue. Even if we raised enough money, the statue couldn't be relocated without a unanimous vote in the House.

There was only one thing to do… write more letters! I wrote a letter to Mr. Gingrich *every other week for an entire year*! Boy, did that try my patience! I sent about twenty-five letters to him before I got a reply. He finally wrote a letter saying that a committee would study the issue.

At that point, I figured that I had better write to every member of the House again. By now I had mailed more than 2,000 letters!

My grandmother helped with postage costs by getting her friends and church groups to donate rolls of stamps to help me with the battle. I got writer's cramp from writing letters and discovered that it takes a lot of work to bring about change. But if you believe in something, it's worth the hard work.

My biggest boost came when I was interviewed on radio and TV shows. Then, a bunch of newspaper and magazine articles came out telling thousands more people about what I was trying to do. As a result of all that attention, I was invited to speak at a fund-raising event for the Woman's Suffrage Statue Campaign in Washington, D.C., in July of 1996. I had never flown in an airplane. My whole family got to go and my brother had a great time. He thought that was a pretty good reward for licking all those stamps!

But the best part was getting to see the statue, even if it was in the smelly old basement. I thought it looked really beautiful. I've heard people say that they think that the statue is ugly. To that I say — it was an ugly time! The three women in the statue have their arms pinned in marble because they were trapped by "slavery!"

I spoke from my heart when I talked to all those people and received a standing ovation for my speech!

After I got home, I continued to write letters. I wouldn't give up! It took women seventy-two years to win the right to vote, but they didn't give up until they reached their goal… and neither would I!

On September 27, 1996, House Resolution 216, the bill to get the statue moved, passed unanimously. My mom and I jumped up and down in our living room when we heard the news. We just kept screaming, "We won!"

The statue stayed in the Rotunda for a year and then was moved to another place of honor in Washington, where everyone can see it.

It will never go back to that awful basement again!

I've learned a lot from this experience… mostly about respecting people who fought for rights that too many people take for granted. I've learned to have more patience. If there is a problem, don't say "someone else will fix it." You have to do it yourself.

I'll turn eighteen in a few years and will be able to vote in the year 2005. When I vote, I'll silently thank Susan B. Anthony for her fight and for helping me discover the power of the pen.

—Arlys Angelique Endres, 13, as told by Carol Osman Brown—

Tough, Sturdy and Triumphant

The mind can have tremendous control of the body;
very few ailments can defeat focused energy and a
determined spirit.
~Katherine Lambert-Scronce

Tears filled my eyes as my parents told me why my arm had been in so much pain during the past three months. "You have leukemia," my dad explained.

I didn't know much about leukemia, but the words still plunged deep into my heart like knives. My parents told me that I had to go into the hospital to have a metal cylinder called a medi-port put into my body. A medi-port has a line through which the doctors would give me medicine to fight the leukemia cells.

Why did this have to happen to me? I wondered.

My whole family went with me to the hospital. My parents told me they'd see me after my surgery. Some doctor hooked me up and made me put on some funky clothes. Then they rolled me into the operating room.

I was so scared. All of the doctors had on masks. They attached sensors to me and assured me that nothing would go wrong. They put a mask over my face, pressed a button and I fell asleep. When I woke up, the surgery was over. My doctor told my parents I would have to come to the hospital every other week to stay for four days so that I could get treatments. I had to do this for one entire year — twelve months!

When we reached home, I couldn't believe how much I had missed it. People brought over presents, balloons, cards and food. My teacher came over and gave me a stack of letters from my classmates. I read them over and over. All of them had cried, especially my friends. I didn't get to see my friends anymore and felt sick practically every day. But I got tons of letters from them all the time, and they kept me going!

I have survived this last year, but I still have a lower blood count than healthy people. I have only two more years of treatments to go, and from now on, the treatments won't be so heavy.

I have been overwhelmed with support and prayer. My mom told the Make-A-Wish Foundation how much I loved castles, and I was granted my wish to see real castles in England and Scotland. My whole family gets to go with me and Make-A-Wish is paying for everything!

I know I didn't get through this by myself. My friends and family have been with me every step of the way. I look back and see how far I've come. I will fight this and triumph.

Even though I'm different than most kids because of the leukemia, I'm as tough as a general leading his men into battle, as sturdy as a wall and as triumphant as a man beating an army. I have been able to do this thanks to everyone who has helped me through, and especially to someone in a high position. Where there is life, there is hope for even the most hopeless.

— Elijah Shoesmith, 13 —

Choices

Peer pressure is a thing
that every child goes through.
But you have to remember
that to yourself you must be true.
Know that there are times to follow
and there are times to lead.
Do what you think is right,
do things at your own speed.
Don't worry about what others think,
don't worry about being cool.
Focus on friendships
and the grades you get in school.

—Jaimie Shapiro, 12—

A Meal with a Smile

*Do your little bit of good where you are; it's those little
bits of good put together that overwhelm the world.*
~Desmond Tutu

At eleven years old, my main concern was money. Where could I get it? What would I spend it on? How much did I need to buy the new must-have thing my classmates either had or wanted just as badly as I did?

I already had a "job" as a sales representative with a kids-based sales company, and I sold wrapping paper and greeting cards with the best of them.

But the more money I got, the more I needed.

On my bedroom floor, I arranged the bills and change from my money pouch to see what I had. I wished it would multiply before my eyes, but of course it didn't.

I went to my mom. Not to ask for money. I received a small allowance each week, and she had been clear I couldn't have a raise. I needed to know my options.

Why couldn't I be older and make my own money? Things would be a lot easier.

"Mom, I need more money," I said, leaning against the kitchen counter while she cooked dinner. "What else can kids do for a job around here?"

"You think you need another job?" Mom asked with a smile. "You could just enjoy the summer like the other kids, you know?"

I shrugged. "I'll still have time for that, but I want to work."

"Okay, let me ask around."

The next day, she had an answer. "Your grandmother will pay you to help her deliver lunch each day to the elderly."

Yes! I pumped my fist into the air.

I couldn't wait to start my new job on Monday after school dismissed for the summer.

When my grandmother picked me up, I thanked her for the job and started peppering her with questions.

"It's simple. We pick up a large container full of hot meals in a nearby town and then we go on our delivery route."

That was easy.

We arrived at the pick-up kitchen and got dozens of little shiny silver trays with slick white lids that were hot when I accidentally touched one on the bottom and not the top corners.

The meals didn't really smell good, but I shrugged and kept going. I didn't have to eat them, just deliver them. This was how I would make money.

After our load was arranged in the backseat, my grandmother drove us to our first stop: a small white house with flaking paint, a blue tarp over a corner of the roof, and an old rusty car in a garage. I took a meal and a small box of milk from the back and walked beside my grandmother to the front gate. She opened it and nodded for me to go in. I trudged along the cracked walkway. Tall grass tickled my ankles.

Did someone really live here? I couldn't imagine that.

The house didn't look nice, but I shrugged and kept going. I didn't have to live there, just deliver food there. This was how I would make money.

In front of the dented metal door leading to the enclosed front porch, I paused, and my grandmother called out, "Mrs. Hershel, we've brought you some lunch."

The reply in a gravelly voice came from my left. "Come on in."

I nearly jumped when I glanced over to see a tiny old woman in the corner looking at me. She sat hunched over in a rocking chair and had more wrinkles than I'd ever seen in my life.

We walked onto the porch. It creaked with each step.

When I drew near to her, she smiled at me, revealing no teeth. Frozen, I stared at the gaping hole that was her mouth, gums flapping, and couldn't look away. Her body reeked of sweat, powder, and stale clothes.

"Who is this nice young lady?" she asked my grandmother, who introduced me.

I just stood there holding the food, unsure what to do. My grandmother guided me inside to place it on her kitchen table.

The house smelled musty and old like the antique stores my mom liked to visit, but I never liked because even breathing in the dusty air made me feel dirty. I held my breath until we went back out onto the porch.

Was this really how some people lived? I couldn't wrap my head around it.

I hid behind my grandmother and peered at the old woman again. I didn't have to stay there long, just give them the food. This was how I would make money.

The next stop was much the same and the next. The houses varied in size and shape, some were nicer than others, but the same wrinkly people waited for their meals. Each person smiled at me and thanked me as I hurried to get out of there. I was sweaty and tired, and my clothes had captured the stench of the food and old houses.

By the end of the day, I guess it was obvious to my grandmother that I wasn't very comfortable about the job anymore.

"You don't have to help me," she said. "I understand if the job isn't what you want to do."

I swallowed hard, thinking of that nearly empty money pouch in my bedroom. Did I want to be comfortable, or did I want the money?

"No, Grandma. It's okay. I'll get used to it." Though, I was not convinced of my words.

"If you're sure, dear."

A moment of silence settled over the car before she spoke again. "For a lot of the people we deliver to this is their only meal of the day."

My eyes widened, and I turned to her. "Their only meal?"

She nodded grimly. "For some of them too we're the only person they see. Many of them are alone. A kind word and a smile go a long way."

I thought about that. What if I was all alone? I couldn't imagine not having my mom or grandmother, my little brother or my friends.

When we were back at the house, my grandmother handed me the money I'd earned. It didn't seem quite as exciting anymore.

"Want to give it another try tomorrow?"

The old woman on her porch came to my mind — hungry and alone. I nodded.

The next morning, I saw each person with all their wrinkles and the rickety houses a little differently. I smiled at each one and greeted them. And after a whole summer, I came to know a little about each one. With those smiles I now saw true happiness in their eyes. And I smiled back too.

I'd like to say that I did something incredible with the money I earned that summer, that I made a difference with it or helped someone.

But I didn't.

The surprising thing is I don't even remember what I bought. And it simply doesn't matter now.

What matters are those people with smiles sinking in their wrinkled faces who brought unexpected joy to my life while I brought them only a simple meal.

That is what stays deep within my heart.

—M.L. Tarpley—

Do What You Love

Dancing's part of my soul. I enjoy it, it makes
people happy, and it makes me happy.
~John Travolta

Growing up, my parents had me try out every sport, from football to basketball to soccer, to name a few. I tried them all. But when my parents signed me up for a hip hop class, dance just stuck. I was so intrigued at everything dance represented, I found myself wanting to learn more about the different styles.

The classes I took, at first, only had girls in them. My parents wanted to show me that there were other guys who danced, so they moved me to a different studio that had an all-boys hip hop class. At first, I was just taking hip hop and breakdancing, never really taking it that seriously. Eventually, I learned that the studio had a team that traveled and went to competitions. That's when I joined the hip hop team.

As time went on, I tried new styles like tap and musical theatre, but I never truly branched out until a teacher named Miss Maria entered my life. She not only introduced me to training technically and improving my dance skills, but she gave me the opportunity to start dancing professionally in the industry.

Growing up as a working dancer and doing what I loved was amazing and fun. However, doing what you love can come with consequences. Males who were technical dancers were not as common when I was starting out, and it wasn't as normalized to a lot of people. Many people, when visualizing dancers, see a ballerina; therefore, elementary school and middle school were not always the easiest of times.

When I was in fourth or fifth grade, I started being more open about being a dancer. I was actually booking jobs, meaning my name was getting known in the dance world and I was earning money through dance. Around this time, a lot of kids in my grade were starting to notice that this was not normal and started to have different opinions about me. I was called names, given looks, and left out of activities just because I was a guy who was dancing.

I remember one time my class was playing tag, and we split up into boys' and girls' teams. When I went over to the boys' team, a kid looked at me and asked me what I was doing on the boys' side. He said that I belonged on the girls' side because that was what I was. I went home and cried to my mom, regretting my choices in choosing to dance. My mom had a conversation with me, saying that if I loved dancing and I was doing what I loved, then why did it matter what anyone else thought? From then on, this conversation changed my mindset. I was confident in being a male dancer and I wasn't going to let someone's opinion stop me from doing what I love.

Going into middle school, dancing was also a very difficult transition for me. I was training a lot and booking dance jobs more often. I was very open about being a dancer at this time because of my confidence, but the middle school I went to was huge, and had a diverse group of people. Middle school was not always easy, I was called names I had never heard of until then, I was asked weird questions, and people would say rude comments about me. This was all because I was a male dancer, and somehow it had still been viewed as weird in society.

I'm not going to lie and say that this did not take a toll on my confidence, but I still had many people who were so supportive of me and lifted me up. I went through a lot of thought and had to get to the point of not caring what others thought about me. Now, I can strongly say that I am confident being a male dancer, and I love doing it.

I have accomplished so much by not caring what others think. I made it on my dream dance team, I was accepted into Joffrey, one of the most prestigious dance schools in the world, and the same year was additionally accepted into another competitive program. I have even been named Mr. Teen Dance at various dance competitions. This goes to show that other people's negative opinions do not matter in the face of success; you choose your own fate.

For anyone who is thinking about doing something they love or just being themselves but is too scared of what other people might think, you are not alone. There will be people who will try to bring you down and judge you, but those people do that regardless, because they aren't happy with their own lives.

There will also be people who support you and love you for who you are. If you are scared to be yourself, don't be! You have one life to live, and you shouldn't spend it in a way you don't want to. I can honestly say that I have been so much happier and confident being a male dancer, now not caring what others think. If you want to be or do something that you love, do it.

— Noah Ross —

Two Tickets to the Big Game

I discovered I always have choices,
and sometimes it's only a choice of attitude.
~Judith M. Knowlton

Two tickets. Only two tickets to the big quarterfinals basketball game.

Three pairs of eyes all focused on the tickets in Dad's outstretched hand. Marcus, the oldest, spoke the question running through everyone's mind: "Only two tickets? But, Dad, which of us gets to go with you?"

"Yeah, Daddy, who gets to go?" repeated Caleb, the youngest.

"Dad, can't you get any more tickets?" I asked. I might be the in-between sister, but I was just as eager as my basketball-crazy brothers were for a night out with Dad.

"I'm afraid not," Dad answered. "Mr. Williams only has two season tickets. He was thoughtful enough to offer the tickets to Saturday's game to me when he found out he'd be out of town this weekend."

Dad scratched his head. "Caleb, don't you think you're a little young to enjoy a professional basketball game...?"

"Am not! Am not!" Caleb insisted. "I know all the best shooters! I know the team's record! I know..."

"All right, all right," Dad finally had to agree. He shifted his focus and tried again. "Jill, since you're a girl..."

Before I could respond, Mom came to my defense. "Don't you dare say 'because you're a girl,'" she said to Dad. "Jill's out there practicing at the hoop with Marcus and all of his friends, and she's better than quite a few of them, too!"

"Okay, okay," Dad held up his hands in a "time-out" signal. "I guess I'll have to figure out a fair way of choosing between the three of you by tomorrow morning. I'll have to decide who deserves it most. Let me sleep on it — okay, guys… and girls?" he added quickly before Mom and I could correct him.

The next morning, Marcus hurried into the kitchen and plopped down at the breakfast table. "Where's Dad?" he asked as he reached for a box of cereal.

"And 'good morning' to you, too," I responded in between sips of orange juice.

"Sorry, but you can guess what I was dreaming about all last night," Marcus explained. "So — where is he?"

"He and Mom went to pick up some books from the library," Caleb answered, digging his spoon into a mound of cereal.

"And he said we should all get started on our Saturday chores as soon as we finish breakfast," I added.

"Chores! He's got to be kidding," Marcus said as he set down his glass of milk with a thud. "How can we concentrate on chores when the big game is a mere eleven hours away?"

"Parents! They just don't understand!" I agreed, popping the last piece of English muffin into my mouth.

"I'm going for the morning newspaper," Marcus announced. "There's probably a preview of tonight's game in the sports section."

"Wait for me!" Caleb added, slurping the last of his milk and dashing after his brother.

The back door snapped shut as the two boys trotted down the driveway. I looked at the breakfast table in front of me: tiny puddles of milk, bits of soggy cereal here and there, a small glob of grape jelly melting in the morning sunlight. *Well,* I thought to myself as I pushed my chair away from the table, *looks like Saturday morning chores start right here.*

A few minutes later, as I was washing off the kitchen countertops,

I heard the familiar "thump… thump… thump" of the basketball bouncing off of the driveway. I glanced out of the kitchen window and saw Marcus practicing his hook shot while Caleb cheered him on. Frustrated, I knocked on the window three times. When the boys looked up, I meaningfully held up a kitchen sponge and dishtowel.

Marcus casually nodded to me and held up five fingers. Taking his cue from his older brother, Caleb did the same.

Sure, five more minutes! I thought to myself. *I'll just bet.* I opened the lower cabinet and tossed an empty muffin package into the almost-full wastebasket. I reached for a twister to tie up the plastic liner bag and carted it out to the garbage container outside the back door.

"He dribbles… he shoots! If I make this next shot, I get the tickets to tonight's game," Marcus teased as he shot for the hoop. "Hooray! Two points! And I get the ticket!"

"Do not!" Caleb shouted.

"You guys, Mom and Dad will be back any minute," I reminded them as I lifted the lid on the garbage container and placed the full plastic bag inside.

"Okay, we're coming in to help," Marcus said, dribbling the basketball around and around Caleb, who tried again and again to steal it. "Just one more minute."

"Yeah, just one more minute," Caleb added as he finally managed to tip the ball out of his brother's grasp.

I shook my head from side to side as I began to replace the lid on the garbage container. Then a flash of white on the inside of the heavy black plastic lid caught my attention. A white envelope… it must have stuck to the lid by accident. But then I noticed that the envelope was actually taped to the inside of the lid, and someone had written the word "Congratulations!" on the front of the envelope, too.

I lifted the flap on the envelope and pulled out a folded piece of paper. "To the one who deserves to go," the paper read, and inside of it was a ticket to the basketball game!

I don't believe it, I thought. *I'm the one that gets to go! But how did Dad know?*

Then I thought back to Dad's comment last night: "I'll have to decide who deserves it most." I smiled. Leave it to Dad to figure out who the most deserving kid really was.

By now, Marcus and Caleb had worn themselves out. They shuffled toward the back door. "Come on, little brother, we'd better get started on our chores if we want to have a chance at getting that ticket to the game."

I turned in their direction and held up the ticket, the note and the envelope. "It might be a little too late for that," I said with a sly grin.

Marcus and Caleb looked at each other with question marks in their eyes, as Mom and Dad's car pulled into the driveway.

That evening turned out to be as special as I'd imagined: Two seats at center court, and a dad and his daughter cheering their team to victory. It was a long-remembered lesson in responsibility from a dad who let his kids make their own choices and earn their own rewards.

—J. Styron Madsen—

Fireplug and Dad

You have brains in your head. You have feet in your shoes.
You can steer yourself any direction you choose.
~Dr. Seuss

used to play football when I was a little kid. Okay, let's face it. I was never really a *little* kid. I was always chunky, hefty, short for my age, pudgy, stout, tubby, round, robust, portly. You get the picture.

In fact, I was so big that I got to play football a whole year ahead of my friends. Our Mighty Mites football league didn't have an age limit, it had a weight requirement. If you were heavy enough, you got to play. I was heavy enough at eight years old.

The only problem was, by the time I turned eleven I was too heavy. You had to weigh a certain amount to start playing, and if you weighed too much, they made you stop.

Not playing would have been just fine with me. I would have been happier sitting at home reading a book.

But Dad was one of the team's big sponsors and friends with the coach, so I figured quitting wasn't an option. I went, day after day, week after week, and year after year... until I was eleven and weighed more than 200 pounds. I thought that would be the end of it, once and for all. And, in a way, it was.

To make sure each kid was under the official weight limit every Saturday, the referees lugged doctor's scales around with them to every game. All of the "chunky" kids had the honor of joining the referees before each game to weigh in.

If the scales tipped past 200, off went the unlucky player's cleats.

Then the helmet and the shoulder pads. Sometimes the jersey and the pants, and even the undershirt and the socks! Coach knew I was heading for trouble the day I had to step out of my underwear just to make weight. So, he came up with a bright idea. The very next practice he presented me with a T-shirt made out of a black garbage bag.

"Put it on," he grunted, pointing out the ragged holes for my head and arms. "Start running around the practice field and don't stop until I say so."

I'd wave at him questioningly after every single lap, while my teammates sat on their helmets and talked — in between laughing and pointing at me, that is.

"Keep going, Fireplug," Coach would grunt around the mushy cigar in his mouth. "Fireplug" was the nickname he had given me. Although no one ever explained it to me, I figured it had something to do with me being shaped like a fire hydrant.

Every day at practice, I had to run laps in that stupid garbage bag. I'd hear it crinkling beneath my underarms as I stumbled through the stickers and weeds lap after lap. My short, stocky legs weren't exactly graceful, and often I'd trip or fall. The other players would laugh, but not as loudly as Coach.

I used to sit in class toward the end of each school day and dream up excuses why I couldn't go to practice. Nothing worked, and so there I'd be, stumbling around the practice field with the sound of my plastic shirt drowning out my ragged breathing.

When the garbage bag T-shirt didn't exactly work wonders, Coach arranged for me to use the sauna at one of the local high-rise condominiums.

I rode my bike there the next Saturday. Coach handed me my garbage bag T-shirt and wedged me into a cedar-lined closet with two benches and a red metal shelf full of glowing hot rocks. He poured water on the rocks to build up the steam, and then shut the door on me with a wicked smile.

Outside the little porthole window, I could see him chomping on glazed donuts and sipping a cup of coffee. My stomach roared. Since it was a game day, I hadn't eaten since dinner the night before.

Nor would I be eating again until after the weigh-in, when, as usual, I would be too weak to do anything much but sit there and pant until Coach shoved me full of candy bars from the concession stand so I could play ball again.

I sat there swimming in sweat and wondering how long this could go on. I'd been trying my best to lose weight ever since I was ten years old. I brought a bag lunch to school and skipped breakfast, but nothing seemed to work. I tried to be strong, tried to be brave, but there I still was… teetering on the brink of 200 pounds and hoping to make it through yet another weigh-in.

Periodically, Coach would pop his bullet-shaped head into the steamy room to see if I was still alive.

I sat there dripping in sweat and realized something was very wrong with this picture. It was Saturday morning, and there I was, sitting in a sweatbox while the rest of the team chomped on Frosted Flakes and watched cartoons. They were still in their pajamas, while there I was in a garbage bag sweatsuit! Why?

Was I being punished for something? Wasn't the running, sweating, hunger and pain enough? What more did they want? I suddenly realized that I'd been knocking myself out for something I didn't even want to do in the first place! It was then that I decided that I didn't have to do it anymore.

My heart fluttered and my stomach flip-flopped, but I finally stood up on wobbly legs and walked out of the sauna. At the time, it didn't exactly seem brave. It just seemed right. It made sense. I had finally realized that there was no law in the world that said I had to keep knocking myself out just so Coach would have another strong player and my Dad could have extra bragging rights!

"Did I say you could get out of there?" Coach bellowed when he returned from the pool deck a few minutes later and saw me sipping on a cup of water and enjoying one of his glazed donuts.

I shook my head, but Coach was waiting for an answer. So I told him.

"I quit," I said in a shaky voice that had nothing to do with heat stroke.

"You quit?" he fairly laughed, looming over me. "You can't quit. What would your dad think? Don't you want him to be proud of you anymore?"

But that was just it. If my dad couldn't be proud of me for just being me, then what was the point? I was a good kid. I stayed out of trouble, made good grades and even made him a Father's Day card every year. Did I have to torture myself, too?

I shook my head and told Coach it was over. All of it. I wasn't going to starve myself anymore. I wasn't going to make myself try to throw up anymore or run around the practice field in a garbage bag dress while the rest of the team pointed and laughed.

That was when he called my dad. But it didn't matter to me anymore. I had finally made up my mind. It was time to be proud of myself for a change, no matter what anyone else thought.

After Coach had explained the situation to my dad, he grunted and handed me the phone. Although my hands were shaking, I was glad I wasn't doing this face-to-face!

"Son," my dad said quietly. "Is what Coach said true?"

"Yes," I whispered into the phone.

"You don't want to play football anymore?" he asked simply.

"I never did," I gasped. Well, if I was going to do this, I was going to do it right.

Dad's laughter surprised me. "Then why did you go through with all of those shenanigans?" he asked. "I thought you wanted to be the next big football star!"

I hung up the phone and headed for my bike. Coach just stood there fuming as I pedaled away.

I started carrying myself differently after that. Respecting myself more. I grew a little, shaped up, learned a lot, and eventually, the name Fireplug just seemed to fade with time.

Except for one night, that is. My family and I were waiting for a table in a local restaurant when Coach sauntered in. He greeted my Dad rather coolly and then eyed me with open disdain. "What's the word, Fireplug?" he asked.

Dad looked at me for an instant, and then he finally corrected

Coach. "You meant 'Rusty,' right, Coach?"

Coach grumbled something through the mushy cigar in his mouth, but it didn't matter. Our table was ready and Dad kept his hand on my shoulder the whole way there.

And no one ever called me Fireplug again.

— Rusty Fischer —

Nice Catch!

When I do things without any explanation, but just
with spontaneity… I can be sure that I am right.
~Federico Fellini

From the moment Kyle heard the loud crack of the Red Sox bat, he was sure the ball was headed over the fence. And he was ready for it. Without ever taking his eyes off the ball, he reached up and pulled it out of the air.

"I caught it!" he yelled to his dad and his grandpa. "And I caught it with my bare hands!"

It was opening day of spring training and they had come out to the ballfield to watch the Red Sox play. Kyle's grandma and grandpa lived near Ft. Myers, Florida, where the Boston Red Sox went in late February to prepare for the season.

Later, on the way home to Grandma's house, Kyle kept his head down. He tried to think of a way to convince his parents to stay a few more days.

"Wish we could go back to the ballpark tomorrow," he said. "Maybe I'd catch another ball to put with my Little League trophies and stuff. And maybe I'd even get some autographs."

"You know that's not possible, Kyle," his dad said. "We're flying out early tomorrow morning."

"I know, I know," Kyle said, rolling the baseball around in his hand. "I just thought you and Mom might decide to stay a few more days. We don't go back to school until Monday, and tomorrow's only Thursday."

"We were lucky to get that flight!" his dad said firmly. "The airlines are booked solid this week."

That night, a huge snowstorm moved into the Northeast. When they arrived at the airport early the next morning, they were told that all flights into Logan Airport in Boston had been cancelled for the day.

On the drive back to his grandparents' house from the airport, it was obvious to Kyle that his dad was upset. It was definitely not a good time to bring up going back to the Red Sox ballfield.

But by the time they were back at Grandma and Grandpa's house, Kyle's dad began to joke about the cancelled flight.

"Another day in sunny Florida isn't so bad," he said. "I'm in no hurry to get back to Boston, where my car's probably buried in snow."

"We could go out to the ballfield again," Grandpa said. "Unless there's something else you'd rather do."

"The ballpark's fine," Kyle's dad said with a grin. "I'd never go against the wishes of anyone with so much power over the weather."

It was mid-afternoon when another loud crack of the Red Sox bat sent a ball flying over the fence. Again, Kyle reached up and caught the baseball in his bare hands.

As he rubbed his fingers around the ball, a small voice from behind him called out, "Nice catch!"

Kyle turned around to see a small boy in a wheelchair. Without a moment of hesitation, Kyle handed him the baseball.

"Here," he said. "You can have it. I already got one."

The grin on the boy's face was a mile wide.

"Thanks," he said. "I never held a *real* baseball before."

Kyle's dad and his grandpa looked surprised — very surprised.

But they were no more surprised than Kyle was himself. He couldn't believe what he'd just done. But he wasn't sorry. He could never forget the happy look on the small boy's face. It was worth a million baseballs.

"I'm gonna get some autographs," Kyle said, rushing off to meet the players as they came off the field.

With three Red Sox autographs in hand, Kyle walked back to the parking lot.

"Think the Red Sox will have a good season?" Grandpa asked.

"They looked pretty good today," Kyle said. Kyle's dad tapped him on the shoulder.

"You looked pretty good today yourself, son."

And three avid Red Sox fans left the training grounds, each carrying with him a special feeling of pride. The proudest of all was Kyle.

— Doris Canner —

The Gorilla Syndrome

wouldn't have believed that I could ever be so embarrassed! I was sweating, my heart was pounding like a bass drum in my head and I felt as though the entire classroom could hear it!

Josh, the cute, blond boy sitting next to me, my secret crush, was looking down at my extremely fuzzy legs! I could feel the heat of his stare. It seemed as though a force field was drawing his dark brown eyes downward to my legs. I swallowed hard and tried desperately to pretend that I was completely enthralled by what the teacher was saying. In reality, she could have been telling me that Martians had invaded Earth, and I would not have reacted. *Oh Lord, please don't let Josh be looking at my hairy legs!*

Time seemed to stand still. The conversation I'd had the previous day with my mother kept whirling through my head like an amusement park ride that wouldn't stop spinning.

"Mom," I said, "Every girl in the seventh grade shaves her legs! I'm the only one who hasn't done it yet! I can't possibly wear a skirt tomorrow unless I shave. I look like some sort of gorilla!"

"Oh, Liz, don't be silly. No one will even notice your legs. I'm telling you, once you shave your legs, you'll have to shave them forever. Your hair will grow back thicker than ever after you've shaved them, and trust me, shaving is not a lot of fun."

Oh, why did I listen to her?! She couldn't possibly know how I feel!!

It seemed an eternity had passed when at last I could feel Josh's eyes moving away from my legs. Inwardly, I breathed a sigh of relief… and then it happened. He said the words that I will never forget as long as I live. "Your mom won't let you shave, huh?"

It was too much. My mouth suddenly felt as though I'd spent forty years in the desert. I couldn't remove my tongue from the roof of my mouth, but somehow, I managed a weak smile and nodded my head.

He gave me an understanding look of sympathy, but couldn't stop his eyes from, once again, glancing down at my very hairy calves that were now wrapped like giant furry caterpillars around the back legs of my desk.

When Josh looked up, our eyes locked, and the embarrassment I felt nearly immobilized me. Somehow, he knew I didn't want to talk about it, and to my great relief, he looked away.

My face felt as hot as a July sun, and I cringed, thinking it had probably turned as red as my hair. My life, as I knew it, was over. My mother had just ruined my life... the sweetest guy in the world had noticed my woolly legs and felt *sorry* for me! *Oh my gosh!!! I can't believe this is happening. He feels sorry for me . . . how embarrassing! How am I ever going to look at him again? How am I going to make my mother understand what this has just done to me? I won't recover!*

I did recover. Slowly, slowly, my pounding heart began to calm down, and little by little I could once again hear the sounds of the classroom around me. I didn't think it was possible, but somehow, I made it through seventh period and made it home again.

After slamming the front door, I made a beeline for my bedroom and proceeded to throw myself back dramatically onto the bed. With one arm slung across my forehead, I closed my eyes against the image of the expression of sympathy on Josh's face as he was looking at my legs. *Ughhh... was this some sort of nightmare or did he really ask me if I was allowed to shave?!*

I rolled over onto my stomach, crossed my traitorous legs at the ankles, and wished I had about a pound of rich milk chocolate and two cartons of hot, greasy, French fries.

Instead, I thought hard about what my mom had said about shaving, thought hard about the consequences... and shaved my legs anyway.

There. I'd done it. My legs were smooth now — except for the half dozen or so cuts. They were shaved though, and I felt extremely pleased with myself.

I did notice, however, that my legs seemed even more pale than before I shaved them, if that was possible. Maybe it was my imagination… no, they definitely glowed. Great, that was just what I needed, even milkier white skin that showed my spattering of freckles even more. *Oh well*, I thought, *at least they are shaved!* I would never have those gorilla legs to look at again.

After pulling on a pair of jeans and a T-shirt, I headed for the kitchen for a long-overdue snack and a phone call to my best friend, Krista.

Although I was exhausted from my ordeal, my sleep that night was restless. I dreamt of Josh and gorillas. He was trying to help me shave their backs and legs. It was absurd, and I was very relieved to wake up the next day. I was also relieved that the weather had turned so cold that wearing a skirt was out of the question. I was able to hide my war wounds with jeans.

I stumbled to my drawer and dug out a stuffed-in pair of jeans. They were only a little wrinkled. As I pulled them on, I noticed something weird. My legs weren't even smooth anymore! I ran my hands down my legs, and then I knew. My mother's words came back to haunt me as I stared at my battered-up, white legs with their newly formed stubble.

Closing my eyes, I sighed and tried to pretend that it wasn't true, but to my dismay, my legs were covered with tiny, black whiskers that were darker than I ever remembered my leg hair being.

I threw myself back on the bed in disgust. *Great, now instead of fur-balls on my legs, I have whiskers that feel as sharp as daggers.*

A week later, I found myself standing in a cluster of giggling girls on one side of the gymnasium at school. It was the school's first dance for the year, and the excitement among my friends and myself was at an all-time high.

Of course, the boys were all on the opposite side of the gym, some trying to look bored, others wrestling around and acting tough. Only a few of the most popular kids were brave enough so far to actually have danced, so much to my dismay, the teacher announced a game where *everyone* would have to be asked to dance.

My heart began to slam in my chest as I realized that I could be left standing until the very last, and I found myself panicking at the humiliation of it all. *I think it's time to go to the bathroom.*

I began making my way through the crowd. Suddenly, a faint scent of spicy cologne filled my nose, as I felt a small tap on my shoulder. Fully expecting to turn and find that it was my friend Krista who had done it, I nearly fainted when I discovered Josh standing only inches from me.

Still unbelieving, I turned my head from side to side, sure that I'd made a mistake. *Surely Josh didn't tap my shoulder… did he?* I had no more than formed the thought when he chuckled shyly, and asked, "Do you want to dance?"

Where was my gosh-darn voice when I needed it? All I could manage was a small smile and a nod. Within moments, I was dancing with Josh… the sweetest, cutest, best dancer in the whole world.

I was still dancing on air that night while getting ready for bed. My smile was huge as I twirled through the hallway and into the bathroom to brush my teeth. Standing in my nightshirt, I suddenly caught a glimpse of my legs and realized that the embarrassment I thought I'd never survive seemed almost laughable… well, almost.

I was better at shaving now. My mom didn't even get mad at me when she found out that I'd shaved against her wishes. She just looked at me and said, "Be more careful next time." I was eternally grateful she didn't make more of a fuss. My dad, on the other hand, was not too pleased that I used his razor…. Well, that's another story.

When I went to tell my parents good-night, I hugged them both extra tightly. I was having a hard time falling asleep. My sister was breathing evenly next to me, and I knew she was already out for the night, but I was still so excited that Josh had asked me to dance.

Suddenly, I felt grateful to my PE teacher for making everyone choose a partner, even though earlier that night I'd been mad at her when she started the game. I smiled into the darkness at the thought and felt satisfied that I had just survived the worst humiliation of my life. With that thought came the realization that Josh must still like me despite my gorilla legs. After all, he asked me to dance, didn't he?!

My smile broadened, and with a satisfied giggle, I rolled onto my side and fell fast asleep.

— Elizabeth J. Schmeidler —

Just Desserts

Do unto others as you would have them do unto you.
~The Golden Rule

"Great dinner, Hon," said Dad, kissing Mom good-bye, then giving a kiss to Sherre, Lizzy and me. "Don't wait up, I won't be home 'til after three."

I was disappointed to see him go. I missed not having dinner together as a family now that Dad had to work nights. He and Mom ate early, leaving the three of us to eat alone.

"Come on and eat, kids," Mom said after homework was done. "It's hamburgers tonight."

We slid into the diner-style booth Dad had made last year before he lost his job as an upholsterer. Little Lizzy was squashed between Sherre and me. The booster seat she had given up since becoming a "big four-year-old" had been replaced with the hips Sherre, now a teen, seemed to have sprouted overnight.

Mom slid a thin hamburger, one by one, onto each bun then — plop, plop, plop — three thick spoonfuls of her tasteless, lumpy mashed potatoes followed.

Our barely audible "Uhhh," was stopped short by a sharp look from Mom.

"Eat all those potatoes, girls," she said. "They're filling and they're good for you." We nodded. Times were tough and potatoes were cheap.

As soon as she left, I took a bite of the hamburger. The smell of heavenly garlic hit my nose. The taste was sheer bliss, juicy and full of flavor. I gobbled it down in four bites.

I risked a forkful of the potatoes, chewed as little as possible and struggled hard to swallow. *Mom must have been absent the day they taught potatoes in her Home Ec class,* I thought.

Sherre and Lizzy were having their share of trouble, too. Sherre gagged and Lizzy looked like she was going to throw up.

I smooshed the potatoes around on my plate trying to make them look less massive. I could dump them in the trash. A pang of guilt shot through me at the thought, knowing how hard Dad worked to put food on the table. Anyway, it'd mean having to pass Lizzy to get to the garbage can, and the little tattletale would tell on me for sure.

Then the idea came to me.

"Look, Lizzy!" I pointed up. "There are footprints on the ceiling!"

"Footprints?" said Lizzy. "Where?" Her gaze followed my finger.

"Up there." I scooped up a spoonful of mashed potatoes.

Plop.

"I don't see anything," she said.

"I see them," said Sherre, picking up my lead and a spoonful of her own. "Look, Liz, over the sink!" Plop.

"I don't see them," Lizzy whined.

"Aw, you missed it," I said. "They're gone."

"I hear too much talking and not enough eating," Mom called from the living room. "No dessert till those plates are clean."

Lizzy turned back to her meal. A puzzled look spread across her face. She took her fork and cautiously poked at the huge heap of potatoes now on her plate. Sherre and I snickered quietly, but Lizzy was silent, unable to take her eyes off the swollen blob.

"I'll be in there in two minutes," Mom said in a loud voice. "You girls had better be through."

Sighing, we re-attacked the potatoes again. Lizzy stuffed her mouth full and managed to get them down with a gulp of water. I choked. Sherre chewed and chewed. Gagging, she spit the whole mess into her napkin.

"Look, Liz," she said. "Those footprints are back!" She pointed to the ceiling. Lizzy snapped her head up. Plop… plop. Lizzy was still looking up when Mom reached the doorway.

"Elizabeth Ellen Mandell!" she said. "What have you been doing all this time? Your sisters are almost done with their potatoes. Yours have grown!"

Lizzy looked at her plate and gasped. Her lower lip quivered and she began to whimper.

"Never mind the waterworks, Lizzy," said Mom. "There are starving people who would love those potatoes. Eat."

Obediently, Lizzy scooped up another lumpy forkful and tried to eat it. Her face turned red. She sputtered. She tried to swallow. I watched with a lump in my throat as she fought to force them down.

Suddenly I felt clammy and sick to my stomach — and it wasn't because of the potatoes. I opened my mouth to speak, to admit to Mom what was really going on. But remembering the torture Sherre had put me through the last time I confessed for both of us silenced my tongue.

Sherre didn't seem to notice my guilt. As soon as Mom left the room, she was back at Lizzy like a hawk on a chicken.

"Lizzy!" She said pointing to a spot behind Lizzy's head. "There they are again!" Lizzy turned around in her seat. Plop.

I picked up my spoon and filled it up with the last of my potatoes, then stopped. *No,* I told myself. *I'd rather eat Mom's mashed potatoes the rest of my life than to watch my baby sister suffer like this.*

I shoveled the potatoes into my mouth and dropped the spoon. It clattered onto my plate. At the sound, Lizzy looked down at her mashed potato mountain. She turned around again to try to find the imaginary footprints, then looked from Sherre to me, a light of understanding in her eyes.

Grasping a spoon in her pudgy little fist, Lizzy began plopping potatoes onto our empty plates.

"Lizzy, are your potatoes gone yet?" called Mom.

"Almost!" said Lizzy cheerfully, loading on some more. "Better eat 'em all up," she whispered to us with a grin. "Or I'll tell!"

— Beverly Spooner —

A Chicken-Noodle-Soup Day

Lying is done with words and also with silence.
~Adrienne Rich

"I think I should stay home from school today, Mom. I'm sick. Really, I am."

I don't believe my fifteen-year-old sister for a minute. She hates school. This is just another one of her excuses to stay home. Again.

Mom isn't as sure as I am. She's a working mom who struggles with guilt for not being home for us. She gives Sandy the benefit of the doubt. Again.

"You can stay home," she says, "but you have to stay in bed. And I want you to eat chicken noodle soup for lunch."

We always eat canned chicken noodle soup when we're sick. It's the only time either of us likes it.

Mom feels Sandy's forehead as she kisses her goodbye.

"You don't feel warm," she says. "Are you sure you need to stay home?"

My dramatic sister lays one hand across her forehead. "I feel dizzy," she says, "and my head hurts. I must have that bug that's going around."

Mom reluctantly leaves for work.

"I'll call you later, Dear," she says as she closes the door.

I have to catch the bus for school.

"Enjoy your day, Sister Dear," I holler over my shoulder, "and get well."

Sandy waves to me from the kitchen window and grins.

She tries her best to look pathetic when I come home from school, loaded down with homework. I hear her scurry into the bedroom we share as I open the door.

"Mom will be home soon. You'd better get your act together," I warn.

Sandy peers at me through drooping eyes.

"I'm feeling a bit better," she sighs.

"Then why are you still in bed?"

"Paying my dues for a day off," she replies.

"Well, save it for Mom," I say. "You're going to need it. I need a snack. What's in the cupboard?"

"Well, I found some donuts, and there's popcorn, and Mom hid a package of candy bars on the top shelf."

"Got you, you little faker. Wait until Mom comes home. This was a chicken-noodle-soup day, remember?"

"Oh, she'll never know."

Famous last words.

When Mom comes home, I'm at my desk doing homework. I open the door a crack so I won't miss anything. Sandy is on the couch, pressing a cool washcloth to her forehead.

"How are you feeling tonight?" Mom begins, in a tone of proper concern.

"Better," Sandy says with only an edge of brightness to her voice. "I think I can go to school tomorrow."

Smart move, Sister, I think.

"The chicken noodle soup must have made you better," Mom says. "Did it taste good to you?"

"Soup always tastes good when I'm sick," Sandy says sweetly.

Liar, I think. *Watch out. You have become an unsuspecting prey.*

"Well, Dear," says Mom, "you just lie there while I get supper. I don't want you to overexert yourself. Are you up to eating your favorite pizza?"

Probably not, I think, *after a day of junk food.*

Sandy manages to say, "I think I could eat a little."

Mom rattles around in the kitchen, stretching pizza dough and filling it with our favorite toppings. I hear her open the trashcan.

I know what's coming next. I think I'll stay right here in my room.

"Sandy, I don't see your soup can in the trash. Where is it?"

If I were you, Sister, I'd confess now. Otherwise, you're done for. But my cornered sister attempts a getaway move.

"I pushed the can to the bottom, so I wouldn't smell the chicken. It was upsetting my stomach."

That's a good one, I have to admit. But Mom's not buying it.

"Poor dear," clucks my predator mother. "I'll get rid of it for you."

"That's okay, Mom. I'm feeling better now. Why don't I empty the trash while you get dinner?"

"No need, Dear. Just relax."

I hear a clatter of cans and bottles in the kitchen.

"Oops," says Mom. "I dropped the trash."

I could help her clean up, but think I'll stay here and begin my essay for English class. I have my topic, thanks to Sandy. I think I'll call it, "What a Tangled Web We Weave."

Mom's voice remains calm and pleasant. Too pleasant.

"That's strange, Sandy. I can't find the chicken noodle soup can anywhere."

There is a long silence. Sandy makes one last attempt to get out of the trap, but she is definitely the weaker one in this predator/prey game.

"I forgot, Mom. I put the can in the bag on the porch."

I know that there are at least four bags on the porch, all tied up, waiting for trash day — just as I know that Mom and Sandy will play this game to the death.

I have finished a draft about the complications of lying by the time Mom calls me to dinner. We sit at the table in silence. Four bags of trash are strewn on the floor.

Mom and I eat pizza, made just the way I like it, and drink soda. There is a special treat in the oven for dessert.

In front of Sandy sits one solitary mug of chicken noodle soup.

— Donna Beveridge —

A Silent Voice

If there are people at once rich and content, be assured
they are content because they know how to be so,
not because they are rich.
~Charles Wagner

The situation seemed hopeless.

From the first day he entered my junior high classroom, Willard P. Franklin existed in his own world, shutting out his classmates and me, his teacher. My attempts at establishing a friendly relationship with him were met with complete indifference. Even a "Good morning, Willard" received only an inaudible grunt. I could see that his classmates fared no better. Willard was strictly a loner who seemed to have no desire or need to break his barrier of silence.

Shortly after the Thanksgiving holiday, we received word of the annual Christmas collection of money for the less fortunate people in our school district.

"Christmas is a season of giving," I told my students. "There are a few students in the school who might not have a happy holiday season. By contributing to our Christmas collection, you will help buy food, clothing and toys for these needy people. We start the collection tomorrow."

When I called for the contributions the next day, I discovered that almost everyone had forgotten. Except for Willard P. Franklin. The boy dug deep into his pants pockets as he strolled up to my desk. Carefully, he dropped two quarters into the small container.

"I don't need no milk for lunch," he mumbled. For a moment, just a moment, he smiled. Then he turned and walked back to his desk.

That night, after school, I took our meager contribution to the school principal. I couldn't help sharing the incident that had taken place.

"I may be wrong, but I believe Willard might be getting ready to become a part of the world around him," I told the principal.

"Yes, I believe it sounds hopeful," he nodded. "And I have a hunch we might do well to have him share a bit of his world with us. I just received a list of the poor families in our school who most need help through the Christmas collection. Here, take a look at it."

As I gazed down to read, I discovered Willard P. Franklin and his family were the top names on the list.

—David R. Collins—

Walking with Grandpa

The power of choosing good and evil
is within the reach of all.
~Origen

randfather was a wise and honorable man. His house was not far from ours, and I would visit him often on my way home after school.

No matter how rotten I had been, I could tell Grandpa anything. My secrets were safe. He always understood. He loved me.

I remember a time when a bunch of us were playing baseball in the field behind Mrs. Ferguson's house. I hit one pitch just right and... *slam!* It was a home run that soared high and away and ended up shattering Old Lady Ferguson's kitchen window! We all ran!

Walking home, my best friend, Tom, asked, "How will she ever know who did it? She's blinder than a bat!" He had a point.

I decided to stop by Grandpa's. He must have known something was up by the expression on my face. I felt ashamed. I wanted to hide. I wanted to bang my head against a tree a thousand times and make the world just go away — as if punishing myself could undo things. I told him about it.

He knew we had been warned many times about the dangers of playing where we shouldn't. But he just listened.

"I was wrong," I told him, with my head down. "I hate myself for what I did. I really blew it. Is there a way out? Will she call the police?"

"Well," he said, "she has a problem, just like you. I'll bet if she knew you cared, she would be sad to know that you're afraid of her.

I'll bet she wishes you would give her a chance… a chance to be understanding. It's your decision," he said, shrugging his shoulders. "Just so I don't say the wrong thing, is the plan to pretend nothing happened? Just keep quiet and carry your little secret around… hide what you're not proud of?"

"I don't know," I sighed. "Things might get worse…."

"Let's think it through," he said finally. "If you were Mrs. Ferguson, what would you do?"

I had been afraid that Mrs. Ferguson would stay mad at me, so I ran. I didn't know what she might do. On the way home I imagined that she was a mean witch chasing me, and the further away I ran, the more gigantic she grew… until finally she towered over the whole town, seeing my every move with an evil eye.

"Well," I said, taking a deep breath, "One solution is to tell Mrs. Ferguson I'm sorry and offer to fix her window."

"If you call her," asked Grandpa, "what's the worst that can happen?" I had to think for a moment. I realized that even if she did not accept my apology, it could not be any worse than seeing the disappointment on Mom and Dad's faces.

Grandpa smiled when he knew I had figured it out.

"Doing what's right is not always easy," he said, handing me the phone. "I'm proud of you." Grandpa did not make me do it. It was always my choice. I knew I had found the best answer, just by thinking it through. That's how Grandpa did things. As it turned out, things were not anywhere near as bad as I had first imagined.

"Owning up to what you're not proud of is the hardest thing of all," said Grandpa. "Choosing to be honest, on your own — even when you don't have to be — makes others trust you and respect you."

Besides, it made me feel really good about myself. No one can ever take that away. *Thank you, Grandpa.*

Mrs. Ferguson and I eventually became really close friends. She was so kind and grew to take a real interest in me. I started doing all kinds of odd jobs around her house after school, which eventually helped me to save enough to buy my first car. She once told me, "Fear can make the smallest things look so much bigger than they really are."

Just before he passed away Grandpa asked me, "Who will you turn to when I'm gone?"

Holding his hand I told him, "Honor is its own reward, Grandpa. And a good teacher lives on through his student. Thank you."

After Grandpa died, everyone was sad. So many people loved him and would miss him.

I still talk to him, in my thoughts. I imagine how he would approach things, what questions he would ask... what advice he might give... whenever there is a problem. His soothing voice is clear and simple.

Grandpa gave me the tools to fix many problems... and cut them down to size.

And most of all he showed me I was brave.

—Uncle Greg—

Chapter 9

Tough Stuff

What a child goes through is hard to explain
We've been through stress, anger, hurt, and pain
Adults know what a child goes through
Because you see, they've been through it, too.

What a child goes through is sometimes insane
Sometimes people offer us drugs like cocaine
And now and again on dark, scary nights
We hear sirens and gunshots because of gang fights.

Death takes family and friends
Divorce takes them, too
Oh, if you only knew
What a child goes through.

—Shannon M. O'Bryant, 11 and Ashley O'Bryant, 13—

Sleepover Sadness

Fall seven times, stand up eight.
~Japanese Proverb

My name is Nathan. I'm ten years old. I like to play video games, play with my dogs, build things, and most of all, I like to play with my friends.

My friends and I are really close. We do a lot together—we play video games, play sports, and go to school together. I enjoy spending time with my friends because they are fun, silly, and kind. We jump on the trampoline and play in my fort.

When I started getting older, my friends and I started going camping, and inviting each other over for sleepovers. That was a problem for me, because I was a bedwetter. I always felt sad, scared, and disappointed in myself for being ten years old and still wearing Pull-Ups. I felt like I was the only one who still wet the bed at night.

Many times, I would tell my friends that my parents would not let me go over to their house for a sleepover. I felt very sad that I would miss out on having fun at night with my friends.

A few times, when I had to spend the night at a friend's house, I had to hide that I was wearing a Pull-Up. My mom helped me hide it in my backpack and I would be very careful to make sure no one saw that I had it with me. Before bed, I would have to take my backpack into the bathroom so I could change, without anyone knowing. I would get a terrible night's sleep because I was scared that I would pee through my Pull-Up and everyone would find out. I was also worried that my friends could hear the noise the Pull-Up made when I moved. In the morning I would go into the bathroom and have to hide the Pull-Up from the night before in my backpack and take it home to throw it out.

My doctor kept saying that I would most likely grow out of it by the time I was thirteen, but that felt like forever, and I didn't want to wait any longer. I tried taking medicine that my doctor gave me, but that didn't help either. I was so frustrated and sad.

Finally, my parents found a device that would go under the sheet at night. If I peed, an alarm would go off. Mom and Dad explained that it might not work, but I said I wanted to try it anyway. It made me feel awesome to try it. The first week I peed every other night. Then I went twenty-five nights in a row without wetting the bed. I peed on the twenty-sixth night and was very disappointed in myself; however, the video that came with it said this was normal. Right now, I have gone another fourteen days without a problem. Now I feel much better about having sleepovers with my friends.

It took some time, but now I feel confident I won't wet the bed again. And If I do wet, I will be sad, but I know that we are all different. Eventually, I won't wet the bed anymore. What I can tell other kids with this problem is, don't give up. You will get through this.

— Nathan Berres —

Ants

Alone we can do so little. Together we can do so much.
~Helen Keller

I am sitting in the grass, feeling alone and so sad. Watching as ants crowd around an old stump, taking bits of food that others have left behind. The sadness, I have discovered, is called depression. It is known as a mental illness.

My vision clouds with tears as I watch the ants crawl into their holes. A figure appears, silently crouching next to me. He looks at me and smiles. I've seen him before. Around the halls and in class. Always paying attention, focusing, answering questions and getting good grades. He doesn't have a "group" in our school either. He wanders, like me.

"Ants are amazing," I say.

He gazes at me, tracing my every move with his eyes.

"Yeah, they're really cool."

He turns back to look at the ants, shifting his stance into a sit on his knees.

"Isn't it interesting how they can carry ten times their weight?" I whisper, mystified as a red ant picks up a cracker three sizes bigger than its own head.

We watch together as the ant heaves the treat down into a tiny hole in the stump, like an alligator dragging its prey into the water.

"My friend got bit by a whole bunch of fire ants once," he says, smiling. "She ran into the cabin to make the burning stop but the only thing inside were two large cans of vinegar. I don't think vinegar helps with ant bites, but she used it anyway."

We both laugh, a sound I didn't expect to hear today. We watch the ants a little longer, sharing facts and funny encounters. I push away my negative thoughts from before. I can tell he has hard times too. He's wearing a hearing aid.

He has different experiences and troubles, yet we're so alike. It's funny how the tiniest things can bring people together. The smallest spark of kindness can change a day. I realize now, we are just like the ants, small things living in a huge world. We are all ants, but together we are one.

— Avery Watterson —

Kelsey

My little sister, Kelsey, was two years younger than me. I can actually remember the day she was born. It was beautiful outside. The sun was out and there was a nice cool breeze. I went into the hospital to see my new sister, but I was too young to hold her.

Four years later, my brother Dakota came along, and by then, I was big enough to hold my new little brother.

Since Kelsey and I were so close in age, we did a lot together growing up. We were typical kids and we sometimes fought like cats and dogs. But there were also days that we were really nice to one another. We used to play games on Nintendo once in a while, but most of all, we loved to play outside.

My sister was the most athletic person in our family. She was a lot faster than me. As we got older, we used to race all the time, but she would usually beat me. We especially loved to swim, so my dad got us a membership at the pool at our nearby church. We loved that pool, especially the lifeguards and the people who would often go there. We would race in the pool, too, and sometimes I would actually beat Kelsey.

My family life was going pretty good, but when I was about eleven I started to notice that my parents argued a lot. My dad was a hard worker and provided well for us, but he drank too much and my mom had no tolerance for alcohol abuse. The madness never did stop, so eventually they divorced.

I thought things would never be the same without my dad living with us and that it would be the hardest thing I'd ever have to go through. I realized that our lives would never be perfect due to the stress and strain that was created. But I tried to stay positive and remember the good times my father and I had. Mom and Dad seemed happier this way, and I knew we'd be okay.

My family and my mom's family have always been a close-knit bunch. My nana and pops were the best! Nana is a really sweet lady and cares for us a bunch, but Pops was my favorite person in the world. He was funny and silly, and he loved me and my brother and sister a lot.

One day, my pops wanted me to come over to watch some John Wayne movies that were on TV. We made popcorn and root beer floats that night. We were up pretty late and had a great time together. I was spending the weekend with them, which I loved to do. The next morning, Pops and I were going to get up early and eat breakfast together. Pops usually woke up at around 6:30 a.m. My nana was up but Pops still hadn't gotten up, so Nana told me to go and wake him.

I went to get him, but I knew something was wrong as soon as I walked in. My pops had died in his sleep early that morning of a massive stroke. I was totally devastated. My whole family was numb and in shock. For months we were all in a sad fog. Still, I tried to stay positive. My pops was in a better place and although I'd miss him my whole life, I knew I'd see him again.

Things were going along all right, but we had our days when it was tough. We did our best to get through them. Then in November of that year, my mom was diagnosed with an aggressive form of breast cancer. She ended up having a major operation on Christmas Eve. My mom spent her birthday, Christmas and New Year's in the hospital. I was so worried about her. I didn't know how I should deal with it. I guess I just dealt with it by trying to be as much help as I could around the house.

My mom went through several extensive surgeries and a massive amount of chemotherapy. She went away to Omaha for a few weeks to undergo treatment. I was so worried about her through those times. I was lucky to have such strong and supportive friends and family through it all.

Finally, Mom came home and was doing pretty well. We had

several false alarms but nothing serious. By July, Mom was feeling good enough to get out with us and have a little fun.

One afternoon, my mom, nana, brother and family friend Tracy went out to play miniature golf and then we went out to eat. We had a really good day. It was the most fun I'd had in a long time.

When we got home, there were tons of messages on the phone machine. My dad's girlfriend left us an urgent message asking us to call her as soon as we got home. When we reached her, she gave us more horrible news. She told us that my dad had died earlier that day of a massive heart attack. My mind was going in all sorts of directions. I had no idea this could happen to my forty-five-year-old father. It was a total surprise to all of us. I did not know what to do or think.

There was a huge visitation for my dad. Then, as a final goodbye, we spread his ashes in Lake Okoboji in Iowa where he always used to say he wanted to be put to rest.

After we got things back on track again and going well, I started back at karate, something that I had always loved doing. Kelsey was excited about starting her first year of middle school and I was going to be in eighth grade. By this time, I'd been through more than most kids had, but nothing would prepare me for what happened next.

On September 3rd, Kelsey and Dakota begged my mom to let them go to the pool. I didn't go because I was mowing the backyard to earn some extra cash. My mom was not going to let them go, but finally they just broke her down. She was very sensitive to the sun from all of the chemotherapy, so she could not go with them. She said they could go for half an hour — just long enough to come back and get me so that I could go to karate.

My mom had just walked through the door and started to change clothes when the phone rang. It was someone from the church. They said there had been an accident at the pool. Mom came running down the stairs to tell our family friend Tracy and me. Tracy left with my mom and I stayed at home. I tried to call my nana and ask her if she knew what was wrong. I needed someone to talk to but apparently Mom called her and asked her to come to the pool. So, I waited at home patiently for a phone call or someone to come and get me.

Finally, the phone rang and it was my nana saying she was on her way to pick me up. When she got to our house, she sat me down and told me what had happened.

My sister, Kelsey, had been caught in the pool drain. The paramedics came, but they could not pull her out. She was underwater for approximately twenty-five minutes. Finally, they were able to get her out and they rushed her to the closest hospital immediately. When she arrived, they worked on her and found a faint pulse after about thirty minutes. From there, she was rushed to Children's Mercy Hospital and that is where she stayed on life support. I went in to see her. She was not the same at all; she was not my athletic little sister anymore. She lived for two days.

Knowing that I would never see her again and having to say a final goodbye to Kelsey was the saddest thing that I've ever been through. We had been together through the toughest times our family had ever known and we had helped each other out. Now she was gone forever, and I was on my own. I knew I had to learn how to help myself out, and to help Dakota, too. If it weren't for my family and friends, I would never have made it through the experience of losing Kelsey.

I think my family and I might have a new start with our lives now. I know it will never be the same without Kelsey, but I think the tragedies in our lives have stopped. Mom is in remission and has gone back to teaching kids with special needs. I'm studying kickboxing and karate and doing really well in school. As for Dakota, he's following in my footsteps and taking karate, too. So far, so good.

One thing I learned from all this is to treat your family with love and kindness. Always give hugs and kisses to them because tomorrow is not promised to anyone. If you do this, then you won't ever have to wonder if they knew that you loved them.

— Shane Ruwe, 15 —

Losing Mom

When I was twelve, my parents separated, and I thought that was hard. Then I realized that something else is even harder: losing someone you love very much.

In my opinion "cancer" is the worst six-letter word in the whole dictionary. My mom was first diagnosed with mouth cancer. She spent Mother's Day in the hospital that year recovering from major surgery. Then, four months later, she was diagnosed with lung cancer. I remember the day so vividly.

When I came home from school that day, my mom's side of the family was there. They were all crying. My mom said, "Come and sit by me," and she started crying, too. My heart began to pound really hard and my eyes filled with tears. I definitely knew something major was wrong. My mom was too upset to explain so my grandpa told me. My mom had cancer in both lungs, and she only had a short time to live. My mom and I just sat there and cried together.

My family had to watch my mom go through so much: chemotherapy, radiation, oxygen treatments and the loss of her beautiful hair. She suffered so much, and we couldn't do anything about it. She couldn't talk without coughing or losing her breath. She was weak, and she was just slowly dying.

We knew it would happen someday, but not as soon as it did. Everything was over in eight months. I came home from school one day, and my mom wasn't there. She was always my first concern when I walked through the door. She had been taken to the hospital in an ambulance. We went up to see her that night. I didn't get my homework done, but I didn't care.

The next day, my brother Robert and I were called out of school because my mom wasn't doing well. I went to my locker and started crying. Two of my friends came out and tried to comfort me. When we got to the hospital, my brother Chris met us at the elevator and told us the grim news. I tried not to cry in front of Mom because it would upset her, and then she wouldn't be able to breathe. I took a deep breath and went in to see her. It was so hard to see her lying there so helpless. I held her hand, and we tried to talk but it was hard for her. I can't even count how many times I told her that I loved her.

When I left her that night, I had the feeling that it was going to be the last time I saw her alive. When I got home, I called her and we talked some more. I remember the conversation word for word. I told her that she sounded better and that I loved her. That conversation was so special.

The next day, Robert and I were called out of school again. I wanted to cry so badly, but I held back my tears. Chris and my dad were in the car waiting for us. I was so scared to face what was in store for us. When we stepped off the elevator at the hospital, I took a deep breath. I just had a feeling that what I was about to hear wasn't going to be good. My sister came out of my mom's room and she was crying. As I got closer, I could see that everyone else was crying, too. I started to shake. My sister came up to me and said, "She's gone. She died." I tried to laugh because I didn't want it to be true. The pain I felt was like no other. My sister asked if I wanted to go in and see her, and I said yes. When it was time for everyone to leave, we went over and gave Mom a last hug. When she didn't hug me back, I knew it wasn't a dream.

Some days I really need my mom. When she died, a part of me died, too. However, I knew that I would have to become an adult very quickly. Sometimes I ask myself, *Why her?* She did not deserve any of the pain that she went through. She fought hard for her children. We meant the world to her, and I know she didn't want to leave us.

I always thought my mom would be here for special things like homecoming, prom, graduation and my wedding day. It's hard knowing she's not going to be. She's never going to know her grandchildren or see Robert and me grow up. I would do anything to have her back. I miss and love her so much.

Very few people consider the true dangers of smoking. They think it is cool because everyone else is doing it. But it isn't. It really isn't.

I'm sure that at least one of you reading this thinks that life would be so much better without your parents. I have a little tip for you: Live life to its fullest and love your parents. It's hard to go on without them.

— Diana Carson, 15 —

Celebrate the Good Days

*Look to your health; and if you have it, praise God,
and value it next to a good conscience; for health is the
second blessing that we mortals are capable of;
a blessing that money cannot buy.*
~Izaak Walton

ancer. It sends chills up my spine as I say it. A six-letter word causes so much pain. I didn't think it would happen to anyone that I knew, until it happened to my mom.

It was in April of what seemed to be a great year. I was in fourth grade with the greatest teacher, Miss DeRosear. It was the year everyone looked forward to because Miss D. was the coolest teacher.

I had just come home from school to find Mom at home. That was odd because she never arrived home before me. Mom was sitting on the couch with Dad. A thousand horrible things started flashing through my mind. What if Grandma had passed away? I did not have the chance to say goodbye. What if my brother was hurt?

As I crawled up on the couch next to Mom, she gave me a kiss and a huge smile, so I relaxed and went on with my normal after-school activities. During the TV show that I always watched after school, Mom started getting phone calls. The calls continued for the rest of the night. Each time the phone rang, Mom rushed to her room. I then knew that something bad had happened.

When Mom came back, I asked, "Mom, why do you keep on leaving the room every time you get a phone call?"

She turned to my sister and me and said, "Girls, I have something to tell you. I have a disease that will make me very sick. I have cancer."

As she said that I felt a sharp pain in my heart. I was thinking, *Why is God taking my mom from me so soon? What have I done?* Little did I know that we were just beginning a very long, painful journey.

The next day on the bus I turned to my friend, Kate. "My mom…" That was all I could say before I started crying. Kate gave me a big hug and whispered, "I know, and I'm here for you." I knew then that Kate would support me.

As other people found out about my mom's cancer, they all had different ways of dealing with it. When my grandma found out about it, she had a difficult time, because to her, cancer was a death sentence. She had lost her husband, my grandfather, to cancer when my mom was only a senior in high school.

Then the time came for Mom to have chemotherapy. Her hair fell out, and she was always sick. I remember all those nights that she was too tired to eat, or she was sick from the chemotherapy.

During the summer, Mom stayed home. On the good days, Mom, Sis and I went down by the pond and made shapes out of clouds. On these days we talked about what we were going to do the next day, week, month or year with Mom. We never talked about losing her.

Support came from many different people and places. When school started again, Mom had to have surgery. I stayed with one of my teachers, Mrs. Stephens. Mrs. Stephens made me rainbow French toast. It always made me feel better: it let me know that someone cared and made time to make something for me. I would feed it to the dog if I had too much or if I wanted the dog to feel good also. Mrs. Stephens was always there for me with a smile, a hug or "it will be okay" advice.

Sometimes I lost hope, wondering, *Am I losing my mother just like she lost her father?* I spent hours just ranting at God, telling him that he could not take her away! I needed her! He just could not take her away!

After a long six months of losing her hair and throwing up because of chemo, my mom took a turn for the better. She slowly started to recover.

On April 5, 1999, my mom became a five-year survivor. When that day came, we had a big party. Friends came from far and wide to celebrate how special Mom is and her victory against cancer!

If you know someone who has cancer, you can help by doing little things. You can stay with them for a while and just chat or do some chores.

Dealing with cancer is so hard. Don't bottle up your feelings. Talk to someone. Chat rooms are available for kids dealing with cancer, and support groups help kids and teens deal with cancer, too. Do not give up!

There will be good days and bad days—some more bad than good. But as I have learned from my mother, celebrate the good days!

—Leslie Beck, 14—

For the Best

It is not only for what we do that we are held
responsible, but also for what we do not do.
~Moliere

It was two days after the tragic school shooting in Colorado, and I was feeling bad about what had happened to the students there. My school began having a lot of bomb threats and it seemed that police cars were there often. I was standing with my friend, Amberly, and her boyfriend when he casually said, "I'm gonna blow up the school and kill everyone." I asked, "Why would you want to do that?" and he said, "I just do," and walked away.

I was scared because no one had ever said anything like that to me before. I found out when talking to other friends that he also bragged about this to other people. My friends told me that I should tell an adult what he had said, but I was too scared, and I made them promise not to tell anyone either.

One day, Amberly and I were talking about what he had said when the teacher overheard our conversation. She took me out into the hallway and made me tell her who had said it and what they had said. At first, I refused to say a word. She told me it really was for the best, so I told her. I felt awful for doing it. I was angry with her for making me tell who said it. I wasn't sure he really meant it and didn't want him to get into trouble.

He got suspended for two days and had two days of in-school detention after that. I sometimes wonder if I had not told, would he have done what he said he was going to do? The guys in Colorado seemed pretty normal to a lot of people. The bottom line is you should never joke around about something as serious as killing people. If you do, responsible people have no choice but to have you checked out to ensure everyone else's safety.

After he was suspended, the whole sixth grade had an assembly. The principal and counselors told the students that there was a kid who was making threats and that he was suspended. I decided later to tell him that it was me who told on him so he wouldn't speculate about who did it. I was surprised to find that he was not angry with me for doing what I did. He was able to get help for his feelings and behavior.

Many people are in the same situation that I was in. If your friend is saying threatening stuff like my friend was, then they obviously need help — soon. It seems like when one school shooting happens, then another one occurs not too long after that. If there were any way that you could prevent one school shooting it could perhaps save your own life and many others as well. If I had to do it over again, I would — because it really was for the best.

— April Townsend, 12 —

My One Regret

Don't ever slam a door. You may want to go back.
~Don Herold

Even though my mom and dad still loved each other, my dad's lifestyle came between them and us. Dad always picked his friends over his family. He owned a bar, rode a Harley, and had other hobbies that I do not feel too comfortable talking about.

My mother and father had been divorced for five years when I went to live with my dad. My mom and I were not getting along. As it turned out, I spent most of my time with my twenty-six-year-old brother. My brother took me to school, picked me up and dropped me off at Dad's house because my dad was still the same and spent all of his time either at work or with his friends.

Pretty soon, I started to miss my mom, so I wanted to move back to live at her house. My dad was really upset with me for wanting to leave, even though I hardly ever saw him. I went ahead and moved back in with my mom anyway. Three months went by without my dad and I speaking a word to each other. It didn't really bother me too much, because my mom and I were getting along, and we had even moved into a new house. Then my whole life changed with just a single telephone call.

My ten-year-old sister and I were the only ones home when a woman called. She did not tell us what was going on, only that my mom should call when she came home.

When Mom returned a few hours later, she called and was told that my father had been in a motorcycle accident and that she needed to call the hospital. When she called the hospital, they told her to contact my dad's family. My mom became hysterical and started yelling that *we* were his family and that she was his ex-wife, and she had his children with her. They still would not tell her anything, except to contact my brother.

I knew that we were too late. I started to cry, but then I stopped. I guess part of me just wanted to hold on to the small chance that maybe I was just overreacting. Deep down I knew that I was not, I just did not want to believe it.

All of us piled into the car and drove to my father's house as quickly as possible. My brother was sitting outside on the picnic table with people all around. When I saw my brother sitting there, I panicked. Right then I knew that he did not have good news for us. My brother squeezed into the car and told us to drive. I can still remember the exact words my brother said — I don't think that I will ever forget them. He said, "Kids, I hate to be the one to have to tell you this, but Dad is dead."

The next few days are still a blur. Everybody tried to act strong. I would catch my older sister locked in the bathroom crying. My younger sister would write messages in her notebook about how she wished that she still had her daddy. I think that I suffered greater than they did. My father and I never had a chance to resolve our problems. I cannot remember the last time we told each other how much we loved each other. He was mad at me when I left his house, and I never had the chance to work things out with him.

The only thing that kept me from going insane was my mother. She told me about dreams that she has had about my father. He talked to her in her dreams. He told her that he is watching over us, and that he loves all of us very much. I want to believe that with all my heart.

I often think about how things could have been different if I had just picked up the phone during those three months and broken the silence between us. I guess I just thought he'd always be there.

The greatest advice that I can give anyone is to always forgive each other — don't let your differences linger over time. You never know what the future will hold.

— Angelia Lee Swift, 17 —

The Perfect Figure

I am as my Creator made me,
and since He is satisfied, so am I.
~Minnie Smith

"Oh my gosh, it looks sooo good on you," exclaimed my best friend. "That color flatters you, and I'm getting it for you for your birthday. After all, it's in two weeks!"

I had gone bathing suit shopping with my best friend. Since we were going into the seventh grade, we needed to look cooler. We tried two-piece suits in hopes that we would get more attention from the guys. We wound up purchasing them, and the topic of conversation came up about going on a diet. The only reason for going on one would be to lose a little bit of our "baby fat." I thought all the guys would like me if I was pretty and thin.

So, I decided to stick to the diet, even though it would be hard because I am a chocoholic. I had always been a big girl. Not necessarily fat, but tall with a solid build. All the courses in school I took were advanced placement and I played many sports. I thought, *A thin, pretty, smart, athletic girl — everyone will love me*. When I would come home I wouldn't snack, and I cut down on my dinner portions. I had cravings for ice cream, but I just looked at beauty magazines and my bathing suit. The craving disintegrated quickly.

My mom noticed when I dropped five pounds. She told me to stop because I could hurt myself. I promised her I'd stop, but I couldn't. My best friend lost about ten pounds and stopped because she knew she looked good. I started getting complimented by my peers at school. I wore my same clothes which kept getting baggier and baggier. Some people would ask me where my lunch was. I lied to them and made up excuses.

Since I lost weight by dropping lunch, I did the same with breakfast. I tricked my dad into thinking that I ate my bagels, but I fed them to the deer. My weight dropped drastically, and my best friend would threaten to tell my parents if I didn't eat. I fooled her so she thought I was eating, but I wasn't. When I looked at myself in the mirror every day, I saw bulgy thighs that had to go.

My gym teacher confronted me about my immense weight loss. I told her I was losing weight, but that it was all through exercise.

Finally, dark circles formed under my eyes, and I stopped physically developing. It was a struggle for me to even walk up my driveway. I couldn't sleep at night, and I wore layers of clothing in eighty-degree weather but I was still cold. That didn't matter. I still needed to be thinner, and I started wondering how many calories were in toothpaste and communion wafers.

About a month and a half after I had bought the bathing suit, I tried it on again and it fell right off me. My mom told me to look in the mirror. I could see my eye sockets, my transparent skin, the dark circles under my eyes, and my cheekbones popping out of my skin. That was the day I realized how skinny I was.

I went to our family doctor and a psychiatrist. My total weight loss was about twenty-five pounds in one month and a week. It took one year for my body to start working normally again.

Sometimes I want to go back to being thin, but I would *never* do what I did again. It's not worth it. Please don't go on diets when you're young. You will regret them. I know I do. Get help right away because you'll slowly kill yourself and suffer greatly. Don't judge and compare yourself to others. Try to love yourself for who you are, not for how you look. Besides, you probably look fine just the way you are.

— Nikki Yargar, 14 —

Pale Dawn of a New Day

Recovery is a process, not an event.
~Anne Wilson Schaef

had always had a feeling of dread deep down within me. When it happened, it hit me with such surprise that you would never know that I predicted it.

At the time, I did not know how lucky I had been. I would lie awake at night before falling asleep, hearing my parents fight and yell at each other. Although neither hurt the other, it always ended up with my mother crying... and that always scared me. I suppose they never thought I could hear them, and they hid their tension from me as much as possible.

One afternoon, my mother told me she needed to talk to me. I never thought of the obvious. My mother sat down next to me on our gray couch with my father on the other side. My mother calmly explained that they no longer enjoyed each other's company and that they would be getting a divorce. As I fought back tears, my mother continued to tell me how they had tried so hard to make it work — for me. They said they never wanted to hurt me. They could never know how much it did. They said that even though they no longer loved each other, it did not affect how much they loved me, and that my dad would move to an apartment nearby, close enough for me to walk to.

I could no longer hold back the tears, and I ran sobbing to my room, slammed the door and collapsed on my bed. I clutched my pillow to my chest. Everything flashed through my head, everything I could have done to make it work. I lay there, never wanting to leave the safety of my room, not wanting to accept my new reality. I stared for hours out my second-story window, not really thinking… not really looking, just sitting out of the reach of my own mind.

I woke up the next morning and trudged to the bus stop. At school, my friends comforted me and I hated it. I was trapped, and everyone made it worse. My friends tried to make me feel better, but they always reminded me of how it had been before. I began to associate the pain of the situation with them and it hurt. I pushed them away, enjoying the solitude.

I found I loved writing, though I shared my compositions with no one. Everything had been turned upside down. No one knew. I only suffered internally. I hid inside myself, remaining the same person externally. My parents, in separate places, acted as though nothing had happened, and that outraged me even more.

My father did not move to an apartment nearby. Instead, he stayed in our house. It was my mother who left and moved to the other side of town.

I was informed my father had fallen in love with a new "companion." It hurt immeasurably to watch my father preferring to hold her hand instead of mine. My mother had found one as well and moved in with him. I would spend long hours at her house waiting to leave, feeling alone and ignored. I thought I would die.

My writings began to be terrible stories of girls in far worse situations than I, making me feel more fortunate. I moved back and forth between homes every week, and when anything went wrong, it was always the other parent's fault. I woke up every morning to meet the dawn, which seemed to be paler and more frail than ever before. Alone, not allowing anyone into my reality, I cried.

Now, two years later, I almost never cry, for I feel that I have cried my share. I have accepted and moved on. I've become closer to both of my parents, and throughout the trials they go through, I now feel involved and helpful. My mother's companion recently left her, and she came to me in friendship looking for support.

But it still hurts quietly somewhere inside of me. I will never forget, and I will always miss how it was. Even though they fought, we were together, and I never appreciated it when we were. As for now, I realize that there is nothing more beautiful than the dawning of a new day and that I must go on.

—Katherine Ackerman, 12—

Chapter 10

Changes

Change is the only absolute
in the world,
the only thing
that you can depend on.
Nothing stays the same.
Tomorrow will come,
bringing with it
new beginnings and sometimes
unexpected endings.
You can hold on to the past
and get left in the dust;
or, you can choose to
jump on the ride of life
and live a new adventure
with perseverance and
an open mind.

—Irene Dunlap—

The Voice Crack

The only thing that's the end of the world
is the end of the world.
~Barack Obama

During my sixth-grade year, I was nervous about many things. I was scared about being a role model on campus. I was scared about going to a middle school the following year. But nothing compared to my biggest fear of all… puberty. I was getting to the age where my voice would start changing. At first, I was excited for my voice to get deeper. But then I learned that before your voice gets deeper, it can sometimes squeak and crack.

The first time it happened to me I was so embarrassed, but to my surprise, my friends did not make fun of me. In fact, they didn't even mention it. That was reality. But in my self-conscious sixth-grade mind I was certain they were going to spend all day making fun of me behind my back. They were not having the same problem controlling their voices.

After my first voice crack experience, I was determined to make sure it would not happen again. At least not in public. So, except for a few strategic times I said, "cool" and "yeah," I stopped talking. My logic was, *If I do not use my voice, it cannot crack.* This worked well, for a while, but there was one issue. I could not go without talking forever. I had to come up with a new solution.

I began clearing my throat before I spoke. Doing this actually seemed to help. It may have just been psychological, but I felt better. I was not having as many voice cracks. Limiting how much I spoke and clearing my voice before I spoke made my recess and lunch experiences much less stressful. Even when my voice did crack it was only my closest friends that would hear. This was great but there was a larger problem. I was way more scared about having a voice crack during class.

There were a couple of reasons why having a voice crack in class was scarier than having one anywhere else. One of these reasons was my class had a whole bunch of new kids that I had never spoken with. I did not want their first impressions of me to be based on a voice crack. Looking back now, it sounds silly, but it was a real concern at the time.

The second, and quite honestly, scariest reason, was the fact that this class had a group of girls in it. This was not just any group of girls; it was the most popular group of girls. To make matters even worse, the girl I had a crush on at the time was a part of this group. This is probably one of the reasons I was so shy in class that year. I had not spoken to girls much. Having a voice crack in front of the girl I liked, not to mention her friends, was a fear that paralyzed me.

Unfortunately, one day my worst nightmare came true. It was about halfway through the year, when I was happy to have made it so long without a bad voice crack incident.

On the day it happened everything was the same as always until I got into class. When I walked through the door the first thing I noticed was we had a substitute teacher. For some people seeing a sub was a great thing, but for me it was a problem. I immediately started thinking about how the sub would need to take attendance. My permanent teacher never had to. Since he already knew each student and where they sat, he just had everyone sit down in their assigned seat, and marked "absent" the students whose seats were empty.

I started to panic. So many thoughts were rushing through my mind I could not think straight. I calmed myself down by telling myself that I only had to say one word. "Here." Easy enough right? Well, I thought so too until my name was called. I did my normal routine; I cleared my throat, took a breath, and said, "here." The only problem was that while saying this, I had the worst voice crack in the history of voice cracks.

The whole class turned to look at me. It felt as if everyone was staring into my soul. There was silence, then the entire class burst into laughter. My worst nightmare had come true, and it was humiliating. I wanted to run out of the class and go home, get in bed, and pull the covers over my head, but I knew that would only make things worse. The class settled down and then continued as normal, but I could not get the thoughts out of my head.

Recess finally came. I was able to find my friends who were in a different class, since thankfully they had not heard what happened. We'd only been playing basketball for a few minutes when one of the kids from my class came and told everyone on the court of my voice crack. Now not only my class knew about my voice crack, but other people were talking about it too. Luckily for me my friends stood up for me and told my classmate to leave. Then they rallied around me and told me not to worry about it.

We kept playing basketball and I thought to myself how that had gone better than I'd expected. School was not too bad after that; everything went on as if nothing happened and I was okay. But when I got home, I could not stop worrying about what the girls thought about it. I figured they had probably made a group chat dedicated to making fun of me. Of course, my chances with the girl I liked were ruined.

Then something unthinkable happened. One of the girls in the group texted me and asked me about it. Surprisingly, the conversation went well, and it led to other conversations. It turns out they didn't care about the voice crack. Since then, I have become friends with most of the girls in that group, and they are all nice.

As for the girl I liked, things could not have gone better. We began "dating" and continued to do so for the remainder of our sixth-grade year, which at that age pretty much means just being friends who are way too nervous to talk to each other. I am thankful that we are still great friends.

I learned that it is important to be positive and to put things in perspective. Even though I thought this was the worst possible situation at the time, it did not have any lasting negative effects. Although everyone laughed at me at the time, and some even talked about me, it wasn't truly a big deal to anyone but me. The fact is that nobody would remember it in the years to come.

— Donald "Trey" Brown III —

The Orange Bike

A friend may be waiting behind a stranger's face.
~Maya Angelou

When I moved to a new neighborhood in the fifth grade it was a hard transition for me. The only thing that helped make it feel comfortable was that we were a few blocks from my grandparent's house.

To make it worse, we had to change our school halfway through the school year. When you move halfway through the school year, your classmates have already established their groups and their friendships. It's hard to break in.

One day my brother and I were playing basketball in the alley outside our garage. A boy rode by on an orange bike. He looked kind, and he nodded to us. We stepped out of his way, but none of us spoke to each other. We didn't think we would see him again.

The next day at morning recess we saw him on the playground. He didn't say anything, but we made eye contact. A few days went by and we saw him again as he rode by on his orange bike. This time he stopped. We found out that he was a grade below me and two grades above my brother. It meant a lot that he had stopped to say hello to us. No one from our new school had really made an effort to befriend us, and we were shy and didn't know how to reach out.

Our new friend made a tremendous effort to include us. He started asking us to go on bike rides around the neighborhood. We slowly started meeting other kids in the neighborhood and realized that some of them went to our school.

The following year, when I went off to middle school, I remembered how uncomfortable I felt not knowing anyone. I made it a point to look for the quiet and shy kids in my classes. Our new friend had shown us how to use kindness toward a new kid. Now my brother and I wanted to reach out to others.

We stayed friends with the boy on the orange bike for years. He taught me to believe in myself and my ability to make new friends. It was just a matter of communication. To this day, whenever I see a bright bike I smile. If it weren't for the kid on the orange bike I don't think I would have formed the friendships that I've been blessed with.

— Vashti Seek-Smith —

My Very First Kiss

was in the seventh grade when I fell in love at the school-bus stop. "Who's that?" I hissed to Annie, my best friend.

"I dunno. New kid. Let's find out," replied Annie. Then she approached him. "Hi!" she dimpled.

Annie never just smiled at boys. She dimpled. She had the cutest, roundest cheeks with a dimple in each cheek. I was so jealous.

"I'm Annie. Did you just move here?" Annie lowered her head and looked up at him through her lashes.

"Yeah," he answered.

"This is my friend, Patty."

He looked at me.

I had never seen eyes so blue… eyelashes so long… a gaze so intense…

I FELL IN LOVE.

Everything you have ever heard about falling in love came true for me at that instant. My legs started to quiver and my kneecaps turned to jelly. I felt like I couldn't breathe very well. I couldn't walk, I couldn't talk, I couldn't even see very well. I just stood there, like the skinny geek that I was, looking at him.

His name was Jerry. He had moved into a house only four blocks from mine. Jerry was shorter than me, but that didn't matter. He didn't have much to say, but that didn't matter either. I was truly in love.

I started riding my bike past his house every day, gliding past the big picture window in the front, afraid he was looking out, yet praying and hoping that he was.

I was miserable and ecstatic all at the same time. I didn't want to share my feelings about Jerry with Annie, because if I made him look too desirable, she would probably want him. And if she wanted him, she would get him.

Then one Friday I got an invitation to a party. I couldn't believe it. It was a boy/girl party. My first. And my parents said I could go. And Jerry was invited.

The party was at Phyllis's house, and her parents had a room for parties that was separate from the rest of the house. Her parents wouldn't be watching us all the time. Annie told me that meant that it would be a kissing party. Perfect. The sweat was already forming under my armpits.

After two hours of eating potato chips, drinking Cokes and listening to our favorite music, someone suggested that we play Seven Minutes in Heaven. Someone else suggested Spin the Bottle. Spin the Bottle seemed much less threatening than spending seven whole minutes making out in Phyllis's garage. We all voted on Spin the Bottle, but you had to really kiss, not like some kind of kiss you give your grandma.

We all sat in a circle: boy-girl-boy-girl. Whoever had the tip of the bottle land on them had to go into the garage with the spinner of the bottle. If you were a girl, and you landed on a girl, you got another turn until you landed on a boy. Same for boys. Couples went into the garage and came back out, some looking weirded out, and some totally grinning.

Then the bottle landed on Jerry. He went into the garage with Charlene. Then, it was Jerry's turn to spin the bottle. It landed on Brian. Jerry spun the bottle again. It landed on me.

I thought I would die, right then and there. I couldn't even breathe. I tried to untangle my legs and stand up, but everything was jelly. I felt every pair of eyes on me. Somehow, I managed to get up and walk into the garage with Jerry. The door shut behind us.

It was pitch black. I could hear him breathing, somewhere in the darkness.

"Patty?"

"Huh?" Nice. Real smooth.

My eyes were getting accustomed to the darkness, and I could see the outline of his face. How was this supposed to happen? Was I supposed to close my eyes or keep them open? If I closed my eyes, how would I know where his face was? If I kept them open, would I look cross-eyed to him when we got close — sort of like the Siamese cats in *Lady and the Tramp?* What if his eyes were closed and my eyes were open? Or vice versa? Should I pucker up my lips, or just let them relax? Was I supposed to breathe, or hold my breath? Was I supposed to move my face toward him, or wait until he moved toward me?

I decided to keep my eyes open until the last minute, then close them as we got close enough to kiss. I took a breath, moved forward and closed my eyes. Unfortunately, so did Jerry. He must have had his eyes shut, too.

KLUNK!!!

"Ow!" we both said in unison. My front teeth and Jerry's front teeth had collided with the force of both of us moving forward toward the other.

"Ow, I think I chipped my tooth," I whispered.

"I'm sorry, I couldn't see you," said Jerry.

"It's okay. I'll live." I ran my tongue over my front tooth. There was a definite chip right in the front. It wasn't very big, but it was there.

"How do we explain this one?"

"I don't know."

All of a sudden I felt like laughing. It had been too much for me: the nervousness of my first kiss, being with Jerry in the garage (in the dark, alone), my chipped tooth. I started to giggle.

Jerry started to laugh, too. Then we heard someone from the other side of the garage door yelling, "What are you guys doing? You're taking too long!" For some reason, that was even funnier than the collision. Then they started pounding on the door.

"Okay, let's go." Jerry grabbed my hand as we opened the door and walked into the room. Jerry and I smiled at each other. Annie looked upset. I was in heaven.

The next day, Annie tried to get me to tell her what happened, but I just smiled. I think she was jealous of me for the very first time.

I'd like to say that it was the beginning of a boyfriend/ girlfriend relationship, but that just wasn't the case. For some strange reason, I started feeling differently about Jerry. I now saw him as he really was: a short boy with bright blue eyes who was my friend. In the eighth grade, I fell in love with someone else.

But every once in a while, when I least expect it, I'll run my tongue across my front teeth and feel the chip in my left front tooth. That's when I remember Jerry — the cutest boy in the seventh grade — and my very first kiss.

— Patty Hansen —

Papa

When you get to the end of your rope,
tie a knot and hang on.
~Franklin Delano Roosevelt

Papa died last night. He was my mom's dad, and I knew him for as long as I can remember.

He told me that if I studied hard and got good grades he'd buy me my first car. He promised. I'm twelve now and the oldest in my family.

I bet he was thinking that the thought of my own car would keep me focused on school. And, of course, if I really buckled down it would take the pressure off Mom.

Mom always said I was born with one foot out the door. Papa knew that. And my quest to grow up quickly and dash out that front door had always been hard on Mom. Papa knew that too, and that's when his voice roared like a lion, "Education, Brian. That's the key!"

Yet, as if he knew what I was feeling, he shook his head back and forth and pretended to whine, "I know, I know, I didn't want to study either." He put his arm around me and whispered, "But you have to do it," as if he were telling me a secret. Our secret. I think he was just trying to help make growing up easier.

I'll never forget the look on Grandma's face. "Your grandfather," she said, rolling her eyes, almost like she knew what he was going to say before he said it.

But once her eyes stopped rolling, she looked right at him, the way Mom looks at us when she wants us to hear her words. She told him to calm down. "Don't get Brian's hopes up," she said.

But Papa wasn't like a lot of people. He meant what he said.

I think his promises sometimes worried Grandma a little. So he just did what Papa always did. He purred like a kitten and snuggled up to Grandma and pinched her cheeks. Then he made a kissing sound with his lips over and over through the air, the way I'd seen him do it a thousand times before. And then he told her how much he loved me.

He used to kiss my brothers, sister, Mom and me that same way. Mom said Papa came from a long line of cheek pinchers. She said it was a family tradition. His father and grandfather did it too. I think it was the Italian in him.

Papa showed me that you can love people in front of others. He was always kissing us and pinching our cheeks. He didn't care who was watching. I remember how all that squeezing used to hurt at first, but we got used to it. I could tell Grandma got used to his way a long time ago. I think Grandma knew that Papa needed to love his family up close.

When Papa came to visit he always wanted to be near us. And he brought us books and magazines because he said we should read every day.

He would sit with us and we would read together. I think he liked to hear our voices. He brought over lots of puzzles, too. He said they were important for exercising our mind. I think he liked to see us learn.

I always felt good about my family after Papa came to visit. His hugs were stronger than anybody's and he liked to laugh out loud with us. He didn't seem to mind our noise. He said we were just being kids. I think he remembered what it was like.

I won't forget the last time Papa was here with us. He came over to hang a fan with a light on it, outside, in our patio. I remember how he worked all day, climbing up and down the ladder, exchanging one tool for another. I helped him for as long as I could, though after a while I got tired. But he kept on working.

He wanted us to be able to eat outside during warm summer nights. He said the fan would help, but it needed to be put in right. And of course, it couldn't squeak.

Last night, the last night I would see him, we all ate dinner together under the light and the quiet breeze from the fan. And not a thing squeaked. In fact, nothing ever squeaked when Papa was around.

Papa always said his tools were his treasures. He never went anywhere without them. I guess he just liked to fix things. I know Mom's going to miss his help around here.

I'm sad that Papa's gone. Today the phone keeps ringing. Lots of people are calling to say they're sorry that Papa died. Mom has put me in charge for a while. She wants me to watch my brothers and sister. She has arrangements to make because Papa died.

Now my littlest brother is looking to me. He says he didn't want Papa to die. He wants to know if he keeps eating those healthy apples, does that mean he won't get old and die?

I don't have an answer for my brother. I'm sorry. He has so many questions. "You're so smart, Brian," Papa used to always tell me. I think I'm not so smart right now.

"Does everybody get old and die?" my brother asks.

"No," I tell him, "that's not the way it always goes. Sometimes people die sooner than that, from other things. That's why Mom holds your hand when you cross the street and makes sure we're buckled up when we drive in the car."

"Then I don't ever want to let go of her hand and I want to live in the car where I'll be safe," he cries.

"I'm not sure that's the right way to live," I tell him.

"Then I want to be a cowboy. Do cowboys die?" he asks.

"Yeah, cowboys die," I say.

"Then I want to be the President. Do presidents die?" he asks, still crying.

"Yes," I nod. "Even presidents die, I learned that in school. It's better to think about living. It's the right thing to do."

Those words just fall out my mouth. Suddenly I realize what Mom means when she talks about doing the right thing. It's kind of like you really only have one choice. I think Papa would say so too.

My brother asks me one more question. "Brian, is Papa going to come alive again and be a ghost?"

"No," I answer sadly, wishing I could still see Papa. "But maybe we'll see him again up in heaven."

"Is that a long drive?" he wants to know. I start to laugh. I feel like jumping up and down, but instead I hug my brother tightly. He feels so small.

"It's a very long drive," I almost shout, "but when we get there and the gates to heaven swing open, I promise you, they won't squeak."

All of a sudden I feel a lot better. I let go of my brother and I can see he feels better too.

I think you can be both happy and sad at the same time.

— Brian Normandin as told by Mary Normandin —

Taking a Stand

It is better to be a lion for a day
than a sheep all your life.
~Elizabeth Henry

The summer before fifth grade, my world was turned upside down when my family moved from the country town where I was born and raised to a town near the beach. When school began, I found it difficult to be accepted by the kids in my class who seemed a little more sophisticated, and who had been in the same class together since first grade.

I also found this Catholic school different from the public school I had attended. At my old school, it was acceptable to express yourself to the teacher. Here, it was considered outrageous to even suggest a change be made in the way things were done.

My mom taught me that if I wanted something in life, I had to speak up or figure out a way to make it happen. No one was going to do it for me. It was up to me to control my destiny.

I quickly learned that my classmates were totally intimidated by the strict Irish nuns who ran the school. My schoolmates were so afraid of the nuns' wrath that they rarely spoke up for themselves or suggested a change.

Not only were the nuns intimidating, they also had some strange habits. The previous year, my classmates had been taught by a nun named Sister Rose. This year, she came to our class to teach music several times a week. During their year with her, she had earned the nickname Pick-Her-Nose-Rose. My classmates swore that during silent reading, she'd prop her book up so that she could have herself a booger-picking session without her students noticing. The worst of it, they told me, was that after reading was over, she'd stroll through the classroom and select a victim whose hair would be the recipient of one of her prize boogers. She'd pretend to be praising one of her students by rubbing her long, bony fingers through their hair! Well, to say the least, I did not look forward to her sort of praise.

One day during music, I announced to Sister Rose that the key of the song we were learning was too high for our voices. Every kid in the class turned toward me with wide eyes and looks of total disbelief. I had spoken my opinion to a teacher — one of the Irish nuns!

That was the day I gained acceptance with the class. Whenever they wanted something changed, they'd beg me to stick up for them. I was willing to take the punishment for the possibility of making a situation better and of course to avoid any special attention from Pick-Her-Nose-Rose. But I also knew that I was being used by my classmates who just couldn't find their voices and stick up for themselves.

Things pretty much continued like this through sixth and seventh grades. Although we changed teachers, we stayed in the same class together and I remained the voice of the class.

At last, eighth grade rolled around and one early fall morning our new teacher, Mrs. Haggard — not a nun, but strict nevertheless — announced that we would be holding elections for class representatives. I was elected vice president.

That same day, while responding to a fire drill, the new president and I were excitedly discussing our victory when, suddenly, Mrs. Haggard appeared before us with her hands on her hips. The words that came out of her mouth left me surprised and confused. "You're impeached!" she shouted at the two of us. My first reaction was to burst out laughing because I had no idea what the word "impeached" meant. When she explained that we were out of office for talking during a fire drill, I was devastated.

Our class held elections again at the beginning of the second semester. This time, I was elected president, which I took as a personal victory. I was more determined than ever to represent the rights of my oppressed classmates.

My big opportunity came in late spring. One day, the kids from the other eighth grade class were arriving at school in "free dress," wearing their coolest new outfits, while our class arrived in our usual uniforms: the girls in their pleated wool skirts and the boys in their salt-and-pepper pants. "How in the world did this happen?" we all wanted to know. One of the eighth graders from the other class explained that their teacher got permission from our principal, Sister Anna, as a special treat for her students.

We were so upset that we made a pact to go in and let our teacher know that we felt totally ripped off. We agreed that when she inevitably gave us what had become known to us as her famous line, "If you don't like it, you can leave," we'd finally do it. We'd walk out together.

Once in the classroom, I raised my hand and stood up to speak to our teacher. About eight others rose to show their support. I explained how betrayed we felt as the seniors of the school to find the other eighth graders in free dress while we had to spend the day in our dorky uniforms. We wanted to know why she hadn't spoken on our behalf and made sure that we weren't left out of this privilege.

As expected, instead of showing sympathy for our humiliation, she fed us her famous line, "If you don't like it, you can leave." One by one, each of my classmates shrank slowly back into their seats. Within seconds, I was the only one left standing.

I began walking out of the classroom, and Mrs. Haggard commanded that I continue on to the principal's office.

Sister Anna, surprised to see me in her office so soon after school had begun, asked me to explain why I was there. I told her that as class president, I had an obligation to my classmates to represent them. I was given the option to leave if I didn't like the way things were, so I did. I believed that it would have been a lie for me to sit back down at that point.

She walked me back to class and asked Mrs. Haggard to tell her version of the situation. Mrs. Haggard's side seemed to be different from what the class had witnessed. Then something incredible happened. Some of my classmates began shouting protests from their desks in response to Mrs. Haggard's comments. "That's not true," they countered. "She never said that," they protested.

It was too much of a stretch for them to stand up and walk out with me that day, but I knew something had clicked inside of them. At least they finally spoke up.

Perhaps they felt that they owed me. Or they realized that we'd soon be at different high schools and I wouldn't be there to stick up for them anymore. I'd rather believe that when they spoke up that day, they had finally chosen to take control of their own destinies.

I can still hear their voices.

— Irene Dunlap —

Just Do It!

The shortest answer is doing.
~English Proverb

My vision is getting worse. I can't even see what is five feet away from me without squinting. I know I need to get glasses, but I refuse to. I'm afraid they will make me look dorky. Besides, I can manage without them. These were my thoughts two years ago, when I was in the sixth grade. An embarrassing experience taught me that what I was thinking was wrong.

School had been out for two months. I was going to go to junior high school shortly, where I was sure that appearances are everything. So the question still remained. *Should I, or should I not, wear glasses?* The question was still in my mind when my family and I attended a wedding late in the summer.

During the wedding, I don't know why, but I felt as if I were ready to explode. Maybe it was the excessive amount of soda I drank prior to the wedding. Immediately after the ceremony ended, I walked quickly to the bathroom. Since it was an emergency and I couldn't clearly distinguish which door was marked boys, I just opened the nearest door and entered the restroom.

Unfortunately, I had entered the wrong restroom. I didn't know this though, at the time, because all I could think about was to accomplish what I had gone there to do.

After I was done, I went to the faucet to wash my hands. *That's awkward,* I thought, after looking around the squeaky-clean restroom. *How come there are only toilets in here? Could I be in the girls' bathroom?*

Abruptly, as if to answer my question, I heard a shrill scream coming from the direction of the entrance to the restroom.

After that incident, I decided to wear the dorky-looking glasses. I didn't really care about what people thought of me anymore, as long as I never, ever, entered the wrong bathroom again.

On the first day of seventh grade, instead of making fun of me, I received compliments from my friends. They thought the glasses made me look more intelligent — more like a grownup.

So if you know something is right, just do it! Don't make premature assumptions the way I did. You can avoid unnecessary embarrassment. It doesn't matter what others think of you. All that matters is what you think of yourself — and that you can see where you are going!

— Son Truong Nguyen, 14 —

I Love You, Lindsey

Time is a dressmaker specializing in alterations.
~Faith Baldwin

My heart drooped as I forced my unwilling body into the car. It would be miles and miles until we reached our painful destination, where we would have to leave Brandy, my older sister. Brandy was leaving home to serve as a volunteer in the Americorps.

My dad revved the car engine and we left the house. Soon, the streets turned into highways, and we were closer to having to say goodbye with every mile. My heart continued to sink lower.

All of the bittersweet memories of growing up with my sister flowed into my brain… from when I was young and Brandy telling me that my troll was evil, to when I copied her every move because I admired her so much, to when the painful teenage years came and her life was too busy for her younger sister. The anger came back to me too: the anger that came when suddenly my life was too immature for hers.

I didn't understand how come my old companion only talked to me when I did something wrong or when I annoyed her. *Why did her new clothes make my childish apparel look babyish?* These questions and many more stayed in my head.

Now I knew that my time with her was very limited. Throughout the ride she made wicked remarks that hurt, but this time I knew what they meant. They still hurt me even though I knew that this was the agonizing way that she pulled herself away from us, in preparation for her leaving us at last.

When we reached the place where Brandy was to stay, we did everything that we could to stall the painful goodbyes that awaited us, until all that was left were the goodbyes. The tears began to stream down my cheeks as she hugged me and told me the words that I hadn't heard in a long time.

"I love you, Lindsey."

I sobbed an answer in response. The family was all tears. We all piled into the car and pulled away. Brandy, still crying, turned her back and walked off. In that one moment, I loved her more than anything in the world. She looked like an adult as she walked away, but as the light from the headlight lit her face, I saw the little Brandy that still wanted to be my friend and still wanted to be a part of the family.

On the long drive home that night I felt as though I had left my heart with Brandy. I couldn't imagine life without my big sister or the endless chatter that Brandy always supplied. Would life ever be the same?

It has taken some time, but now I know that life goes on, even though Brandy isn't here. She is always with me because a part of her is in me and always will be.

— Lindsey Rawson, 12 —

My Best Friend

We had been best friends since fourth grade. Me and Patty. Patty and me. Just about everywhere we went, people knew we were best friends. She taught me how to play pool in her cool, dark basement, and I taught her how to play basketball on my asphalt driveway. But the best part about having a best friend was taking turns sleeping over on Friday nights, sharing secrets over popcorn and soda, year after year after year.

Then in eighth grade everything changed. Or, I believe I changed and Patty didn't. Suddenly, boys became more than pals to me and my interest in make-up and clothes surprised even my mom. I couldn't believe Patty started the first day of school wearing the same pigtails she had worn forever. I had the latest hair fashion. I felt so confused and guilty at the same time. What was happening? Other girls seemed more interesting than Patty, and I wanted their approval. I felt restless and bored every time I went to her house now.

I started avoiding her and making excuses. Finally, during the middle of the year, as we were sitting on my front lawn, the words burst out. I said, "Go home, Patty, and don't come back." I ran into the house crying and sobbing. Mom sat me down and I told her everything. I'll never forget her words. She said, "Friends will come and go in and out of your life forever. You are changing and it's okay for both of you to make new friends. What's happening is hard but perfectly normal." Hearing the word "normal" was just what I needed.

The next day, the word was out at school and classmates picked Patty's side or mine. The rest of the year was tough — I missed having a best friend but I also started enjoying the new "me" that was emerging.

Patty became captain of the girls' basketball team while I got the lead in the eighth-grade spring play. We spoke to each other but only on the most superficial terms.

Time healed a lot of the awkwardness, and over the next few years we clearly went down separate paths. Still, when I saw her in the halls of high school, I felt a strange sadness and longing. I thought if I went back and "fixed" everything between us, we could somehow start all over as friends. But that was a fantasy. Our differences were too great, and I could only hope she understood.

I'll always remember the years Patty and I were best friends, but Mom was right. Friendships can change, and we have to let them go when it's time.

— Tamera Collins —

You Know You're Growing Up When...

You can't fit in the baby swing at the park.

Kirsten Gunderson, 8

You manage to squeeze yourself into your old hiding space but you can't get back out.

Rachael Pavelko, 12

You can go on the roller coaster because you pass the height mark.

Kelsey Gunderson, 10

You realize the world does NOT revolve around you.

Lindsay Carlson, 14

You start getting more phone calls than your mom.

Kim Riddle, 11

Instead of getting up at the crack of dawn to watch cartoons on Saturdays, you sleep until noon.

Lauren Aitchison, 11

Food tastes just as good with a lot less ketchup.

Amanda Long, 10

You realize it's YOUR underwear that your mother is hanging on the clothesline for all the neighbors to see.

Janelle Breese-Biagioni

You go to the movies and you can see something not made by Disney.

Alex Blake, 9

Boys and girls no longer have cooties! (I don't know if I'm there yet.)

Amaelia Macoritto, 12

The goofy-looking neighbor kid who plays football with your brother comes over and asks if you're home, not your brother, and he has suddenly transformed into a handsome prince!

Ashton Howe, 13

You stop giggling at the word "kiss."

Katy Coleman, 13

You no longer crawl in bed with your mom and dad during thunderstorms.

Annie Barkley, 13

You tell your mom that you're too old to be holding her hand while walking in the mall.

Emily Skees, 13

You won't take a bath with your younger sibling anymore.

Keley Katona, 15

The waitress no longer assumes you want crayons and a kid's menu.

Kaleigh Cronin, 10

You are trying on thousands of clothes just to go to the skating rink (acting like your big sister).

April Randes, 16

You are asked to say the blessing at a family gathering.

Craig Lee Watrous Jr., 10

Your daily vitamins switch from Flintstones to vitamin C.

Jennifer Luptak, 11

Eclectic Wisdom

Life is given as a gift,
So wonderful and new.
We need to live it day to day,
Being careful as we do.
For life can give us many years,
Or only months or days.
Each moment must be savored,
And used in special ways.
Stop and take a moment,
To help the poorer man.
Or teach a child something,
Lend a helping hand.
Small things take but minutes,
And one thing is plain to see:
Great rewards return to you.
Give the best of life; it's free.

— Meghan Beardsley, 16 —

How My Parents Ruined My Sixth Grade Life

Gratitude turns what we have into enough.
~Author Unknown

My parents have never really been strict, but they've always had more rules than "literally everybody else in the whole entire world," or so I thought when I was in sixth grade. They always make fun of me and say, "You act like we are ruining your life!"

No dating, no staying up late, no make-up, and no phone. Those were some of the rules. That last one was particularly devastating.

During the fall of sixth grade, I tried to persuade my parents to let me have a phone with the same tactic that I used for virtually everything: "EVERYONE else has one!" Every time I attempted this, I walked away deeply saddened by the fact that my totally genius argument didn't convince them.

My argument did seem to be true (for once). There were hardly any other kids who didn't have a smartphone. In other words, my parents ruined my entire life.

Was I being a little dramatic?

Probably.

Okay, okay.

I was being very dramatic.

Like the majority of sixth graders, my FOMO (Fear Of Missing Out) was off the charts. I would always think, *If I just had a phone, my life would be so much better!*

Near the end of the fall, I decided that "Operation Cell Phone" was a failure. Don't get me wrong, the phone was definitely still mentioned. Quite a lot, actually. But I gave up the notion that it was a possibility.

Fast forward to Christmas morning! The single best day in the whole entire year! Well, except for my birthday. And Halloween. And the last day of school. But that's not the point.

I was, as I would've said then, SO SO SO SO SO EXCITED! I opened my gifts, which weren't too lame. All of a sudden, there was only one gift left under the tree. (Yes, I'm in one of those lame families where everybody has to take turns opening Christmas presents.) The gift was mine.

Crinkle crinkle everyone heard as I unwrapped the gift.

"YOU GOT ME A PHONE?!?!?!"

Yesiree, a real-live phone!

Well, sort of.

It had… a keyboard. And a tiny, tiny, tiny screen. The screen wasn't a touchscreen. It had no Google, no Snapchat, no Spotify. I was so incredibly excited, however, that there was no room left for disappointment. I quickly e-mailed all of my friends to get their numbers. (Yes, e-mail. How else was I supposed to chat with anyone? I mean, my options were very limited. But not anymore!) Best. Christmas. Ever.

Unfortunately, I quickly found out that my phone has limits. A lot of 'em. No group chats, emojis, very slow connection, insanely low-quality pictures, only fourteen-second videos, and a pretty old-fashioned design. Most kids were hoping to get the iPhone 11, and I ended up with what felt like the iPhone negative 11.

I still have the same phone, halfway through my seventh-grade year. Whenever someone sees it, their first reaction is typically something along the lines of "Is that actually your phone? Wow. I feel bad for you."

And while it would definitely be nice to have the latest iPhone, or even one that's just a few years old (hint hint, Mom and Dad), I've gotten used to it. There are definitely worse things in life than not having a fancy, brand new hand-held cellphone.

I still have all the other rules that I mentioned earlier. Maybe you feel the same way, like everyone else is allowed to do something that you're not. I've learned not to make it such a big deal. It's really not. And I'm fine.

—Peyton Webb—

Two Weeks

How could I ever be lonely when I am with
my own best self?
~Anoir Ou-Chad

March 13, 2020. That was the beginning of what was supposed to be a two-week hiatus. I am of course talking about the closure of schools due to COVID-19. I remember that day as if it were yesterday.

We had all known school would shut down soon; we were just wondering when. We thought it would be fun to have a couple of weeks off. We began making jokes, saying, "Who's gonna take one for the team?" We figured if one of us got the virus the school would definitely have to shut down.

When the Los Angeles Unified School District announced the shutdown, we were in our fourth period class. I was using the school's laptop for an assignment, so I searched for news of the coronavirus in Santa Clarita Valley. And there it was, an article saying some high school students in our district had contracted the virus. I announced this to the class, some excitement in my voice as we knew what would happen next. No more than five minutes later our teacher received an e-mail from the principal: this would be our last day of school for two weeks. We all cheered and jumped out of our seats. But how wrong were we.

The rest of my seventh-grade school year was done online. I was happy about it; I would FaceTime a friend in the morning and we would finish all of our schoolwork by 10 a.m. And that's how life went for about two months.

During that time nothing was getting better... the virus was just increasing, I was isolated from my friends, and for the first time in my life, I felt truly alone. The days were not all sad though. I went on bike rides with my brother and I got closer to my family. There was a void in my happiness, though, one that only my friends could fill. I had never spent so long without seeing my friends in person and it was definitely getting to me. The video games and late-night FaceTime weren't enough.

I remember thinking to myself at night how badly I missed them, how I had actually enjoyed school and missed it. I wasn't getting to have a normal early teenage life. However, over the summer something happened. My neighbors became more important than ever. In my neighborhood there were about nine kids: I was the oldest, and there was a girl going into eighth grade like me, three siblings at the time going into fourth, fifth, and sixth grade, as well as another sixth-grade boy and a fourth-grade girl. The nine of us played outside from afternoon to night that summer.

Prior to that I had felt I was too "cool" to hang out with them. But those kids were one of the reasons I lasted that summer. In the summertime I did see friends but not as much as I needed, and that's where my neighbors came in.

By the beginning of my eighth-grade year I was able to see my friends again. Unfortunately, about a month into the new school year, the coronavirus numbers started rising again. I was no longer allowed to see friends. By Christmas break I was at my lowest. My friends had begun hanging out again, but I wasn't allowed to go. That tore me to pieces. Just the thought of not being able to see my friends while they were all hanging out really bothered me.

I began going to bed extremely late. Staying up all night and waking up at 4 or 5 p.m. This not only caused my mental health to suffer, but it made it hard for me to get to sleep. My worst night, I went to bed at midnight and lay restless for four hours. I remember at around three in the morning, tears began streaming down my cheeks. I wanted to sleep and I wanted my friends.

I realized how much I depended on my friends for my happiness, and that I needed to learn to be happy with just me. When I was finally able to see friends again a few months later, I was anxious, but I knew I didn't need them anymore for me to be happy. And now to this day, I still carry that knowledge with me. No more crying over missing sleepovers, and no more long nights thinking about what it would be like if I were there with them. It is crazy how "two weeks" off turned into me finally being able to find happiness within myself.

—Caleb Matthew Sperber—

Calm and Confident

*If I head into a meditation with my mind a little
scattered, I always come out of it feeling
more clear and calm.*
~LeBron James

I've been playing basketball since I was six years old. I started to take it seriously when I was in the sixth grade. I train multiple times a week with a trainer and a travel basketball team. My goal is to get a scholarship to college and open doors to different opportunities in my adult life.

When playing basketball games and tournaments sometimes my nerves get the best of me. It seems lately I feel nervous in a way I never have before because it's getting way more competitive, and I'm overwhelmed by the pressure. I don't want to let anybody down, especially my parents who have invested a lot of time and money into my basketball. In addition to my parents, I also don't want to let down my trainer, who is also a mentor; he pushes me to be better in basketball and in life. I also want to impress and show my worth on the court to my coaches.

When this nervousness sets in my game changes from good to bad. I feel in control when I'm not feeling the pressure. When nerves get the better of me, my shots become inconsistent, and I make bad decisions and plays. My trainer always tells me that it doesn't matter how skilled you are, if you play nervous all the skill goes out the window and you end up playing horribly.

One day my mom suggested that I should meditate before my

games to see if it helps me play better. As you might expect, I thought my mom was crazy, so I did some research on the Internet to find out how athletes calm their nerves. What I found was a lot of popular athletes like Lebron James, Kevin Durant, Kyrie Irving and many other athletes meditate to calm their nerves and to help them play more focused. I also saw that most good athletes have pre-game routines that include meditating, breathing exercises, and stretching. I was surprised at how many professional athletes do these types of activities before a game.

On the day of my next game, I decided to give meditating a try right before the game. I meditated for about fifteen minutes and I honestly felt like nothing happened. I was doubtful that it would help. But surprisingly, when I went into the gym to play, I could tell I was way more focused and not as nervous as I felt previously. I ended up playing a great game that day. I scored a lot of points and made a lot of good plays happen. I was playing like I would play at the park when I'm training, much calmer and more confident.

I'm getting ready to enter high school and I plan on trying out for basketball. I'm hoping this new tool helps me earn a spot on the team. Maybe it will even be my secret weapon as it is very competitive in high school and beyond. Seeing how much meditating significantly helped me with basketball I feel like it might be able to help me during other times in my life where I feel unfocused or not as confident as I need to be. I guess my mom isn't that crazy after all.

— Landon Dean —

Tippy

I was late for the school bus and rushing to get ready. My dog, Tippy, ran past me. *What's your big hurry?* I wondered, annoyed. It wasn't like *he* was late for the school bus like I was. When he got to the front door, he lay down in front of it — his way of asking to be petted. I ignored his shameless begging for affection, hurdled over him and sprinted for the waiting yellow bus.

That afternoon, I jumped out of the bus and dashed up the driveway. *That's odd,* I thought. Tippy was usually outside, barking an entire paragraph of "hellos" as soon as he saw me come home. When I burst through the door, the house was quiet and still. I dumped my coat and backpack on the floor. Mom silently appeared. She asked me to sit down at the kitchen table.

"Honey, I have some sad news that I need to tell you. This morning, while you were at school, Tippy was hit by a car and killed. He died instantly, so he didn't suffer. I know how much he meant to you. I'm so sorry," said Mom.

"NO! It's not true!" I was in shock. I couldn't believe her. "Tippy, come here! Come on, boy!" I called and called for him. I waited. He didn't come. Feeling lost, I wandered into the living room. He wasn't on the couch, so I had no pillow for my head while I watched cartoons. Mom called me for dinner and I rambled to my place. He wasn't hiding under the table, so I had to eat all of my dinner. I went to sleep that night, but I didn't cry. I still couldn't believe that he was gone.

When I got off the bus the next day, the silence grew deafening. Finally, my sobs bubbled up and erupted like lava from a volcano. I felt like I was also going to die from having my insides shaken apart, and I couldn't stop crying or end the thoughts that kept going through my head. *I should have trained him better. If I had been home, I could have called him away from the road. I didn't even pet him when I left. How could I have known that was my last chance?* I cried until I felt hollow inside.

My parents bought a new dog named Tinker Belle. I didn't care. I was busy giving hate looks to people speeding in their cars. *They shouldn't drive so fast that they couldn't stop when they see a dog in the road.* My parents still got the silent treatment from me. *Why hadn't they made sure that Tippy was tied up?* I was mad at Tippy for getting killed, and I was mad at the entire "dog kingdom" for not knowing enough to stay out of the road.

I didn't share my dinner with our new dog. She was too small to be my pillow for television, and her bark was squeaky. When she begged for attention, I pushed her away. I spent a lot of time alone, feeling sorry for myself and wondering, *Why did this have to happen to me? What am I going to do now? Why did Tippy have to die?*

Time passed, and against my will, I started to understand some things. It felt like waking up a little at a time. I realized what little control any of us have over what happens to a dog. Sure, we can train them and tie them up and do everything right, but bad things can still happen. And, in spite of us, good things can happen too. That's life. The best way to deal with the hard times is to figure out what I need to do for myself to get through them when they come, and to remember that hard times pass.

I also discovered that my capacity to love didn't die with Tippy. I became awfully lonely when I was trying to harden my heart. I began to realize that there were good things about Tinker Belle that were different from the good things about Tippy. I couldn't rest my head on her little body, or pretend to ride Tinker Belle the way I had done with Tippy, but I could fit Tinker Belle into my backpack and carry her around.

I learned that I need to pet my dog whenever I can — and to really enjoy my time with her! Now I pet my dog slowly when I have the chance and quickly when I'm in a hurry, but I never leave the house without petting her.

I now deeply understand the "Circle of Life." Everyone is born, everyone dies, and that's the way it is. If dogs never died, there would be no room for others like Tinker Belle... and her five cute puppies!

Best of all, I realize that Tippy left behind all of my good memories of him. And they come to me every time I call!

— Christine Armstrong —

Never Put Rocks in Your Mouth

When I was in the sixth grade, my teacher asked our class the question, "What does 'doing the right thing' mean to you?" She asked us to think about that question over the weekend, and to talk to our parents or anyone else we thought might have a good answer. By Monday, we were to turn in an essay on what "doing the right thing" meant, and be prepared to live up to our answers.

The entire weekend, I wracked my brain trying to come up with something that would impress my teacher and be easy to live by. I talked to my parents, called my grandmother and asked my next-door neighbor. I even asked the mailman! Everyone had good answers, but I didn't feel like I could live up to them.

By Sunday afternoon, I hadn't written my essay. To make matters worse, my parents said we were going to my Aunt Cindy's house. That usually meant that I would have to entertain my cousin Andrea while my parents visited after dinner. Andrea was four and a major pest.

Just as I predicted, my parents told me to play with Andrea while they visited. I turned on the television and found a Disney movie for Andrea, and then I sat down and started to write my essay. I still didn't know what I was going to write about, but it was due the next morning and this was my last chance.

Soon I felt a pair of eyes on me. It was Andrea.

"What are you doing?" she asked.

"I have to write an essay about what doing the right thing means to me."

Andrea laughed. "That's easy," she said.

"Okay," I said, thinking, *What could this smart aleck four-year-old possibly know that all of the adults who I had asked hadn't already come up with?*

"Tell me the answer," I said smugly.

Andrea cleared her throat and stood up.

"Doing the right thing means being nice to your family and friends. Doing what your mommy says. Never lie. Eat lots of fruits and vegetables. Don't eat dog food. Take a bath when you're dirty and wash your own private parts. Don't watch icky movies with kissing and stuff. Don't waste water and electricity. Don't scare the cat. Don't ever run away. And never, never put rocks in your mouth."

I stared with astonishment at my little cousin. Then I jumped up, grabbed Andrea and gave her the biggest hug I could. Not only had Andrea answered a very tough question for me, I could easily live by all of her rules. All I had to do was be nice, not lie, keep myself clean and healthy, not scare cats, and never, never put rocks in my mouth. Piece of cake. So when I wrote my essay, I included the story about Andrea and how she had answered my question.

Two weeks later, my teacher returned everyone's essays. I received an A+ along with a little note my teacher had written at the top: "Always do the right thing — and give Andrea an A+, too!"

— Shirley Barone Craddock —

The Moment I Knew I'd Never Be Cool

From their errors and mistakes, the wise
and good learn wisdom for the future.
~Plutarch

My older sister was born to be liked. She came out of the womb with a cute face, blond hair, a sense of humor, athletic ability, and what my mom called the "gift of gab." She went through her childhood with lots of friends, lots of parties and lots of attention. I wanted what my sister had: popularity.

I studied her for years and never came close, so I turned to kids my own age for role models. Jen, the girl I always sat next to in school, threw her blond hair around, showed off her dimples, put her head to one side when she asked for favors and was easily voted most popular in class. *Okay,* I thought, *I'll try her tactics.* I threw my brown hair around, smiled without dimples, put my head to one side and asked my teacher for a pass to the bathroom. She looked at me and said, "Why are you doing that with your head? Don't you feel well?"

That was my cue to try for cool instead of popular. I'd do anything to escape my lack of social status. Cool kids always acted as though they had the world under control, maneuvering around obstacles and adults with ease, and never cracking under pressure. My big chance came when a new girl moved to town and into my class. Nothing seemed to ruffle Tiffany. She was cute, trendy, and best of all, she liked me.

Our friendship lasted four weeks—just long enough for me to

learn that Tiffany took European vacations, went skiing in Aspen and bought clothes at Neiman Marcus. I'd never been outside of Illinois, on skis or anywhere but the Sears preteen department. We were only eleven and she'd already picked out the car she'd get for her sixteenth birthday. Tiffany was way too much for me. I crawled back into my familiar invisibility...

Until I met Mandy. Mandy's middle name was "rebel." She and her brother, Kevin, smoked cigarettes and stole money out of their mom's purse. *If popularity and cool are out of reach,* I thought, *I'll take rebellion over facelessness.* I was soon hanging out at Mandy's house, where no adults were ever around to notice what we were doing. I puffed cigarettes, pretended to shoplift, and felt powerful for the first time in my life. I did crazy things my parents never suspected, and had a great time bragging about it to other kids. I could feel my status rising. Then Kevin was arrested and sent to a detention center. Never wanting to end up like him, I pitched my cigarettes and headed back into obscurity.

By eighth grade, I was desperate. I tried out for cheerleading at my small school, and by some miracle, made it onto the squad. My head swelled like a melon. *I must have absorbed popularity and coolness without realizing it,* I thought. I took this tiny piece of status and ran with it.

At first, being popular and cool seemed to be easy. I tolerated, agreed with or laughed at the nasty comments of the cool girls who stayed that way by pointing out the uncoolness of others. Things like, "Look at Dana's hair. Think she used a hedge trimmer?" or, "Can you believe those shoes Lauren wore last night? She must have borrowed them from her grandmother." Guys weren't spared. "Oh, Tyler. What a crater face!" and, "Yeewww. Bryce actually thought I'd be seen with him in public!"

The better they were at cutting people to shreds, the faster those girls seemed to rise above the masses. Like stand-up comics, they pointed out other people's flaws and made the crowds roar. *Why,* I wondered, *were put downs cool? They made my stomach cramp. Was it who said them? The way they were said?*

Okay, I decided, *I can say nasty things about other people for the sake of personal success.* I picked a time and place for my initiation. A budding friendship with the Faris twins gave me a stage. Sara and Shauna were way cooler than I'd ever be. They'd been hanging with guys since seventh grade.

My debut came after church. The three of us were standing around waiting for rides home. I listened to them rip first on girls and then on guys. One guy in particular took the brunt of their hits: first his clothes, then his voice, then his brain, then his looks.

"I know what you mean," I volunteered, as Shauna turned up her nose at the mention of the poor guy's hairy arms. "Some guys are real apes..."

As the words left my mouth, a not-so-good-looking guy drove past in a blue convertible. *Perfect opportunity,* I thought. I pointed to the driver, "...like that guy — red-haired and u-g-l-y." I made chimp sounds as I watched the car turn into a nearby driveway. Instead of agreement, I heard nothing from the twins. It was like I was standing on the ocean bottom with my ears plugged. I turned slowly to see Sara and Shauna with necks stiff and eyes impaling me on an invisible stake.

What? What? my confused brain was pleading. *What'd I say?*

The answer slithered out of Sara's mouth as the twins turned their backs and walked toward the blue convertible. "That red-haired and u-g-l-y ape is our brother."

The rest, as they say, is history. My journey to cool stalled right there in front of church. With face burning and ears ringing, I'm sure I heard an otherworldly voice whisper, *You'll never be popular, cool, or anything else your heart won't let you be. Start looking inside, instead of out.*

It took me a while to get what those words meant. But once I stopped trying to be like other people, life got a whole lot easier. I'm even growing up to be someone I really like.

— D. Marie O'Keefe —

Kindness Is a Simple Gift

In this world we must help one another.
~Jean de La Fontaine

My family and I were taking a well-deserved vacation to Disneyland. I had never been there before and was eagerly anticipating experiencing the magic.

There was another reason that this trip was special. My father was a workaholic who worked long hours. I longed to spend time with him. I wanted to be able to sit down with my father, who I loved more than life, and just talk. It always seemed like there was never time.

The day finally arrived when I was allowed to pack my clothes. I chose only my favorite outfits. I threw in my autograph book and then muscled the suitcase zipper around the overflow of clothes. I set my suitcase on my comforter and smiled. I was ready.

I didn't get any sleep that night. I lay in my bed and stared out the window. I knew that my father's work was going to be left at home, finally.

After a brief breakfast we hit the open road. It was all smooth sailing for the first couple of hours until I unexpectedly felt a sharp jerk. We coasted to the side of the road, and my dad said something about the engine being shot. We were in the middle of four lanes of traffic, so he decided the easiest thing to do would be to flag someone down and get a ride into town.

An hour later, my dad was still waving his hands at each and every passing car but it wasn't doing any good. Not a single soul would stop to assist my helpless family. Finally, Father gave up and decided to walk into town. I was certain it was a very long distance. I pleaded with him to stay and try again, but he was deaf to my pleading. He just said that he wouldn't let anything ruin this trip for me. My heart ached as he put on his coat and began to walk away from our car. My dad has a back problem, and he was too stubborn to admit that he wasn't in any condition to even walk a couple of miles.

Then I saw a figure out of the window. It was a lone trucker. I looked around for his rig. I didn't see it until I realized that his truck was parked on the other side of the road. He had walked across four lanes of traffic to get to us. The feeling I felt at that moment is indescribable. I was truly touched that this man cared so much. Not one other person had taken time out of his or her own selfish life to stop and see if everything was okay, but this man was different. He didn't even know us, and he didn't expect anything in return.

Father got his ride back to town, and our car was repaired. My visions of Mickey were rekindled, as was my faith that angels do exist. Because of that man's actions, my father and I had the opportunity to grow close again, and I still cherish my genuine Mickey Mouse autograph.

None of this would have been possible if that man hadn't given us the gift that he did — the gift of kindness.

— Michael Oknefski, 17 —

Our Christmas Secret

Admitting errors clears the score and proves
you wiser than before.
~Arthur Guiterman

I t was Christmas Eve when my sister and I decided to open our presents before our mom got home from work. She usually came home about an hour after we got home from school, which we thought was plenty of time to sneak a peek at the gifts under the tree. Since my sister was older, and that put her in charge, she opened the first gift while I was ordered to stand guard at the big picture window in our front room. I was to report any suspicious activity or persons, namely our mother.

I was so excited that I could barely stand still. I also couldn't keep my eyes on the window very long. My head moved from the window to my sister and back to the window again. I felt like I was watching a ping-pong match.

"All right!" my sister shouted. She pulled out a jewelry box. "You know what that means, don't you?"

I jumped up and down. "Yeah, it's my turn!"

"No," she said. "It means that there must be some jewelry under here." I watched my sister rummage through the presents under the tree trying to find one she thought was small enough to be a necklace or earrings.

"Hey, that's not fair!" I whined, stomping my foot.

"Are you watching for Mom?" is all that she said. I couldn't do anything except stand guard as she opened present after present. Finally, when my sister's curiosity was satisfied and she had finished wrapping her last present back up, we traded places.

My heart hammered so hard that it felt like my chest was moving in and out. My sister reminded me to be careful so I wouldn't tear the paper, and to wrap the present back up the same way that I had found it.

After unwrapping a few presents, I found it faster to open one end of a present and peek inside. "Cool! Mom and Dad got me headphones for my stereo!"

I pulled the headphones out of the box and was about to put them on when my sister shouted, "Quick! Wrap it back up! Mom's coming!"

My heart hit the floor along with the headphones when I heard what sounded like glass crushing. I knew it was my mother coming down our gravel driveway. My body was as frozen as a snowman.

"Come on!" My sister's face was as white as the paint on the wall.

I shoved the headphones back in the box but my hands were shaking so much that I tore the paper trying to wrap it back up. My sister was yelling at me, which only made my hands shake more. I heard the jingle of keys and the doorknob rattle. I thought I was going to wet my pants! My heart pounded harder as I tried to get the tape to stick.

"Just shove it under the tree and put some presents on top of it!" my sister shouted as she ran to stall my mother.

I had just finished burying the package with my headphones in it when my mother came into the front room. I jumped up and said, "Hi, Mom!" She smiled at me and said, "Hi," back, but didn't appear to suspect a thing. My heart began to slow as I took a deep breath. That was close. Too close!

On Christmas morning, my sister and I smiled for pictures and gave award-winning performances when we opened our presents — again. "Headphones!" I exclaimed. "Thanks, it's just what I wanted." After everything had been opened, my sister and I looked at each other, and our eyes met. Our secret was safe, but somehow Christmas morning didn't feel the same.

My sister and I never opened our Christmas presents early again. I don't know if it was that opening our gifts for the second time just wasn't as much fun as the first time, or if we came too close to getting caught and didn't want to think about what our mother would have done to us.

I also learned something that year about my mother. I found out that she wasn't as dumb as I thought she was. Maybe it was the lack of squeals on Christmas morning or the torn wrapping paper that tipped her off. For some reason, all of the packages for our birthdays, which she usually hid at the top of her closet shelf, never appeared. I never did find out where she hid them.

—Lori Menning—

What I've Learned So Far

Never try to get corn off the cob with a fork.
When playing in the gym, beware of steel beams.
Never let guys in your room on an overnight school trip.
The condiments at meals are not toys.
Before you give a kid Listerine, make sure that he knows not to
swallow it.
NEVER throw up in a vent.

Melissa Amyx, 14

Don't try to baptize your neighbor's cat, especially with a hose.

Marleigh Dunlap, 13

Some teachers are there to teach and that's all, but others are there
to watch and help you grow.

Janne Perona, 13

Everything you do in your life cannot be taken back.
Family is the most important gift of all.
Be true to yourself and it won't matter if others aren't true to you.

Nikki Chance, 15

Don't be afraid to make new friends and expand your relationships
with other friends.

Reanna Grissom, 12

Don't trust anyone who knows how to give a wedgie.

Sylvia Lares, 9

If you have something bad to tell your mom, tell her when she's on the phone.

Brennan Shaw, 11

Never let a stain from the past make a mark on your future.

Jillian Graham, 12

Read lots of stuff written in the 1700's; it'll make you smarter.

Dena Soffer, 10

Never put your tongue on a really cold metal pole.

Joshua White, 12

Never eat unsweetened chocolate. Yuk!

Dylan Dudley, 7

If you give your enemy a second chance they might turn out to be your best friend.

Mandy Tallant, 12

Always pretend you understand what the Spanish teacher is saying

Tarek Audi, 15

Never trust your fifteen-year-old uncle to make dinner.

George Preston, 14

Never eat prunes, no matter what your grandma says.

Melanie Hansen, 12

Never fall asleep during a field trip if your friends have toothpaste with them.

Filipe Romero, 13

Don't use words that you don't understand to impress someone. It can be very embarrassing.

Chastity Sezate, 13

Make sure to look at yourself in the mirror before you leave the house, especially if you're going somewhere important.

Carol Rodriguez, 13

Don't let older siblings get the best of you; that's just what they want.

Gladys Lau, 12

You can't run away from your fears, unless it's a wasp.

Michael Betancourt, 12

If your dad asks you, "Do you think I'm an idiot?" carefully consider your answer.

Liz Hansen, 14

Your food ends up in your lap when you sit too far away from the table.

Cory Price, 9

With my wheelchair, I can run faster than anyone else in my class and I can write faster than anyone with my computer.

Becca Yurcek, 10

When your parents yell at you they still love you.

Santana Hubert, 10

Pay attention in class. That way, when the teacher calls on you, you won't make a goof of yourself and have to ask, "What was the question?"

Courtney Stewart, 12

Sometimes it's nice to be important, but it's always important to be nice.

Kaleigh Cronin, 10

Never play with a baby right after it finishes eating.
Don't bother your cousin when she is on the phone with a guy.

Jade Mason, 13

When something bad happens to you, think about someone out there who may have a bigger problem.
Never underestimate the power of love and friendship.
Never laugh with a piece of chocolate in your mouth.

Melissa Quincosa, 13

Don't eat noodles when you are wearing your retainer; they get stuck in there and it's really hard to get them out.

Ashley Fannon, 13

Even if dinner looks disgusting, it doesn't mean it will taste that way.
Have boys for friends, not just for boyfriends.
No matter how much I learn, there is always stuff I don't know.

Chelsey Rice, 8

Having had over nine surgeries by the age of fourteen, I will never again take for granted the gift of walking.

Vanessa Cupo, 14

If you want to make a difference, get off your butt and do it.

Danielle Relue, 13

Begging works, but don't rely on it. You don't always get what you want.

Melissa Lansford, 13

Play the hand that God has dealt you to the best of your ability. You never know what the next card will be.

Jacqueline Christy, 13

When you are waiting for your mom to finish her haircut, don't spin on the chair or you'll throw up your lunch.

Lorin Padgurskis, 10

Never play basketball by your parents' new car.

Kaitlyn Sweeney, 12

Don't flush the toilet when your older sister is in the shower getting ready for a date.

Weston Dunlap, 10

It takes years to build up trust, and seconds to destroy it.

Dijana Atikovic, 12

When you are cleaning your room, don't shove stuff under your bed, in your closet or under your dresser. You just end up cleaning those places, too.

Eddie Holtz, 11

Who I am is not what I have but what I try my best at.

Julie Lundgren, 11

When you are sick or sad, laughter is the best medicine.

Aaron Snyder, 11

Keep dreaming and you may be writing the next *Chicken Soup for the Soul* book.

Jason Trusso, 11

Afterword
The End

This is it, no more, no more
Now your days will be a bore
You're out of your mind, going crazy too
Sigh! Now what will you do?
Without this glorious book to read
The sequel to it is all you need.

— Paige Holland, 10 —

We hope that the stories and various pieces in this book have become something more to you than written words. Our highest desire is that they now give you perspective, courage, hope and especially the ability to laugh through awkward moments should you encounter some of these same issues in your preteen years. Thanks for reading.

We are pleased to introduce you to the writers whose stories appeared in the original *Chicken Soup for the Preteen Soul*. These bios were the ones that ran when the stories were originally published. They were current as of the publication date in the year 2000.

Meet Our Original Contributors

Kim Aaron is a braille specialist working with blind and partially sighted children. She has been married for seventeen years to a television news reporter and has one son, Adam, who is an honors student. She volunteers in her community, and in her spare time, rides an eleven-year-old mule named Bob. You can reach Kim at #3 Maple Tree Ln., Cross Lanes, WV 25313; 304-776-0403; Jaaron2255@aol.com.

Denise and Rett Ackart live in California. Denise is currently working on a series of children's books and enjoys spending time with her husband and two sons, Rett and Rhys. Rett is an active twelve-year-old who enjoys soccer, basketball, snowboarding and drumming for the junior high school jazz band. They can be reached via e-mail at mongo@tco.net.

Katherine Ackerman is a thirteen-year-old from Florida. She enjoys traveling, writing, painting, drawing and sculpture. Katherine is also involved in many different sports including canoeing and backpacking and is on her school swim team.

Sara Alfano, age twelve, lives in Pennsylvania and has been writing poetry for several years. Her favorite pastimes are reading, basketball, softball, listening to music and hanging out with friends. She loves animals, especially her dog, Sadie, and her cat, Tweety.

Apryl Anderson is a seventeen-year-old from Washington. She loves to sing, dance and play baseball. Apryl dreams of going to college and becoming a kindergarten teacher and a model.

Christine Armstrong is an attorney who lives with her husband Roger and their son Randy in a farmhouse in the Minnesota woods. In addition to writing, her hobbies include reading, making handmade books, jewelry and quilts. Christine has continued to open her heart to a variety of animals over the years including ducks, hamsters, parakeets, dogs, cats, a chinchilla and even a goat. Reach her via e-mail at Chris99337@aol.com.

Whitney M. Baldwin is a thirteen-year-old from New York. She is a dance competitor and loves to read and write poetry. Whitney would like to thank Mr. Sherry for being the first to inspire her to write.

Meghan Beardsley is sixteen years old. She has studied ballet for thirteen years and has toured with a professional ballet company. Meghan is an avid soccer player and has traveled extensively. Her previous writing acknowledgments include the Sperry Award for an essay and a poem published in *Celebrate — New York's Young Poets Speak Out.*

Leslie Beck is a high school sophomore in Missouri. She enjoys playing the flute and running track. As a freshman, she was Rookie of the Year on her softball team. Leslie aspires to be a veterinarian and own her own practice. She dedicates her story to her grandmother who was not here to see Leslie's mother win her fight against cancer.

Lisa-Dawn Bertolla lives in Essex County in the south of England with her dog Harry and Colin the goldfish. She has always had a passion for writing. Her latest project is a book of short stories, poetry and Haiku. Lisa-Dawn feels that writing transcends international boundaries and brings people together. Contact her via e-mail at lisa-dawn@skynow.net.

Donna Beveridge is a primary literacy specialist. She loves early mornings, sing-alongs, children's books, new journals, her grandchildren and family stories. Her first children's book, *Henry,* was published in 1999 for the educational market. She has also published books for teachers. Donna can be reached at P.O. Box 1635, Windham, ME 04062, or via e-mail at DLBeveridg@aol.com.

Carol Osman Brown is a freelance writer and photographer whose work has been published in many magazines and newspapers. She speaks at writing conferences and teaches writing at Arizona State University and Rio Salado College in Phoenix, AZ. You can contact her at cobrown@aztec.asu.edu.

Megan Brown is a thirteen-year-old who published two books by the third grade. She runs track, takes dance class and plays soccer, basketball and the electric guitar. She lives with her parents, sister, brother and pet dog, Bailey, and enjoys being with her friends and talking on the phone.

Courtni Calhoun, a thirteen-year-old eighth grader from Texas, is a GATE student who plays alto sax, holds first chair in her school band, won second chair in an all-region competition and has been a majorette for the past two years. Winning fifth place in a state writing competition and being published is proof of the impact that her teacher, Mrs. Barrow, has had on her life. Courtni is a dedicated Christian and is active in her church.

Doris Canner has three grown sons and four grandsons. She resides with her husband in New Hampshire on Lake Winnipesaukee. When she's not surfing the Internet, Doris enjoys reading and listening to music. Her love for children and for the written word has been the motivating force behind her passion for writing children's stories. Currently, she's working on a biography for young readers. Doris can be reached at 9 Campfire Cir., Alton, NH 03809.

Diana Carson is a sixteen-year-old from Pennsylvania who loves to write and with a few poems already published and her story in *Chicken Soup for the Preteen Soul*, it shows. Diane enjoys playing volleyball and would like to major in journalism and minor in theater in college.

Rachelle P. Castor grew up in a family of twelve children. She is married to her favorite guy, Doug, and they are the parents of three amazing boys. She has taught preschoolers and is now writing children's literature. Rachelle can be reached at rpcastor@aol.com.

David R. Collins combined two careers, teaching English in Moline, IL, for thirty-five years and writing books for young readers. Many of his articles and stories sprang from his classroom experiences, as did "A Silent Voice." Named "Outstanding Illinois Educator," Collins has won recognition from the American Legion, the Veterans of Foreign Wars, the PTA and the Junior Literary Guild. A prolific biographical writer, he now writes full-time and makes author visits to schools. He can be reached at 3404 45th St., Moline, IL 61265, by e-mail at kimsuess@aol.com, or by calling 309-762-8985.

Tamera Collins is a busy mother of two, ages six and seven. This is her second published piece; the first, a children's story, *Emily's Coat,* was featured in the literary review, *O' Georgia.* Tamara is a former mathematics teacher who enjoys golfing with her husband, tennis, reading and her cat, Cleo. She can be reached at 14290 Morning Mountain Way, Alpharetta,

GA 30004.

Shirley Barone Craddock is the published author of two children's books and several magazine stories. She is an artist and has received the People's Choice Award from the North Valley Art League. Shirley loves to write in such a way that will stimulate a child's mind and entertain them to silliness and surprise. She can be reached at 1703 Victor Ave., Redding, CA 96003; 530-223-2584; tigerknot@thegrid.net.

Cynthia Ross Cravit is a freelance writer who has written primarily for children's magazines. Recently, she completed several chapter books and is working on a middle-grade novel. She resides in Northern Michigan with her husband and three children, all of whom have enormous influence on her writing.

Krissy Creager is a sophomore from Arizona, where she lives with her parents. She likes playing basketball, soccer, running track, writing stories and poetry and doing normal teen stuff like hanging out with friends. She enjoys listening to and giving advice to friends. Krissy hopes to either become a physical therapist or a counselor, in order to make a difference and help others.

MaryJanice Davidson has written several critically acclaimed novels, but this is the first time that she has been able to write about the fire. She lives in Minnesota with her husband and children, about twenty miles from the site of the fire. "The Best Christmas I Never Had" is her first published short story. For information on her books, visit Mary's website at www.usinternet.com/users/alongi.

Leigha Dickens is a thirteen-year-old who lives in South Carolina. She enjoys writing stories and poetry, reading, gardening, and some sports and is also in the "Imaginations" drama group at her school. Leigha hopes to make a career out of writing.

Noah Edelson is a director/writer/producer for television and film. His credits include producer/writer for Nickelodeon and NBC, among others. His short film, 78, premiered at the 1997 Sundance Film Festival. An award-winning poet for his children's verse, Noah is also founder of Mighty Oak Press, committed to publishing "books for kids to grow on." He lives in Sherman Oaks, CA, with his wife Valerie, his daughter Hannah and his cat, Mister. Contact Noah at MightyOakPress@aol.com.

Arlys Endres, thirteen, enjoys synchronized swimming, softball, old music, old movies and hanging with her friends. She also plays violin, clarinet and the piano. Arlys loves animals and has four cats, two dogs and a hamster. She is also a member of the United Neighbors Association, a community watch program that includes painting over graffiti and taking down Christmas lights for the elderly.

David Ferino is a thirteen-year-old living in Illinois. His favorite pastimes include playing the guitar, skateboarding, golf, soccer, basketball, theater and art. He is involved in speech tournaments, where he has received several first-place medals. David has also had his artwork hung in a college art museum but feels that his greatest accomplishment is being published in this book.

Russell (Rusty) Fischer is a former teacher who now writes for a small publisher in Florida. He is proud to be able to share his story with other children all over the world. Although he still struggles with his weight, he has a new "coach" in his beautiful wife, Martha. You can contact Russell via e-mail at mfis245583@aol.com.

Christine Fishlinger is seventeen and lives in New York with her parents and brother. She enjoys reading, writing, soccer, track, working on school plays and hanging out with friends. She looks forward to being a senior, and to going away to college.

Nicole Fortuna, age eleven, lives in Illinois, with her mom, grandma and little brother. She is in the sixth grade and is involved in the school newspaper, yearbook, gymnastics, softball and band. Her teacher, Lisa Anco, encouraged Nicole to write her story.

Kelli Frusher is seventeen and from California. When not at home singing, dancing or reading you can find her hot-air ballooning, white-water river rafting, dirt biking, snorkeling or horseback riding. She has written mini-novels about her experiences, as well as poems. Kelli would love to make it on Broadway or the radio.

Eugene Gagliano is the father of four children, a published author and teacher who shares his love of reading and writing with his second-grade class at Meadowlark School in Buffalo, WY. He lives with his wife, Carol, at the base of the majestic Big Horn Mountains. His fiction book, *Falling Stars,* will be released this year. You can reach him at 20 Hillside Dr., Buffalo, WY 82834.

Barbara L. Glenn is a writer, horseback riding teacher and 4-H Horse

Project leader. She began her freelance writing in 1989 and has published articles in magazines such as *Horse Illustrated, Horse Power, Stable Kids* and *Children's Playground*. She owns three horses, a Great Dane and two cats. Barbara enjoys art, traveling, photography, music and the company of her two girls, Ginny and Amy.

Uncle Greg is Greg Hall, a father, uncle and businessman living in Los Gatos, CA. He is the author of numerous stories for kids of all ages. You can visit his website at www.unclegreg.com, or call 408-366-9812.

Mia Hamm is widely recognized as the world's best all-around soccer player. In the 1996 Centennial Olympic Games, she proved it by leading her team to Team Gold in front of eighty thousand screaming fans in Athens, GA. Never in history had so many spectators come out to watch a women's sporting event. Then in 1999, Mia's team won the Women's World Cup while more than 40 million viewers watched in the United States alone. Mia was the youngest player ever to play for the US National Team at age fifteen and has been U.S. Soccer's Female Athlete of the Year for five consecutive years. Her awards and accomplishments tell only part of the story of this remarkable athlete. Through the Mia Hamm Foundation, she supports two causes: promoting women's athletics and raising funds for research and awareness of bone marrow diseases. Each year, Mia hosts the "Garrett Game" in honor of her brother, whom she lost to complications from aplastic anemia, a form of bone marrow disease.

Cynthia Marie Hamond, Secular Franciscan Order, has had stories published in nine books. Six of them are *Chicken Soup for the Soul* books. Her story *Goodwill (Chicken Soup for the Kid's Soul)* was seen on the *Chicken Soup for the Soul* television series. She enjoys speaking to various groups and school visits. You can reach Cynthia at P.O. Box 488, Monticello, MN 55362; or e-mail her at Candbh@aol.com.

Laurie Hartman is the director of licensing of *Chicken Soup for the Soul* Enterprises, Inc. She loves writing, reading, horseback riding and her job with the "best people to work for on the planet." Laurie is also the mother of one incredible son, Connor, who shares her love of writing at the tender age of ten, hoping to be a contributing author to Chicken Soup for the Soul one day himself. You can reach Laurie via e-mail at laurieh@chickensoup.com.

Lauren Elizabeth Holden, age thirteen, lives in Georgia with her parents, kitten and dog. She enjoys reading, writing, tennis, boating and hanging out with her best friends, Leslie, Lauren and Salley. A very special teacher, Joi Cox, helped Lauren develop her love for writing. Lauren continues to write and has submitted numerous entries for her school's writing fairs.

Paige Holland is eleven years old. She loves to read, swim, ski and write poetry. Paige began writing stories in kindergarten and now has three of her books in her school library. Paige lives with her parents, her sister Caitlin, brothers Robby and Patrick, and Gwenith, the dog.

Megan Jennings is a high school student from Kentucky. She enjoys writing poems and true life stories. Megan is a straight-A student, the secretary of her local FFA chapter and an employee of an auto parts store. Megan loves animals and owns four dogs, two horses and two donkeys. She loves the outdoors, horseback riding and hiking.

Lou Kassem was born in the mountains of East Tennessee and inherited a talent for storytelling. In 1984, she put her talent on paper, publishing the first of eleven novels. Being an author is a career that she loves. Her hobbies are reading, traveling, golfing and mountain hiking with her husband. You can reach her at 715 Burruss Dr. NW, Blacksburg, VA 24060, by phone at 540-552-2241, or e-mail her at Lmk1931@aol.com.

Michael Kavalinas, sixteen, swims, does karate, works part-time and loves science. He is a lifeguard and has done volunteer hospice work. Michael still misses his dad and thinks about him all the time.

Ryan Kelly, age eleven, lives in New York with his parents, sister and maternal grandparents. When not in school, where he is on the wrestling team, he likes to play Playstation and swim, and he is a huge Pokémon fan. Ryan would like to thank his parents and Miss Finnegan for the inspiration they gave him in writing his story.

Ashley King is an eleven-year-old who plays on her school's soccer team and participates in band, choir and drama. She likes to express her feelings through writing. She would like to thank her friends and family, and especially, her mom. A special, heartfelt thanks goes to her sixth-grade teacher, Ms. Oderman, who encouraged her to write to her fullest extent. But most of all, she wants to thank God for putting the words in her heart.

Barbara Lage is a library media specialist for an elementary school in Omaha, NE. She has been a media specialist for a middle school in

Iowa and worked as a librarian for a Japanese college in Honolulu, HI. She likes kids and books. She has three children, Jo Anne, Mark and Amy, with her husband, Pete. She can be contacted at 759 N. 130th Plaza, Omaha, NE 68154.

J. Styron Madsen writes to make kids laugh, think, feel, and most importantly, to realize that they can make choices. She writes in front of her antique Macintosh surrounded by seven dogs, all adopted from local animal shelters. You can e-mail her at mad03@execpc.com.

Karl Malone is a ten-time NBA All-Star player and the 1997 Most Valuable Player in the league. He was also the co-MVP in the 1993 All-Star game with teammate John Stockton. Voted one of the fifty greatest players of all time, he has truly earned his famous nickname, "The Mailman," for Karl Malone never fails to deliver. He was a member of the original "Dream Team" that won the Gold Medal in the 1992 Barcelona Summer Olympic Games. Malone lives in Utah with his wife and six children. He enjoys hunting, fishing, camping and riding his Harley in his spare time. A giving man, Malone supports the Special Olympics and many charitable causes through the Karl Malone Foundation.

Anne McCourtie lives on a farm in Kansas with her husband John, six horses, three cats and a dog. She has written short stories, poems and puppet plays. Her favorite things include writing, dancing, gardening and crossword puzzles. She has enjoyed many occupations, such as teacher, bookkeeper and photographer's assistant. For the past nine years, she has worked with people with developmental disabilities. You can e-mail her at amccourtie@holtowks.net.

Karli McKinnon is a sixth-grade student living in Ontario, Canada. She loves creative writing and wants to be a journalist when she grows up. She has been swimming competitively for eight years and playing piano since she was five. She likes reading, writing, skating and spending time with her friends and family.

Lori Menning is a preschool teacher, mother of twin boys and author of *One Was Not Enough*, a children's picture book published by *TWINS Magazine*. She lives with her family in Memphis, TN.

Leslie Miller is a fifteen-year-old whose hobbies include fishing, drawing, and writing poetry and short stories. She looks forward to having a career as an author and poet after college. Her writing inspirations are

Jewel and her mother, Patti.

Kathleen M. Muldoon has written for children's magazines for many years. She is the author of one picture book entitled, *Princess Pooh*. When she is not writing, she enjoys reading, taking long walks and playing with her cat, Prissy. She can be reached at mink@texas.net.

Son Truong Nguyen, age seventeen, loves to write. He encourages everyone to pick up a writing instrument and "just write for the sheer enjoyment of it," and go out there and live your life to the fullest.

Aubrey Nighswander lives in Ohio, on the south shore of Lake Erie. She is active in her junior high Pen program and an editor for the school newspaper. Aubrey enjoys a wide variety of activities and is very competitive in soccer, swimming and sailing.

Brian Normandin is a sophomore in California. In addition to hanging with his friends, he spends his spare time collecting and trading basketball cards and working a part-time job.

Mary Normandin began writing four years ago and draws the inspiration for her stories from her family life. Mary resides in Southern California with her husband and four children, where she volunteers at her kids' school and chauffeurs them to their various activities.

*NSYNC, which includes Lance Bass, J. C. Chasez, Joey Fatone, Chris Kirkpatrick and Justin Timberlake, have obtained global stardom. Their self-titled 1998 debut album sold more than ten million copies and yielded four number-one singles: "I Want You Back," "Tearin' Up My Heart," "God Must Have Spent a Little More Time on You" and "Drive Myself Crazy." Even while touring nonstop and doing more than three hundred concerts in the last year, they recorded hits with other artists including Gloria Estefan and Alabama and released a Christmas EP, *Home For Christmas*. *NSYNC has won numerous awards including a 1999 American Music Award for "Best New Pop/Rock Group," embarked on some solo projects and recorded a new album, *No Strings Attached* for Jive Records.

Ashley O'Bryant is a fourteen-year-old honors student. Some things she likes to do for fun are reading, shopping, spending time with family and friends, but especially talking on the phone. She is always willing to lend a helping hand and enjoys serving others. Her career goal is to be a psychologist.

Shannon O'Bryant, age twelve, loves to play soccer. It is her favorite sport because it keeps her active and it's fun. Her favorite foods are pizza, barbeque ribs, artichokes and corn. She enjoys expressing herself through poetry and making home videos.

D. Marie O'Keefe, a Wisconsin freelance writer and former librarian, now knows that it's way cooler to give time and energy to family and friends than to becoming what others think is cool. Her passions include dogs, parrots, fly-fishing, protecting endangered plants and animals, and collecting books. She also enjoys photographing wildlife, encountering wild grizzlies and wolves, digging for dinosaur bones and riding in hot-air balloons.

Michael Oknefski is a senior in high school who plays on the school golf, basketball and baseball teams. He is a member of the National Honor Society and has been nominated to "Who's Who" among high school students for three consecutive years. Mike will major in engineering at Penn State University in fall 2000. You can e-mail him at davo@ncentral.com.

Daphne M. Orenshein is a full-time kindergarten teacher in Los Angeles, CA, and a distributor for DKFL publishing company. Her hobbies are reading, basketball, photography, dance, singing, event planning and keeping her husband on his toes. She has three terrific book-loving, Lego-building, cooking-helping, Marco Polo-playing, in-your-face little boys.

Susan Overton was born and raised in Denver, CO. She resides in Seattle, WA, and is a manager at Andersen Consulting, where she specializes in the area of international e-commerce. Susan enjoys biking, snowshoeing and running. She continues to be an advocate for child literacy by supporting programs that put books in the hands of children. She credits her parents and siblings for always providing guidance, eternal optimism and patience in her many crazy ideas. You can reach her at v-acsuso@microsoft.com.

Jonathan Piccirillo is a junior in Pennsylvania. His hobbies include soccer, drama, music, debate, travel, creative writing and spending time with friends. Jonathan became interested in writing from his creative-writing teacher, Mrs. Aiello. He plans on pursuing an English or arts degree in college.

Kathy Kemmer Pyron is a devoted wife and mother of four children, three dogs and two cats. When time allows, she writes children's stories for picture books and magazines. Kathy has been published in *Highlights for Children* and *The Flicker Magazine*.

Lindsey Rawson, age thirteen, enjoys writing poetry and short stories. She spends much of her time dancing, acting in plays, helping people and hanging out with friends. Lindsey hopes to make the cheerleading squad next school year.

Julia Wasson Render is a former elementary teacher who now works for a company that helps very young children build literacy skills. In her spare time, she contributes to *Partners for Schools* and *Partners for Parents*, two newsletters just for parents of preteen kids. Her inspirations are her daughter, Lindsay, and sons, Aaron and Jake. Julia can be reached at 1916 Grantwood Dr., Iowa City, IA 52440.

Michelle Richard is a sixth grader in Louisiana, where she lives with her parents and three younger brothers. Her interests include reading, visual arts, acting and composing songs. She is also an active member of the Girl Scouts. Michelle would like to thank all of her friends for their support, especially Amber and Brittany.

Nicole Ritchie is a ninth grader from Texas. She belongs to two dance groups and has been jazz dancing for nine years. She plans on attending college after high school.

Nadine Rogers has been writing picture books, magazine articles, educational material and chapter books for eight- to twelve-year-old children for ten years. Current educational titles coauthored include a set of three books called *Directives* (Humanics Publishing Group) and a book of Constitution puzzles (Royal Fireworks Press). She writes a monthly column in a local newsletter called "Grammargram." Nadine enjoys playing duplicate bridge and tennis in her free time. She can be reached at 2403 Greenhorn Rd., Yreka, CA 96097-9467.

Shane Ruwe is a fifteen-year-old from Missouri. He is a black belt in the martial arts and enjoys bow hunting, football, baseball and golf. He likes writing mostly nonfiction stories and also writes some fiction. Writing "Kelsey" helped him express his feelings about his family's tragedies.

Mary Ellyn Sandford is a happily married mother of seven. She has been published in several magazines, *Chicken Soup for the Kid's Soul* and is currently working on a middle-grade novel. She is the head director of Ministering Metacarpals, a traveling puppet performance team. When teachers didn't encourage her desire to write, she spent lots of time with heroines like Anne Shirley, Jo March and Laura Ingalls. You can contact Mary Ellyn at 4507 Chelsea Ave., Lisle, IL 60532 or via e-mail at wfkig@quixnet.net.

Hope Saxton lives in Ontario, Canada, with her husband and two sons. She began writing stories and poetry as a child, and her love of writing has carried her into the present. Her work has appeared in many magazines, as well as *A 6th Bowl of Chicken Soup for the Soul*. Hope is currently working on her fourth novel. She can be e-mailed at hope_saxton@hotmail.com.

Elizabeth J. Schmeidler is happily married to her husband, Gary, and feels blessed to have her three sons, Jerome, Paul and Roy. She started writing three years ago and since has written a Christian romance mystery entitled *Forget Me Not*, as well as a collection of poetry and three children's books. Her second novel is in the works. She also enjoys singing at church and at weddings and funerals. Elizabeth can be reached at 508 W. 32nd St., Hays, KS 67601.

Judith Burnett Schneider, a former research organic chemist, is the mother of three. She is the author of *Write Well & Sell: Changing Life's Simple Stories into Sales* and is a contributing author for the book *Plastics Recycling*. Judith is also host of Critique Retreat for Writing Women. She teaches workshops at bookstores, her local community college and through her Internet writing classes. Judith welcomes feedback via e-mail at jbswrites@sgi.net; or mail P.O. Box 207, Ingomar, PA 15127.

Bunny Schulle has more than fifty published stories, articles and plays for children and young adults and has received several writing awards. She taught English as a Second Language through adult education and has volunteered in the Listen to the Children program. Currently, she is writing a preteen mystery novel and enjoys spending time with her granddaughters. She can be contacted at 106 N. Dory Rd., North Palm Beach, FL 33408.

Mark Schulle is a classical guitar instructor in Florida. He is the owner of the Gainesville Guitar Academy where he shares his love of music with children and adults. Mark also enjoys boating, reading and hiking.

Amy Severns, age fifteen, has enjoyed writing for many years. Her poetry can be found in the International Library of Poetry's Anthology entitled *Seasons of Happiness*. She is also an active softball player, musician (playing the bass guitar and the clarinet), and website designer. More of Amy's writing is available on her personal website located at www.manifest-angel.com/roses.

Jamie Lauren Shapiro is fourteen years old and lives in Virginia with her large family and dog named Max. She loves writing poetry and often uses it as a way of expressing herself and communicating with others.

Elijah Shoesmith is a freshman in high school who enjoys writing adventure stories, reading action books and playing computer games. He aspires to write adventure books for teens. He would like to thank God, his family, the Oraras, the Boyds, Jason, Josh and Rachel for their support.

Makenzie Snyder is a nine-year-old from Maryland who enjoys gymnastics, ballet, drawing and making things. She has been twirling baton since she was four years old and won first place in Dance Twirl competition at the national championships. She has two older brothers, a dog and two cats. She can be reached at Children to Children, 3262 Superior Ln., PMB# 288, Bowie, MD 20715, or at the website, www. childrentochildren.org.

Beverly Spooner wanted to be a writer since the age of seven. Throughout her preteen and teen years, she was an avid journal writer and poet. In her late twenties, she became a contributing writer for *The Topanga Messenger,* a local newspaper. She is now a freelance writer living in Illinois with her artist/husband Michael, son Philip, and dogs, Snowy and Rembrandt.

Monte Stewart is a journalist living in Calgary, Canada who became a *Calgary Herald* staff writer in 1987 and has covered sports (including the National Hockey League and the 1998 Winter Olympics). He serves as president of Falcon Press, the publishing company that produced his critically acclaimed book, *Carry On: Reaching Beyond 100,* the inspirational autobiography of centenarian Tom Spear. His freelance articles have appeared in such publications as the *Toronto Star, Profit Magazine, The Hockey News* and *San Jose Mercury News.* He enjoys hockey, golf, reading and traveling. You can reach him at monstr@telus planet.net, or phone him at 403-284-4292.

Angelia Lee Swift is a freshman at Tennessee Technological University who enjoys creative writing, reading and hanging out with her friends.

She looks forward to contributing to society by becoming a published author. You can contact her at P.O. Box 2490, Cookerville, TN 38502, or via e-mail at aLs9514@tntech.edu.

Stephanie Taylor, age eleven, enjoys skating, shopping and talking on the phone with her friends. She owns a dog named Ginger and two cats named Tiger and Mittens. Her favorite subjects in school are history and science. Her website is www.dogvest.com.

Lauren Thorbjornsen is a freshman at her high school where she serves on student government. She is a member of the swim and soccer teams and enjoys traveling, shopping, music and being with her friends.

April Townsend is thirteen years old and likes reading and writing. She wants to be a middle-school English teacher or a psychologist because she enjoys listening to people and helping them with their problems.

Megan Weaver is a thirteen-year-old from Georgia who has been writing and illustrating short stories since she was eight. She is active in her church and loves art, sports, tap and jazz, and playing the piano. Megan plans to write a book someday and maybe become a doctor or veterinarian.

Nikki Yargar, age fourteen, plays lacrosse, softball and basketball and loves swimming in the summer. Music and her friends are important to her. In her free time, she likes to write in her diary and work on her scrapbook. She is very close to her parents, three brothers and two sisters.

Megan Youpa, fourteen, enjoys playing softball and hanging out with her friends. She started writing poetry to express her feelings to the world and to show others how she feels. Megan would like to thank her English teacher, Mrs. Always, for introducing her to poetry.

Meet Our New Contributors

Emily Andrews graduated college in May 2021 with a degree in mathematics and a minor in STEM education. She has plans to teach middle-school math. Emily enjoys traveling, reading, and spending time with friends. She is also a loving dog mom to her two dogs, Winnie and Sunny.

Donald Brown III is known as Trey by his friends. He lives in Southern California and after making the honor roll eight consecutive quarters, graduated middle school in spring of 2021. He is a Christian who enjoys playing sports, video games and eating burgers from In-N-Out.

Landon Dean is fourteen years old and lives in Southern California with his family. Landon is an honor roll student, plays acoustic guitar and loves the game of basketball. Landon is most proud of the work he does as a mentor to kids with special needs.

Hazel Gonzalez is twelve years old and lives in Canada with her mother, younger sister and their cat, Bowie. She loves nature, art, and reading. In the winter she cross-country skis and in the summer, she hikes and bikes. She is an avid baker and makes beautiful cakes for every occasion.

Kyahna Hammond, who grew up in a small town located in British Columbia, always had a passion for sharing her life stories and experiences in a humorous yet touching way in hopes of one day reaching a young reader who may be going through a similar circumstance and wanting someone to relate to.

M. Eliza Hryniewicz grew up in Chicago with five other siblings. After graduating high school, Megan left her hometown to join AmeriCorps where she discovered a love of humanity. Megan has done four years of service working with those who experienced incarceration and homelessness across the U.S.A.

Emma Kaefer lives in California with her parents, grandparents, younger sister, and hamster (Potato). When she grows up, she wants to help save elephants and be a singer. She loves hanging out with her friends, art, baking, Harry Potter, writing, playing soccer, softball, and ukulele. She hopes to make a difference in the world.

Robin Lanehurst grew up in St. Louis, MO and is currently writing from Houston, TX where she lives with her wife, son, and a small menagerie of pets.

Elijah LoMonaco is a fourth grader. He likes to read, write, hang out with his friends, skateboard, and play video games. He lives in California with his family.

Kenedi Morgado is eleven years old and loves to write all kinds of stories. She plays softball, does archery and has a passionate love for horses. She wants to be a farmer and a writer when she grows up.

Seema Patel-Trivedi received her Doctorate in Pharmacy degree from the University of Maryland in 2009. She has always had a passion for writing and has written children's books in the area of diversity. She lives in Houston, TX with her son and husband. She enjoys travelling and exploring other cultures.

Noah Ross is fifteen years old and has been dancing for twelve years. He has attended many different dance courses and is a stellar high school student. Noah hopes his lessons in life can help others because he loves to inspire people and help them find a happier way of life.

Vashti Seek-Smith is the founder of Seek Fitness, an in-home personal training business that caters to the needs of the more mature population. She is married with three children. Vashti enjoys serving others and writing. She hopes that her writing will always build others up according to their needs.

Julia Sonntag is currently attending Indiana State University, double majoring in Insurance and Financial Services. After graduation, she is eager to start her career with the goal of owning her own insurance agency. This is Julia's first published story, but she intends to continue improving her writing abilities.

Frances-Amelia "Frankie" Spadoni is a high school freshman in Santa Clarita, CA. She plays tennis for her school, and when she is not on the courts she is painting or crafting. She loves her time with her family and their three dogs, Packers, Hawkeye and Lambeau.

Caleb Matthew Sperber was born in Tarzana, CA in 2006. He attended school in West Hills, CA before moving to the Santa Clarita Valley in fourth grade. Caleb loves sports, especially basketball and volleyball. He loves to read and write and is working on his second book.

Author **M.L. Tarpley** writes stories of adventure, friendship, and fun that transport kids to amazing places across the world. She is an award-winning journalist and world traveler who lives in Louisiana with her husband and son. Learn more at www.mltarpleybooks.com.

Thirteen-year-old **Avery Watterson** has been writing since the second grade. At age eight, her heart for philanthropy led her to win the top fundraiser award for Bear Necessities Pediatric Cancer. In 2020, Avery and her twin sister were featured in *NBC Nightly News with Lester Holt: Kids Edition* for their "Kidshope" campaign.

Peyton Webb is a junior high student who enjoys reading, writing, and the arts. Her favorite things to do are hang out with her friends, visit coffee shops, and travel. She loves to sing and is learning to play the guitar. She dreams of using her skills as a speech writer or a novelist one day.

Abigail Williams is studying environmental studies and English. She enjoys the beach, shopping, travelling, and spending time with friends and family. She hopes to travel the world and write about her experiences. She thanks her professor, Ana Maria Spagna, who inspired her to write and pursue an English major.

Kobe Williams is a freshman honors student in Seattle, WA. He has two loving parents and a six-year-old little sister. A few of his hobbies include exercising, playing sports, and video games, exercising being a favorite. He hopes to grow up to be a lawyer or an architect.

Kaiwen Zhang is a high school student in San Jose, CA. He is in the class of 2024, and enjoys playing basketball, listening to music, and hanging out with friends in his spare time. He also loves to write short stories and articles.

Thank You

We owe huge thanks to all our contributors and fans. Barbara LoMonaco, D'ette Corona and Laura Dean read the original book to familiarize themselves with this wonderful title. Editor Laura Dean read all of the new submissions and narrowed down the selection for Associate Publisher D'ette Corona and Publisher and Editor-in-Chief Amy Newmark.

Amy edited the new stories and shaped the final manuscript, as D'ette Corona continued to be Amy's right-hand woman in working with all our wonderful writers. Barbara LoMonaco, Kristiana Pastir, and Elaine Kimbler jumped in at the end to proof, proof, proof. And yes, there will always be typos anyway, so please feel free to let us know about them at webmaster@chickensoupforthesoul.com, and we will correct them in future printings.

The whole publishing team deserves a hand, including our Senior Director of Marketing Maureen Peltier, our Vice President of Production Victor Cataldo, our Executive Assistant Mary Fisher, Editor Jamie Cahill, and our graphic designer Daniel Zaccari, who turned our manuscript into this inspirational, supportive book for preteens.

Chicken Soup for the Soul

Changing lives one story at a time®
www.chickensoup.com